What reviewers have said:

*"This is potentially of interest to anyone concerned with how we grow up, how we are shaped, and how the way that young people are drawn into whatever religious faith into which they are born, how this supposedly, avowedly benign process is enacted can have deeply malign effects on the individual and so on society in general. It tackles — head-on — an important and pressing subject… it's vital stuff. It's about how we safeguard young people, how we grow up, how we interact with others."*

—KARL FRENCH—
Literary Reviewer

*"Awesome how far Augustine's tentacles of guilt and sinfulness reach. Alone among the world's civilised nations, Britons are allowed to physically punish children because unelected bishops sitting in the House of Lords advocate it."*

—CAROLYN THOMPSON—
Reader

*"It takes us directly to a seemingly real situation with flesh and blood people. The menace in the good father's every action is tangible, and what isn't said adds to the sense of danger."*

—ALAN WILKINSON—
Literary Reviewer

# WHY PUNISH ME?

## AUGUSTINE'S SINFUL LUST UNWRAPPED

Michael Moloney
& Lorna Graham

*To Dad, to whom I owe more
than I realised until it was too late to thank him.*

# CONTENTS

# ILLUSTRATIONS

# ACKNOWLEDGEMENTS

Acknowledgements must begin with thanks to Pope Francis who prompted me to start writing when I read in February 2019 that he had dubbed his critics 'friends of the devil'. Most of the words in the following pages were written later. Ruminating on my parents' years of futile, stoic suffering kept me writing and focussed on achieving closure. The book was made possible by many helping hands, but especially the trailblazers and scientists whose star labours my modest contribution relies upon. They completed the challenging, and often fascinating, research studies without which there could be no discussion. These include the National Secular Society, Humanists UK, teams of academics and scholars, and indeed all of the sources mentioned in my references.

Lorna Graham, who edited and commented as the manuscript progressed, made a contribution to the work far in excess of the chapters she authored. Special credit must be given to my wife who tolerated an entirely undeserved lack of attention for months on end. (That said, I recognise more praise will be needed to get me back in favour.) I am particularly grateful to the book designers WordZworth and IngramSpark the printers, who between them have honed the process of publication so that the many obscure technical processes are comprehensible to a novice, or at least made manageable.

Finally, thanks to you, my readers. Whatever your beliefs, my hope is that after scanning these pages you feel as passionate as I do about the value of an open education for all British children. Today, children in some schools are being insidiously misinformed.

To properly safeguard our young and defend our liberal way of life for the future, religious studies should be taught from an objective, critical and pluralistic viewpoint so that children are well placed to make up their own minds what to believe and what to doubt.

# FOREWORD

Every week we are contacted by members of the public from all backgrounds annoyed, angered and aggrieved by the inappropriate imposition of religion in their schools. In England three in ten live in areas with little or no choice but a faith school and every year 20,000 pupils are assigned faith schools against their families' preferences. Every week we hear from those locked out of suitable local schools by discriminatory admissions. We speak to parents shocked to find their children being directed to pray in schools or proselytized to in religious education. We speak with teachers facing religious discrimi-nation in employment, or uncomfortable with evangelical visits and pupils experiencing discriminatory sex education. We deal with the extreme examples that can only be called indoctrination and a large range of more subtle problems arising from the privileging of religion.

As coordinator of the 'No More Faith Schools' campaign I am happy to write this brief foreword for the authors, both members of NSS and committed to our goal of removing the connection between religion and state. The evidence of harm presented here should give the government cause to reconsider funding schools organised round and promoting exclusive religions.

Around one in three publicly funded schools in England & Wales are faith schools, i.e., they have an official religious designation or ethos. Scottish and Northern Irish schools are still strongly divided along sectarian lines. Abuses of children's rights are common in religious schools beyond the state sector. While we do not oppose independ-ent private religious schools, we are increasingly active in challenging schools where the most basic standards of secular education and even health and safety are often sacrificed in the prioritisation of faith formation.

Our principled opposition to faith schools, comes not from any antipathy towards religion but from our support for children's independent right to develop their own beliefs free from religious discrimination or control. Principles we are glad to see supported by many people of faith, but fiercely resisted by the religious establish-ment.

The authors of this book have taken aim at that establishment and their arguments will be persuasive to any open-minded reader. Two lines of their argument are particularly relevant to our campaigning.

The first is that the religious establishment that plays such a large role in state education – spearheaded by the Church of England – is increasingly disconnected from the population it seeks to lead. Yet the Church relies on this persona of kindly teacher of the nation and heart of the community to justify its role in education. This disconnect – seen in the consistent and dramatic decline in church attendance, and a growing majority of non-religious citizens – makes the increasing role of religion in schools even more incongruous. Many are driven away by the Church's institutional homophobia and ideas about 'sin' which are deeply disconnected from the moral zeitgeist. The hypocrisy of this moralising while the Church remains mired in safeguarding and clerical abuse scandals, with more than 100 cases of clerical child sex abuse reported every year, is clear for all to see. Time and again such lax safeguarding is enabled by the state authorities' continuing deference engendered by the Church's establishment status.

Secondly, we increasingly view children not as vassals or property of their parents, but as independent rights holders. Modern pedagogies view the purpose of education as enabling self-actualisation, prepar-ing children with the knowledge and skills to take their own path in life. The idea of education focusing on obedience and moulding unruly children feels like a relic of the last century. But the ideas that children are inherently sinful, that they need instruction to follow the correct path, and that parents choose children's beliefs, are kept alive, albeit often in a weakened state, by religious influence over education.

*Alastair Lichten*

Head of education, National Secular Society

# INTRODUCTION

*Wilt thou forgive that sin where I begun*
*Which was my sin, though it were done before?*
*Wilt thou forgive that sin, through which I run,*
*And do run still, though still I do deplore?*
*When thou hast done, thou hast not done,*
*For I have more.*

—*A HYMN TO GOD THE FATHER* BY JOHN DONNE—

Whether or not religion spawns tension and violence around the world is an issue that has been exhaustively discussed elsewhere, and is beyond the modest ambitions of this book. What I hope to do is show how the teaching in certain schools can disadvantage children who are, as I was, imaginative and impressionable. Having a sensitive nature is a positive attribute: it is what makes us human. However, sensitive individuals are especially susceptible to corrosive feelings of guilt and shame. These feelings are sharpened by the relentless burden of culpability imputed by Augustine of Hippo, one of Christianity's foremost saints. St Augustine deemed all humans inherently depraved and sinful, from birth. We will look at Augustine's fourth century teaching and the subjective effect of the drill and doctrine imposed on infants in some faith schools today. Modern thinking, and the new research that we will review, challenges Augustine's dismal verdict on the human condition. We will explore the state's long collaboration with the church, which ensures Augustine's archaic preoccupation with sinfulness continues to be ingrained into the minds of all British infants. Reviewing evidence of the influence

Augustine's ideas have on the long-term mental well-being of apostates, we discover that this group is widely misrepresented in academic research endorsing religious belief. Finally, noting that clerical child sexual abuse (cCSA) continues to bedevil church institutions today, we consider whether instruction in Augustinian theology might play a role in cCSA. From time to time, I will intrude with examples from my own experience as a follower and former acolyte. I will show how Augustine's sin-centred teaching stimulated and sustained a negative mental schema that I endured for much of my life.

A friend of mine shared an instructive story. He said, 'My dad hated seeing people baring an open mouth. When I was a boy, he often used to say that if a fly gets in your mouth, your teeth will turn black and fall out. I am in my forties now, and I know that he was joking, but to this day I close my mouth if I see a fly. It's instinctive: half the time I don't realise I'm doing it.'

The founder of my old school, Cardinal John Henry Newman (recently canonised and now St Newman), put the idea another way. He wrote in his school notebook, 'Train up a child in the way he should go, and, when he is old, he will not depart from it.'[1] Reading the reports of evasiveness by the Vatican in response to the disclosures of cCSA,[2] I thought back to my childhood and the religious education (RE) that I had undergone in schools. Existing literature offers implausible rationalisations for cCSA, while my memory of school drill in rites and rituals offers an explanation that I find persuasive, and it reaches back in history to implicate that keystone of Western Christianity, St Augustine. It occurred to me that teaching Augustine's ideas might inadvertently build a favourable grounding for the subsequent exploitation of a child.

St Augustine, whose literature informs Christian faith, was a tormented man writing in unenlightened times. A revered doctor of the church, he is held up as a role model for healthy spiritual development. Yet, as bishop of Hippo, he advocated a dubious moral code and he wrote disgusting tracts about infant sexuality. Later, when we examine his life, we will review the historical background that

2

helps explain this apparent paradox. We will evaluate the soundness of his ideas, which are not just tolerated but compulsorily taught to infants as definitive in Britain's schools.

As soon as I could speak, my mother told me what all infants in Christian households are told, that I was born with original sin and I had been baptised to wash the sin out. Later in life I learned that original sin is Augustine's mark of guilt for concupiscence (sexual lust),[3] which by his decree is ineradicable. In his autobiographical works, Augustine wrote of 'filth' and the 'itch of lust in infants',[4] declaring that babies are born stained with guilt from original sin, the sin of sexual lust. He reframed baptism to do away with the sinful flesh, but he held that lust is not removed.[5]

When I started my own family, Augustine's idea that children are contaminated by the lust of their parents in conceiving them was hideous and repugnant. In the Augustinian view, a baby is not innocent and unsullied, with potential for self-determination. Rather, a child is born in sexual sin and needs external regulation for the rest of its life to control its lustful impulses. Most Christian adults take a blithe view of original sin and many will be unfamiliar with the significance of the rite of baptism. However, St Augustine's teaching is required reading for church men and women who learn that baptism does not entirely cleanse original sin. Sexual lust is dampened down but some concupiscence remains in a baptised infant, a doctrine endorsed in the catechism of the Catholic Church.[6]

Teachers and parents might overlook or ignore the sexual connotations, but we will see how clergy focus their lives on scripture. The overwhelming majority of priests and vicars I meet seem kindly and well meaning, yet they insist children are born marked with the stain of original sin.[7] If they did not believe Augustine's doctrine that there was sin from carnal guilt in little children that needed acknowledgement and forgiveness, they would not solemnise baptism, because sacramental grace to douse lust would be superfluous.

Augustinian theology is the bedrock of Christian faith in the Western Church, inculcating notions of personal guilt and sin. RE is required and funded by the government, and schools in the UK are obliged by law to promote Augustine's fatalistic doctrines.[8] In fact, only 60% of primary schools currently comply,[9] but in these schools RE helps shape the lives of nearly one half of British infants.[10] These children are having their life chances affected by reciting unhelpful prayers like the ones we will review in chapter two. Infants are told they were inflicted at birth with the stain of original sin. As these children grow up, clerics, supported by teachers and childcare workers, reinforce the disgrace they administered by getting children to perform Augustine's penitential admission of wrongdoing and making them beg for forgiveness and mercy.[11] Chapter 3 draws attention to how impressionable infants are inculcated with these unhelpful ideas. Reviewing primary school curricula, we find Augustine's hairshirt ritual of self-inflicted guilt and censure is still recited by infants in faith schools.[12] Receptive young minds are repetitively weighed down with his ancient creed of mock sinfulness and self-blame.

Teachers on both sides of the Atlantic used to put dull pupils in a corner and make them wear a pointy **dunce cap**. This practice of open humiliation was scrapped 100 years ago. Yet today the state supports schools that publicly shame children with Augustine's contrived guilt. In 1927, British philosopher and Nobel laureate Bertrand Russell declared 'People in church debasing themselves and saying they are miserable sinners, and all the rest of it, seems contemptible and not worthy of self-respecting human beings.' Nearly a century later the cradle of Russell's intellect still requires infants to be indoctrinated in these self-abusive terms. The pages that follow examine the background to this shameful tradition, how it is enforced and propagated in today's schools, how it inhibits some children and how it might tempt acts of cCSA. Here we unravel how discriminatory government appointments ensure the perpetuation of Augustine's negative creed.

My RE was actually Augustinian indoctrination, similar to that in many faith schools, and as you progress through these pages it will become clear why I take pains to make this distinction. Shrewd intellectual critiques of religion by Anthony Grayling, Richard Dawkins, Victor Stenger, Daniel Dennett, Sam Harris, Dan Barker and the late and much-lamented Christopher Hitchens, among many others, fill the bookshelves. But these great men cannot speak for those who spent years being indoctrinated and drilled, as I was, in Augustine's undignified ideology.

RE was plain and simple in my schooldays, but for today's schoolchildren it is technically sophisticated. Demand for religious content is sufficient to sustain commercial producers offering slick media presentations, including Augustine's penitential pleading. Using well-conducted research studies we examine how school drill and doctrine instils Augustine's potentially disturbing ideas in young minds. Then we look at some of the measurable outcomes in affected Western societies. I will argue that Christianity's Augustinian teaching can have enduring and far-reaching effects on some children into adulthood. We will compare his primitive ideas with recent scientific discoveries and then review compelling evidence that the attitude of adults towards children is shaped by Augustine's unsafe teaching.

Almost all children (99%) schooled in Britain today will go on to renounce religion soon afterwards, as I did.[13] Unfortunately, apart from the wasted hours of misspent lesson time, repudiation does not promptly disengage the billions of neural connections made in the brain during a child's formative years.[14] I, and countless other apostates, have experienced distress caused by the RE we received in childhood. Little rigorous research has been published regarding the lifelong effect of instilling Augustine's ideas in young people.[15] Indoctrination of minors as a factor contributing to mental ill-health is surprisingly lacking from that literature which does exist. The possible effect of sustained drilling on the minds of receptive infants has not escaped notice entirely, but research presents particular challenges. In extreme cases, RE gives rise to trauma,[16] but the milder upset borne by others is unrecorded and quietly disregarded. We will look at the work that has been done and the difficulties involved in the study of religion. Comparing diverse cultures, we see how

Augustinian guilt is so prevalent in Western societies it has become normalised. Here we will learn why existing literature claiming benefits for religiosity is unreliable, and we hear about a surprising inhibition reported by psychologists to explain why this field of study is shunned by academia.

The mental scars inflicted by my upbringing in a Roman Catholic (RC) community still mark me. Following my parents' alienation at the behest of a priest, my mother sent me to a Catholic boarding school where I encountered abuse. Reading the many reports of child exploitation and sexual abuse and reflecting on my own experiences, I was moved to speculate why the Christian community appears to hold an unduly liberal attitude towards the mistreatment of children. It is not just clerics who shock us with their abuse of children. Nuns also seem disposed to mistreat young people, as the unmarried mothers-to-be care homes scandals noted here show. Examining the literature, we question why some ecclesiastics seem to have a disdainful view of children, typified by my indecent clerical beating overseen by nuns, described in chapter 6. We review speeches by bishops in the House of Lords to discover why the English, unlike other secular populations, continue to permit children to be physically punished in the home.

Augustine's version of the ritual known as penance, also called confession or reconciliation (meaning reconciliation with God, not with the victim of wrongdoing), is morally questionable. His doctrine, discussed in chapter 7, teaches children a moral code of mock culpability, secretive disengaged justice, and arbitrary retribution, which conflicts with the principles of fairness accepted by enlightened societies. I recall the sense of ambivalence and the moral limbo I experienced in my adolescence as I struggled to resolve the confusing beliefs I had been indoctrinated with – beliefs that I did not value and did not own.

Followers deem that when a priest forgives transgressions, he stands as Christ, in person. We look behind the Latin phrase **in Persona Christi**, the title given to Catholic priests by the pope, meaning that a priest stands 'in the person of Christ', which allows priests to forgive sins. Although generally associated with Catholicism, all Western denominations offer to forgive transgressions without thought or consideration for the aggrieved party. Christians are accountable only to a confessor for wrongdoing and the confessor is compelled by canon law to absolve the penitent if they are contrite and accepts a penance, usually prayers to the saints. If a believer is sorry and has confessed, forgiveness is guaranteed by canon law regardless of any moral or judicial considerations. Those who find comfort in religion can develop ethical blind spots or maladaptive feelings of guilt, and we will examine these issues as we progress. We go on to consider enlightened concepts of decency and fair play compared with Augustine's ancient philosophy. We explore contemporary approaches to wrongdoing which displace Augustinian ideas with evidence-based methodologies. Government research demonstrates the superiority of progressive judicial systems like restorative justice.

We have considered Augustine's readings on the doctrines of original sin, penance and sacrifice. In chapter 8 we are ready to sift the moral lessons these ideas teach our schoolchildren. Augustine thought humans were born wicked and predisposed to being bad and sinful. He taught that only the Christian God can distinguish right from wrong. Acts of goodness can only be achieved by means of God's grace, and forgiveness is His sole prerogative. We look at game changing advances made by British researchers in identifying the source of human morality and we find Augustine was wrong. Far from his doctrine of preordained human wickedness, science reveals we are born with a socially positive and valuable sense of cooperation and fair play. This valuable sense of right and wrong that has evolved in humans predates Augustine by thousands of years. Telling children that they were born wicked and are predisposed to evil is not only potentially harmful, it is also dishonest.

Examining psychologists' assessments of Augustine's state of mind, we take time out here and allow ourselves to speculate upon why he took the view he did. Aided by expert study, this light-hearted digression offers a fascinating theory that could account for Augustine's dark psyche. No other country in the world demands all its children be indoctrinated in outdated Augustinian values. We uncover the sordid reason why the British state alone continues its headlong charge in a direction opposite to the wishes and needs of the majority of its citizens.

In the course of my research for this book I have encountered thousands of accounts from adults articulating feelings of exploitation and betrayal by their evangelical schoolteachers.[17] Like me, these individuals were too naïve to demur as infants. Now, many express a view like mine; that their schooling punished them. Here we review some of the disturbing ideas and images infants are being exposed to in faith schools. It is hard to disagree with Dawkins when he claims that religious indoctrination is a form of child abuse.[18] Dawkins was criticised by Augustinian apologists for insulting people who have endured physical child abuse, but having been abused mentally and physically myself I can speak from both sides of the argument. However, the term **abuse** is contentious and I prefer to describe religious indoctrination as a form of punishment. According to Merriam-Webster, punishment is 'suffering, pain, or loss that serves as retribution'.[19] Indoctrination in Augustine's ideas undoubtedly punishes some children, and the evidence for that claim is contained in these pages, which recount my childhood experience.

Reviewing judicial reports and criminal records, we look at the backgrounds of convicted child sex offenders and the personal histories of the world's most notorious distributors of child pornography, to identify a correlative influence. With caveats regarding data collection and acknowledging international and cultural inconsistencies in defining child abuse, we move on to investigate recent records of 'darknet' internet child pornography. Then we compare that data with countries where Augustine's followers are dominant.

Chapter 11 trawls through the many theories that have been posited to explain the aberration that is cCSA. We have noted the remarkable paucity of rigorous research in this field. In the absence of clear evidence, the cause of clerical cCSA is open to speculation. A report commissioned by the Catholic Church itself implies that nearly three quarters of victims of predatory clerics fell within the range that would identify the abusers as paedophiles, according to the clinicians' manual. We consider whether the Augustinian theology nuns and clerics are taught regarding infant concupiscence might be a factor in cCSA. Could Augustine's doctrines on infantile guilt and culpability be unconsciously moulding the attitude of clerics towards young people? The church's report goes on to confirm that the indoctrination clergy receive in seminaries is a factor in cases of cCSA. Here is testimony from the church itself, admitting the far-reaching influence of Augustine's unsafe ideas.

In the last few decades, the Christian communion has been confronted with an avalanche of cCSA cases from around the world. Most claims involve Catholic priests, but thousands of Church of England (C of E) clerics have also been implicated in cCSA. Although the Catholic community has the most cases of abuse at the time of writing in March 2021, cCSA has been uncovered throughout the Christian communion, despite having been carefully concealed by ecclesiastics at every level of authority. The C of E has been obliged to deal with thousands of complaints of cCSA and has taken desperate measures to cover up cases of abuse.[20,21,22] Finally, analysing the latest government statistics, we assess whether clerics are more liable than others in society to sexually abuse children today.

Recent high-profile lawsuits and harrowing testimony given to public inquiries have kept the issue in the headlines. Meanwhile, cover-ups continue to surface, and victims' groups say the churches have not done nearly enough to guarantee reform and safeguard children. Church history is laden with prevarication and evasion in dealing with cases of cCSA.[2] Despite multiple demands for change to Church procedures and practices, safeguarding has been erratic and half-hearted. We explore evidence that ever since Augustine, cCSA has bedevilled the Church, while ecclesiastics have carefully papered over cases within their ranks.[23] Evidently, little has changed and new cases are still being reported. In November 2020, the UK Independent Inquiry into Child Sexual Abuse (IICSA) reported that the crisis is 'far from a solely historical issue', adding that more than 100 allegations of cCSA had been reported each year since 2016.[24]

I am indebted to Lorna Graham who wrote the final chapters of this book. With 26 years' experience of teaching in primary schools and in secondary religious education, Lorna writes with authority about infant proselytisation and the current obsolete connection between the state and religion. Media attention has rightly focused on radicalisation, highlighting the danger posed to society by fanatical religious indoctrination. Less attention has been given to the routine teaching in state-funded primary faith schools that Lorna explores. Some readers have expressed doubt that the practices described in these pages are relevant today. Lorna corrects this misconception with accounts of her primary school classroom experience, and parents themselves describe intensive faith indoctrination.[25] Ofsted reports give a disturbing picture of how primary school RE lessons are being conducted today.[26]

Sex and Relationships Education (SRE), recently introduced into British schools, is not as widely taught as some might think. In fact, many schools do not publish a policy on SRE and others neglect to cover the subject fully or misrepresent the facts.[27] For an annual subscription of £456.00, Ten:Ten Resources will provide lessons to meet the government's requirement for objective relationships, sex and health education (RSHE) '…through the prism of Catholic RSHE'.[28] In other words, RSHE will be delivered in an explicitly distorted, faith-friendly form. Chapter 12 highlights the omissions and inaccuracies that result from schoolteachers failing to present the facts of life clearly and objectively. The failure to give comprehensive information on this important topic is liable to put young people at a serious disadvantage when they leave school.

Before progressing further, it is useful to clarify the lexicon used by professionals in the field. The terms **child grooming, child molestation, child sexual abuse** and **child sexual exploitation** (CSE) might be used interchangeably by the media, but there are important distinctions. Grooming is the process whereby an adult prepares a child to ease the way for sexual abuse. Molestation is an outmoded term; child sexual abuse is more precise and is the preferred term to describe an adult using a child for sexual stimulation. According to Google Trends (trend.google.com), child sexual abuse is slowly becoming the more popular search string. CSE is an umbrella term, which covers all child sexual abuse including prostituting, trafficking and underage marriage.

The NSPCC says, 'When a child or young person is sexually abused, they're forced or tricked into sexual activities. They might not understand that what's happening is abuse or that it's wrong. And they might be afraid to tell someone', and 'Abuse is sexual touching of any part of a child's body, whether they're clothed or not.' The Sexual Offences Act 2003 defines inappropriate touching as sexual assault if (a) the touching is intentional, (b) the touching is sexual, (c) the child is under 16. The Act goes on to define touching as sexual if a reasonable person would consider that, (a) whatever its circumstances or any person's purpose in relation to it, it is because of its nature sexual, or (b) because of its nature it may be sexual and because of its circumstances or the purpose of any person in relation to it (or both) it is sexual. Touching includes touching, (a) with any part of the body, (b) with anything else, (c) through anything.[29]

Thus, the boundaries for what constitutes child sexual abuse are wide but clear and detailed. Bearing in mind the context, and the relationship between clergy and altar boy, any touching other than hand to hand is inappropriate and therefore could meet the criteria for sexual assault. If I were to cite simply **abuse** or another general term when relating the incidents I encountered I might be alluding to any number of acts, varying in gravity and harm. Since there could be uncertainty, I have made a point of particularising the behaviours I witnessed or experienced and I trust the reader will understand the necessity for my accounts to be graphic and detailed.

From the time I could hold a pen, I have kept a diary in which I scribble anything that catches my interest. Although my notes were never a strict chronological record of events, some of my early writing survives to trigger memories of my boarding school days. These recollections provided a starting point for laying out the evidence in the following pages with the authenticity of someone with a lifetime of involvement in the Christian community. With the Vatican decrying critics of the Church as 'friends of the devil',[30] I felt spurred to record my experiences to highlight the effect that Augustinian indoctrination has had on my life and on the lives of others.

Many of the issues raised here are not new. Countless luminaries have discussed failures in the school curriculum, and secular groups bristle with letters from former faith school pupils voicing their concerns. I will examine these concerns from the perspective of my personal experience inside and outside the sacristy to shed light on the interaction between clerics and children. Lorna focuses attention on state-funded faith schools where some children might be affected by the same guilt and moral confusion that has scarred many of us. We noted earlier that today over one million infants are undergoing similarly unhelpful schooling. Nearly all of them are likely to reject religion later. This book gives many good reasons for government to stop financing and promoting religion and end the Church's outdated participation in education.

A YouGov/Daybreak survey in September 2010 found that school performance was the factor highest rated by parents when considering schools for their children. The religion of the school was rated as an important factor by fewer than one in ten people.[31] Over many years, opinion polls have consistently found that a majority of taxpayers do not want to fund faith schools. In June 2014, The Guardian reported a survey by Opinium showing that 58% of voters believe faith schools, which can give priority to applications from pupils of their faith and are free to teach from the perspective of their own religion, should not be funded by the state or should be abolished.[32,33] Safeguarding should start with separating the state from religion so that schools do not indoctrinate young people and risk preparing them for possible abuse. Many Christian individuals and institutions carry out valuable charity work, but compassion, altruism and good-will are pervasive human values that span doctrinal boundaries. The good work done by some Christians does not compensate me, and millions of others, for the life-changing sectarian indoctrination that we endured. For those readers who think faith schools have a benign religious function, I hope that the personal experiences I describe and the research explored in the following chapters will give them cause to think again.

Given the wealth of positive assessments of Augustine already lining the shelves, a critical evaluation seems perilous, but I will depict the man as I see him. Every step of the way I have referenced my work with original material or other reliable evidence that supports it. Unfortunately, this has led to a rather overblown reference section, but better that than have my readers left doubtful. I would like to think that the ideas within are couched in terms accessible to all. That being the case, I apologise in advance if some viewpoints are perceived to be excessively polemical. I hope the reader will forgive any impertinence, given my background, and understand that no disrespect is intended.

The National Secular Society (NSS) (*https://www.secularism.org.uk*), Humanists UK (*https://humanism.org.uk*) and many other groups campaign vigorously for an end to religious influence in the education of young people. More information on many of the topics discussed in this book is available on their websites. Whether or not you believe, as I do, that all children in Britain should enjoy their right to receive a broad and balanced education, free from indoctrination or discrimination based on ethnicity, religion or belief, you might like to contribute to the debate at *www.mike-moloney.com*.

# 1

# THE WICKEDNESS OF ST AUGUSTINE

St Augustine, Bishop of Hippo, is probably the most influential theologian in history, alongside St Paul. His texts have been translated into numerous languages and his ideas have been pored over, quoted and debated since his death in 430 AD. Not only was he one of the most prolific authors in antiquity, but more of his output survives than any other writer of the period, most of it studiously catalogued in his own vain hand. As a result, his is the best-chronicled life of any figure from ancient history. The passion and fluency of his writing gives an extraordinary insight into the man and the ancient world he inhabited. He was proclaimed a Doctor of the Church by Pope Boniface VII in 1298. Yet, his most famous series of books, *Confessions*, declares his own lust and wickedness, and we will examine this contradiction in a moment. Augustine's productivity is only surpassed by the huge number of books describing and dissecting his life and literature. There is even a scholarly journal devoted to the study of St Augustine and his psyche.[34] Theologians, classicists and historians all acclaim his intellectual genius, although some historians have questioned the accuracy of his accounts. The most successful advocate in history, 1.2 billion people all over the world still follow his ideas 1,600 years later. Augustine's large oeuvre and the quality of his prose are the key to his enduring power. However, despite the volume of literature, there is much we don't know and we should bear in mind that almost everything we do know has been sourced solely from the testimony of the writer himself.

Of the abundance of biographies on the bookshelves, those by Christian followers are not always objective. Rowan Williams, the retired archbishop of Canterbury, has written a fawning tribute rather than a thoughtful study of the man.[35] Celebrated historian and classical scholar Robin Lane Fox is more detached and measured in his assessment. A declared atheist, he nonetheless admires Augustine's 'restless intelligence and his exceptional way with words'.[36] With such profusion of worthy literature available, created by others far better equipped than I, a detailed life story is unnecessary here. We are interested in Augustine's ideas on sin, not so much in the man. A brief profile is needed to provide some context for what follows, but my view of Augustine differs from most conventional readings and I will explain why in due course.

St Augustine was born in A.D. 354 in Thagaste, Numidia (modern day Souk Ahras, Algeria) into an upper-class family. The name Augustine is a form of the title Augustus, which was given to Roman emperors to underscore their status and venerability. His mother was a Christian and his father a pagan, albeit one who converted to Christianity on his deathbed. Augustine was of mixed-race ancestry, but Latin seems to have been his first language. Although they were high-born, his parents were not wealthy and they scrimped and saved to give their son a first-class education. He studied grammar at Carthage, the great city of Roman Africa where he later taught rhetoric. The word 'rhetoric' comes from the ancient Greek rhētorikē, which means 'art of the spoken word'. In antiquity, rhetoric was defined as 'the faculty of observing in any given case the available means of persuasion' (Aristotle). In other words, Augustine's talent was similar to that required for today's public relations specialist or spin doctor. In Roman times rhetoric was an essential skill for politics, as it is now, but also for law, which was an honourable profession for a Roman gentleman.

Decoding the lines of Augustine's stylish prose, we note he admits to being a philanderer. One of his mistresses soon gave him a son whom they named Adeodatus, meaning 'Gift from God'. The mother was of a lower social class and Augustine never married her. Her name is unknown; his writing omits the names of many people, perhaps those he considered unworthy. He claims he was faithful, but after 14 years, when he was 28, Augustine abandoned her for a 10-year-old heiress. They could not get married because his new love was too young, but before she came of age he dumped her anyway and headed for Rome to further his career. Augustine was raised a Christian, but he renounced Christianity in his teenage years to become a Manichaean, a trendier religion at the time. Manichaeans believe in a spiritual world of powerful dualistic forces for good and evil (light and darkness) in eternal opposition. (Manichaeanism is still practiced in some parts of China). Later, when it became fashionable and suited his purpose, he would return to Christianity, as we shall see. Now, the influential Manichaean contacts he had acquired through his opportune spiritual rebirth arranged a plum job for him in Milan as imperial professor of rhetoric. Regardless of the hand-up, Augustine must have been a gifted orator; Milan was the de facto capital of the Western Roman Empire.

What we now call child sexual abuse was customary in Augustine's time and locus. Pederasty, i.e. sex between high-born men and pubescent boys, was common in Milan. In modern times, the age of consent has been raised and pederasty is illegal, but in antiquity the threshold for sexual consent was drawn at a much earlier age.[37] A woman was considered a man's social inferior, and as such she could never compare to another man, let alone 'a sweet smelling boy'.[38] Originating in Crete in the eighth century BC, what we now call child sexual abuse spread in ancient times, and sodomy was widely practised by adult men on boys throughout the Roman Empire, as shown in art of the period. Such is the Warren Cup from the first century AD, a Roman artefact now in the British Museum. (Fig. 1.) The Warren Cup is decorated in relief with explicit images of a bearded man sodomising a young boy.[39]

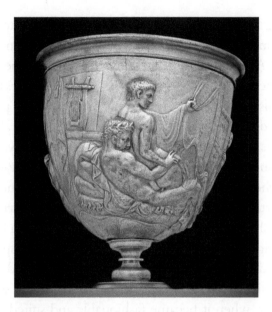

**Figure 1. The Warren Cup 15BC–15AD**

(Curtesy of © Trustees of the British Museum)

In ancient Greece the pederastic man-boy relationship had been part of the aristocratic social and educational system: an intimate relationship that aided the mentoring of a pre-adolescent boy, the eromenos, by an older male, the erastes. Pederasty continued into Roman times, albeit less openly because Greek culture was considered inferior. Romans perceived sexual expression in terms of the binary roles adopted, 'penetrator-penetrated' or 'active-passive' rather than 'adult-child' or 'male-female.'[40] Males being the active penetrator, partaking in a relationship as a passive individual in Rome was considered dishonourable for a man. Ground rules were established about when a boy should be entrusted to a rhetorician, and the character of the teacher would have been validated in order to protect the boy's virtue.[41] Attitudes were changing and even before Augustine, legislation had been enacted to protect free-born minors from sexual activity where boys took the passive role.[42] Although minors were not legitimate targets for penetration because it violated Roman sexual mores, the practice was so well established that the law was widely ignored.[43] Railing against 'sexual sins', John Chrysostom, a contemporary of Augustine wrote, '…there is some danger that womankind will become in the future unnecessary with young men instead fulfilling all the needs women used to.'[44]

Apart from technically illegal relationships with free-born boys, Roman citizen men commonly enjoyed sex with young slaves, and freed minors were also available as potential passive partners of a pederastic relationship.[45] Slaves were a viable option for a citizen man to have sex with, as long as they were his own slaves, because any shame brought down upon them was an inherent part of their subordinate status.[43] Additionally, even though slaves could gain their freedom and move into the libertini (freedman) class in Rome, they were often indebted to their former masters and obligated to continue providing them with sexual favours. It should be noted here that infant sex has never been normal or acceptable, either today or in Roman times. Young boys being sodomised would be postpubescent.

Most of what we need to pin Augustine down is contained in the series of books he called his *Confessions* and there is no better place to make a start. Confessions is a devotional prayer to God and also a confession and expression of sorrow for sinfulness. (Some scholars have claimed he was writing a confession of his faith, others suggest his purpose was to convince the reader that his beliefs were truly Christian. Augustine's contemporaries were mistrustful of him as an ex-Manichee and suspicious of his brilliance as a rhetor.) Consisting of 13 books, written in Latin before AD 398, *Confessions* is regarded as the earliest surviving Western autobiography. It is incomplete, as it was written when Augustine was in his early 40s, and he lived well into his 70s, but it is the only comprehensive record of a life from the fourth and fifth centuries. Because little else remains from this period, any writers concerned with ancient history are obliged to turn to Augustine for support. Copied and quoted from manuscript to manuscript, Augustine's *Confessions* have fed his legacy throughout the medieval period, creating an aura of authority around him.

Augustine has been quoted countless times, enhancing his influence and giving him weight as a reliable source.

But brilliant prose is no indicator of truth or legitimacy in what is written. Penmanship should not confer authority, and the scarcity of literature from the era should not validate his ideas. The elapse of 16 centuries since Augustine's death limits the validity of his opinions in modern times. The world has progressed and people are more civilised, better educated and healthier, at least in advanced societies. Most modern cultures have abolished the primitive customs of Augustine's time. Following enlightenment, the goalposts have been moved forward and today the age of consent throughout the UK is 16.

Notwithstanding the passage of time, for classical scholars Augustine's *Confessions* is an impressive achievement, described by several as a 'Christian masterpiece'. Despite the weight of scholarly endorsement, I see Augustine's works from a different perspective, and here I must declare my prejudice. Force-fed Augustine's introspective denunciations of sin and his avowals of subjugation and self-loathing, daily throughout my childhood, I feel less enthusiastic. I approach *Confessions* with a mixture of nausea and misgiving. I sense a dark side to Augustine.

For me, *Confessions* are Augustine's discourse with his personal God, his conceptualisation of his own superego. Boring through endless treatises on his sinfulness and lust, the reader is blitzed with self-flagellating tracts on guilt and repetitious protestations of remorse. The word lust appears 44 times, sin or sinners more than 100 times, mostly self-accusatory, but as we have noted earlier, sometimes he directs blame for sin and lust at infants. Describing himself in infancy, he writes 'weltering in filth and scratching off the itch of lust...my infant tongue spake freely to thee' (Book IX, p128). Claiming 'no one is free from filth in (God's) sight, not even an infant whose span of earthly life is but a single day' (Book I, p9), he continues 'The only innocence in infants is the weakness of their frames; the minds of infants are not innocent.' (Book I, p10). Later he declares '[infants] being yet little ones and carnal' (Book XII, p213). We noted that pre-pubescent sex was unacceptable in Roman culture, yet Augustine penned letters to the British monk Pelagius repeating his claim that infants are carnal.[46]

For the sake of clarity, in the Latin original, as in the English translation, the words **libido** (lust), **cupiditatem** (desire) and **sordes** (filth) do not necessarily have sexual associations. One might have a lust for food, or power or even fresh air. The three most common words for negatively connotated desire in Augustine's works, 'concupiscentia', 'cupiditas' and 'libido', have several interpretations which have been intensively analysed by Augustinian scholars. Bonner suggests 'sinful longing'[47] whereas Lössl suggests 'carnal hankering.'[48] The Latin **carnales** is similar in meaning to the English word carnal, and Augustine repeats the word 35 times in his *Confessions*. In the case of infant concupiscence, the context makes clear that Augustine is referring to sexual lust. The words he uses when describing his own sexual lust are similar to those used when describing the lust he sees in infants.

The average parent will readily accept that infants can be naughty, perhaps sinful even. A parent describing infants as carnal, weltering in filth and scratching off the itch of lust suggests sexual deviance. Could a perversion, since censored, have tempted Augustine to fantasise about infant sexuality? To me, the father of two delightful daughters, present at the birth of each of them, these descriptions of filth and lust in infants burst out of the page. Augustine had offspring but he and I have very different views of children. I read my daughters to sleep from a child's storybook when they were infants. As they fell to slumber, I saw purity in their well-scrubbed faces, blushed lips and dark lashes. I am at a loss to understand how their innocence could be corrupted into 'wickedness and filth', much less into carnal desire, but this is what Augustine wrote, and it is what Western Christians are required to accept.

Some academics have picked up on the sinister quality in his writing. Augustine has been eagerly and thoroughly psychoanalysed. His possible Oedipal crisis;[49] homosexual urges[50] and narcissism[51] have all been detailed, discussed and dissected. Augustine admitted mental torments, writing about his desires fighting between themselves. He complained, 'They tear the mind apart by the mutual incompatibility of the wills' (Book VIII, page 149). In the year 386, when he was 31 years old and in the throes of one bout of existential anguish, Augustine wrote that, prostrate and weeping bitterly over his uncleanness, he heard the voice of a child repeating the words 'tolle lege' meaning 'take up and read.' He thought that the voice was coming from a nearby house: he was not sure exactly where (Book VIII, page 126).[4] He could not tell if the child's voice was that of a boy or girl, but the phrase echoed over and over in his head. It seems likely this episode came to him as a daydream, or it might have been a literary invention.

Augustine tells us that he picked up a copy of the Bible – presumably he was still daydreaming – and it fell open at a passage that exhorted him to turn to Christ and '…make not provision for the flesh, in concupiscence.' Augustine took this message from his subconscious as a mandate to reform. Some writers view *Confessions* as a pronouncement of Augustine's conversion to Christianity, but he does not mention Christianity or Manichaeanism. As Lane Fox and other historians point out there is some doubt that Augustine ever in fact converted to Christianity at all and the mental turmoil that preceded the episode of resolve that he described seems overdone. We noted earlier that Augustine rejected Christianity in his teenage years. At the time of the *Confessions*, in 382, the Roman emperor Theodosius I issued a decree of death for all Manichaean monks. This seems a more likely motivation for Augustine's sudden endorsement of Christianity. Soon afterwards, in 391, Theodosius declared Christianity to be the only legitimate religion for the Roman Empire. The evidence is circumstantial, but it suggests that Augustine's apostasy from Manichaeanism might have been more a conversion of convenience and self-preservation than a genuine change of heart. After all, he had chosen to turn away from Christianity when it suited his circumstances.

Augustine writes in a tormented manner, describing sexual desire or libido as a disease, obsessing over the wickedness of carnal lust and claiming that infants are cursed with sin and lust. His inexhaustible preoccupation with rejecting his own sinfulness and sexual lust is bizarre. According to his biographer, Possidius, Augustine spent the last days of his life weeping over his sins. No other society, nor any animal, repudiates sex as Augustine does. His effusive remonstration against the '…itch of lust' he perceives in his infant self is suspicious. To paraphrase Shakespeare's Queen Gertrude 'The (bishop) doth protest too much, methinks.' I have no professional training but I cannot help spotting that Augustine's neurotic diatribe against lust exhibits features associated with a specific mental disturbance.

Reaction formation is a clinically recognised defence mechanism in which a person perceives their true feelings or desires to be socially, or in some cases legally, unacceptable, and so they overplay their opposition in an attempt to convince themselves and others that the reverse is true. Here is a scholarly description of the disorder:

> It's believed that reaction formation develops as a way to cope with the pressure and stress caused by the original feeling that they have identified as being bad and with the possibility of their true feelings or desires being discovered. For example, if a person has a particular sexual fetish that they feel is shameful, they may take every opportunity to condemn those who share the fetish in order to demonstrate to others that they are 'normal'[52]

*Confessions* is generally interpreted by theologians as a religious term for Augustine's confession of faith. However, the intense rant about his sinfulness seems less a pronouncement of religious conversion and more an admission and ousting of his demons. Nobody had called a book *Confessions* before, but in the Hebrew scriptures confessions of sins were already well represented. In Roman law a confession before a judge was considered to have the same effect as a judgement, and for Augustine, 'confession' (confessio in the original Latin) meant an accusation of oneself. There seems little doubt Augustine was accusing himself of lust: we have noted that he mentions lust 44 times. What is less clear is the focus of all this lust. Researchers have suggested that if Augustine's conversion was not from Manichaeanism, perhaps it was a rejection of homosexual lust. Some commentators have suggested Augustine might have been homosexual or bisexual, and we have noted that in Augustine's time the distinction between homosexual and heterosexual was blurred. In Book III Augustine writes of his unholy loves. 'To Carthage I came, where there sang all around me in my ears a cauldron of unholy loves. I loved not yet, yet I loved to love, and out of a deep-seated want, I hated myself for wanting not.' Some have interpreted his reference to 'unholy loves' as homosexual loves, but homosexuality was not unholy in Rome during Augustine's time, at least not for men taking the dominant or penetrative role.

After he left Milan in 390, his writings show an increasing degree of internal torment. Reflecting on the content of his literature, he might have had a preference for infants rather than adults. Paedophilia, sexual activity or attraction to underage minors was certainly unholy. It seems at least possible that Augustine might have been a paedophile (paedophiles are not necessarily child abusers – see chapter 11). We have noted his peculiar references to the lust and filth he saw in infants. According to the FBI the single most common rationalisation of all paedophiles is to blame the victim. Law enforcement officers, investigating cases of child sexual exploitation, emphasise 'The offender may claim he was seduced by the victim, that the victim initiated the sexual activity, or that the victim is promiscuous or even a prostitute.'[53] Recent reports suggest that the church would certainly have suppressed any evidence of paedophilia that might have existed from Augustine's time. His writings do not refer directly to paedophilia, and knowing his writing would be circulated, perhaps he was not willing to broadcast his compulsive weakness. Or he might have been so mortified by his loathsome appetite he could not bring himself to point directly to the true focus of his lust, a common attitude of paedophiles. He alludes to his possible compulsion when he says he was prompted to give up his sinful lust by a child. Augustine's writings repeatedly accuse children of sexual desire; now he tells us that a child told him to mend his ways. His account of this messaging is dreamily vague: he was not sure where the voice was coming from or whether it was that of a boy or girl. Why did he choose to imagine a child prevailing upon him to give up sinful lust? Was this a child he had been attracted to, or one he was tempted to sexually abuse?

Psychologists tell us that paedophiles often hate themselves for their repulsive behaviour, but they cannot help their urges. Researching this possible connection, I found echoes of Augustine's writings in the recorded testimonies of convicted paedophiles. In correspondence directly with Dr Hammel-Zabin, (a prison therapist) Alan, (a convicted paedophile) admits sexually abusing more than 1000 boys. Alan was a boy scout leader and a deacon in his local church. He never shows remorse in his letters, but he does say he despises his compulsion.[54] Augustine's conversation might not have been a religious conversation away from Manichaeanism to Christianity, but a conversion away from his paedophilic urges towards celibacy. Augustine already believed in God. 'The "name of Christ",' as Augustine's acclaimed biographer Peter Brown puts it, 'had always been present in whatever religion he adopted.'[55] Lane Fox agrees. 'It is a conversion away from sex and ambition.' (p289).[56]

Whether or not Augustine was a paedophile is, of course, a matter of conjecture. What is not in doubt is that Augustine's view of infants was depraved, as our review of his writings confirms. To support his cause Augustine coined the word concupiscence, signifying 'physical desire, especially sexual longing or lust,' to describe exactly what he meant. The expression comes from the Church Latin verb concupiscere: the first syllable, con- (meaning with) + cupi(d)- (meaning desiring) + -escere (a verb-forming suffix denoting beginning of a process or state). He stipulated that newborns are concupiscent and that their sexual desire manifests itself into infancy, childhood and beyond. He insisted it cannot be removed by baptism or any other means. He repeated his view about infant lust in letters to the British monk Pelagius as we noted earlier.

The custom of papal canonisation had not yet been established when he died in 430 AD, but Augustine was made a saint by popular acclaim. Augustine's numerous theological, philosophical and spiritual works helped lay the foundation for much of Christian thought until the present time. Attitudes have rightly changed in 1,600 years, but perhaps less so for priests according to experts Thomas Doyle, Richard Sipe and Patrick Wall, co-authors of *Sex, Priests, and Secret Codes: The Catholic Church's 2,000 Year Paper Trail of Sexual Abuse.*[23] Child abuse by clerics stretches back unbroken through Augustine's time and Western Christianity remains tainted with his distorted view of children. Modern standards of moral conduct transcend Augustinian scruples, which are out of step with enlightened ethical values. In the next chapter and in those that follow we will look at how Western mores continue to be influenced by Augustine's outdated and abhorrent ideas.

# 2

# THE DARK IMPRINT FROM AUGUSTINE'S SIN OF SEXUAL LUST

My Bible storybook in primary school showed a picture of Adam and Eve with a drawing of a serpent and Eve holding an apple. I was not old enough to associate original sin with sex, not even when the text explained that 'Original sin is the carnal sin of Adam and Eve revisited upon new-borns'. The Bible story of creation will be familiar to most Britons. For those readers whose memory fails them, the Old Testament traces the beginning of life on earth as it was understood about 3000 years ago (Genesis 3:1–8). Briefly, the story goes like this.

A superhuman being, God, created a perfect world. He made Adam and put him in a beautiful garden called Eden. Adam was told he could do anything he wanted, except eat fruit from the tree of the knowledge of good and evil (life and death). Adam got bored and so God provided a female mate, Eve. Eve was tricked by a serpent into eating the forbidden fruit from the tree of the knowledge of good and evil. She tempted Adam with some of the fruit and he ate it too. (The taking and giving of fruit is seen as a metaphor for the sex act.) After they had disentangled themselves, Adam and Eve realised that they were naked and hid themselves in shame. Because of their disobedience, Adam and Eve fell from God's grace and were banished from the Garden of Eden into the imperfect world we all inhabit. The defiance of these first humans is the source of the so-called original sin that has tainted mankind ever since.

Science has shown that the biblical creation account is not literally true: the story is a fable and Adam and Eve are not historical figures. Far from man falling from a perfect world, evolution explains that life on earth is constantly advancing and improving, becoming better adapted to its environment. Even conservative scholars agree publicly that the Genesis account of creation is genetically impossible. Dennis Venema, a biologist and senior fellow at the Christian group BioLogos Foundation admits, 'With the mapping of the human genome, it's clear that modern humans emerged from other primates as a large population – long before the Genesis time frame of a few thousand years ago. And given the genetic variation of people today, scientists can't get that population size below 10,000 people at any time in our evolutionary history.' In chapter 12 we read that this clarity of evidence does not stop some faith schools dishonestly teaching creationism as a valid theory, as parents also testify.[25]

Nothing in early scripture speaks directly of original sin. The biblical basis for the doctrine is found in the New Testament where Adam is identified as the man through whom death came into the world.[57] Psalm 51:5 states that we all come into the world as sinners: 'Behold, I was brought forth in iniquity, and in sin my mother conceived me.' The concept of an original sin was first mentioned by Irenaeus, Bishop of Lyons, in the second century. In the third century, Origen wrote that 'Every soul that is born into flesh is soiled by the filth of wickedness and sin…'[58]

Controversy flourishes among Christian groups as to the exact understanding of original sin. According to doctrine, babies come into the world bearing the wrath of God because they are born with a sinful nature. Critics from all sides have condemned the doctrine's apparent contradictions and the imputation of guilt on newborns. Original sin is a stain of filth and wickedness which will, left unbaptised, justify God in condemning a baby to eternal banishment from heaven, and all for a sin never actually committed. That idea contradicts our sense of justice. We had no existence before our birth, so we could hardly have done anything wrong before we existed. Further, claiming that babies are born with the stain of sin is to charge the creator, God, with creating sinners. How can humans be sinners when they are created in the likeness of a perfect God, and so on.[59] The idea of a baby incurring blameless guilt raises a multitude of unanswered questions concerning the origins of evil in the world, but the earliest Christian writers all agree on the fundamental doctrine of original sin and the remedial effect of baptism.

History had to wait until Augustine for original sin to proclaim its association with sexual lust. We noted in the previous chapter what Augustine thought about infant lust. He considered the Bible story was incomplete and added his own licentious spin, claiming that original sin was not just about disobedience towards God, but included the libidinous lust felt by Adam and Eve, which he called concupiscence. Augustine equated the beginning of sexual desire with Adam and Eve's mythical act of human disobedience. Despite controversy over the roots of original sin and baptism, there is general agreement that before St Augustine no one had connected either original sin or baptism with sex. It was Augustine who asserted that every child is born guilty of original sin arising from the sexual lust of Adam and Eve. Now we will look at how a split in the established church resulted in Western Christians seeing infants in Augustine's sexually culpable terms while everywhere else in the world babies are born spotlessly innocent.

Augustine fought fiercely with his intellectual contemporaries to connect concupiscence with original sin. According to Augustine's teaching, humans are born lusting to be bad. In his later work *The City of God,* Augustine argues God is source of all goodness. He reasoned that since the absence of good is evil (Manichaeism) so humans must be evil without grace from God. We cannot be good and gain salvation, which grants admission to heaven and life hereafter, without the aid of God's grace. In order to receive grace, you have to join the Christian Church. The British monk Pelagius rejected Augustine's concept of original sin and insisted that babies are not stained by Adam's sin. Humans can be good and obtain salvation by the exercise of their own free will alone, and do not require the help of divine grace.[60] If people can be good on their own account, they might consider they have little need of the Catholic Church. At the Council of Ephesus in 431 the Catholic Church sided with Augustine, condemning Pelagianism as heresy.

The Eastern Orthodox Church accepts that the first human couple disobeyed God in the Garden of Eden, but not that this disobedience involved sex. Eastern Orthodoxy never adopted Augustine's idea that babies inherit original sin. According to the Eastern Church, sexual intercourse occurred after the Fall and babies are not stained with sexual guilt. Only in Augustine's account did the first parents decide to disobey God and give way to lust, originating the sexual sin that is inherited by all Christians in the Western Church. Although 1054 is the date usually given for the beginning of the Great Schism between the Eastern and Western branches of the Catholic Church, the rot started with Augustine. According to Augustine and the Western Churches, we all share this unmerited, misogynistic and carnal sin of the fall of the mythical first humans, from the time we are born. In his book *Conversions to Confessions,* Lane Fox has pointed out that the foundation of the doctrine of original sin accepted by the Church was probably based on a mistranslation by Augustine.

Nevertheless, in 1546 at The Council of Trent, the Catholic Church formalised Augustine's idea that the original sin deserved through Adam and Eve's sexual lust is transferred from generation to generation by propagation – that is to say during the act of sexual intercourse that leads to conception. The Council explicitly ruled out the possibility that original sin was transferred by 'imitation', in order to discount the idea that human beings just copied the example set by their parents and others.[61] This sexual formulation of original sin was accepted by Protestant reformers such as Martin Luther and John Calvin, and thus passed into most of the leading Protestant Churches.

For 1,600 years, original sin, with its subtext of guilt and shame about sex, has been sustained by Christian doctrine and handed down through the generations. This unpleasant Augustinian slur continues to infect babies today, who are pronounced tainted by their parents' carnal lust in the act of conceiving them. The nature attached to original sin by Augustine is clearly stated in Christian rites and rituals, and original sin remains an article of faith in Western Churches. Followers confirm they think babies are born sinful every time they declaim their tenets of belief. Christians recite various versions of the Nicene Creed, but all denominations include the line '…one baptism for the forgiveness of sins.' That Christians really do believe in the inherent sinfulness of babies is further shown when they have their babies baptised.

According to doctrine only the Virgin Mary was free from stain of sin, although scripture is somewhat ambivalent.[7] The title Immaculate Conception was conferred on the mother of Jesus because having been inseminated by a ghost, albeit a Holy Ghost, she was free from concupiscence and clean of stain from original sin.[62] (In recent years churches have been swapping **Holy Ghost** for **Holy Spirit**, presumably because the term ghost had gained awkward connotations in fiction. The King James Bible typically refers to Holy Ghost, the Catechism of the Catholic Church (CCC) says Holy Ghost and throughout the twentieth century that was the term used.)

Let us return to Augustine's preoccupation with the filth and lust he saw in infants. Not only did Augustine claim that babies are concupiscent, but he insisted that this lust in the baptised infant '…is not removed all at once, so as to exist in it no longer.'[5] His teaching that some concupiscence remains in infants is also a tenet of Christian doctrine.[6] Some Christians might be unaware that their religion considers infants sexually lustful, but Augustine's ideas are central to the faith and required study for novitiates. The doctrine has been variously reinterpreted by modern reformers, but there is general agreement amongst theologians today. All humans in the Western

Church are stained with the guilt of Adam's sinful lust, which is transmitted by sexual intercourse and is only partially removed by baptism. These beliefs might affect the attitude of clerical men and women towards children. That could go some way towards explaining why child abuse is more prevalent amongst clerics, and we will examine the evidence for this more fully in chapter 11. A wayward priest, indoctrinated with the notion that infants are already soiled by the carnal stain of original sin, might see minors as valid targets for sexual predation, if not wilfully then perhaps subliminally. It might lower the psychological barrier, making it easier for a cleric to violate the innocence of a child, or it might tempt a cleric to fantasise that children really are concupiscent.

In 2018, the Pennsylvania Investigating Grand Jury reported one case of cCSA where a priest raped a young girl, got her pregnant and arranged an abortion. The bishop expressed his feelings in a letter:

'This is a very difficult time in your life, and I realize how upset you are. I too share your grief.'

But the letter was not for the girl. It was addressed to the priest, the rapist.[63] Even taking account of 'ingroup favouritism,' that is the bishop's natural inclination to favour his colleague, this cold dismissal of the abused girl is extraordinary. Apparently, the bishop believed the girl had seduced the priest. If he accepted Augustine's claim that children are concupiscent that would help account for his unsympathetic attitude and the implicit misattribution of blame in his letter.

All clergy will be familiar with Augustine's teaching on the connection between infantile sexual lust and original sin. At a recent hearing of the UK child abuse inquiry, Christopher Jamison, abbot primate of the English Benedictine Congregation, said that the reason monk-priests had perpetrated abuse was because their training focused too much on doctrine. There should be no doubt that clergy take their faith seriously and some clerics who have abused children believe the ideas with which they have been indoctrinated.[64] In Pennsylvania, a priest forced a nine-year-old boy to give him oral sex and then rinsed out the boy's mouth with holy water 'to purify him'.[65]

Scholars suggest that Western society is especially disposed to regard children as erotic. They point out that our culture has 'enthusiastically sexualised the child while denying just as enthusiastically that it was doing any such thing'. Child pageants in the United States, Western social media and certain spheres of the pop music industry are seen by many as sexually charged, and inappropriately so, for minors.[66] Surprisingly the literature does not attempt to make a connection between the doctrine of infant concupiscence or the unhealthy doctrine of penance, and this libertine, exclusively Western attitude. The trees are less apparent when we are ourselves trapped in the forest.

There is no merit in inflicting original sin on newborns, either for the child or for parents and fellow Christians. The only obvious benefit is to the Church's leaders, in helping to maintain privilege and power over their flock. My long-standing connections with Catholic and Anglican communities suggest that Christian churches are especially autocratic and authoritarian institutions. It seems that ecclesiastics uphold Augustine's doctrine of original sin for their own good and for the good of the Church, at the expense of infants. In the previous chapter we examined the historical basis for infants being considered sexually aware by the Church and later we will look at the shadow this dark side of the doctrine might be casting. My parents would not have believed me to be guilty of sexual lust the moment I came into the world. Nor is it likely anyone else in the community into which I was born believed babies are defiled with sexual lust. However, in validating my baptism they all accepted, and assisted in perpetuating, that perverse judgement laid against me by St Augustine and confirmed by Christian doctrine.

After the Reformation, the C of E retained most of the core Catholic beliefs including the doctrines of penance and original sin and many of the rites and rituals that go with them. The C of E Book of Common Prayer includes the lines '...the flesh lusteth always contrary to the spirit; and therefore in every person born into this world, it deserveth God's wrath and damnation.' The Presbyterian view is stated in their Standards: 'It must always be kept in mind that original sin in its wide sense includes both guilt and depravity. In this sense it includes the whole state of sin in which men, descended from Adam, are born. In its narrower sense it denotes hereditary depravity as distinguished from imputed guilt.' In recent years the Catholic Church has stepped back from claiming that original sin inflicts guilt on children, but babies continue to be baptised because the church still considers they are 'Born with a fallen human nature and tainted by original sin'. These Augustinian punishments of sinfulness, guilt and the wrath of God are being inflicted today upon children in some faith schools, as evidenced in chapter 12.

Nominal Christians might not realise that the story of original sin related above is the exclusive preserve of the West, with all the characteristic Latin shame and anxiety that has been shaped by it. We have noted how children are sexualised in the West compared with other cultures. In his acclaimed book, *Born Bad*, historian James Boyce explains how Augustine's ideas continue to influence the Western view of human nature in multiple subtle ways.[67]

Boyce claims the legacy of original sin takes many forms, including the characteristic self-reproach of Western people – the feelings of guilt and inadequacy associated not with just doing wrong, but with being wrong. He overlooks the contribution that years of ritualistic self-castigation in childhood might make to our propensity to feel guilty and inadequate, but Boyce rightly points to the distinctive discontent of Westerners. Our advertising offers hope of wholeness, happiness and virtue, by purchasing this new merchandise, adopting this new lifestyle or accepting this liberating advice. Trendy diets, self-improvement programs or gym training all help counter our feelings of guilt and inadequacy associated with being inherently blameworthy. These subconscious feelings of guilt and inadequacy are the legacies of St Augustine's obsession with sin that has been hard-wired into our infant neurons.

In no other culture are humans understood to be born bad; no other society considers its members permanently corrupted from birth. Nor do any creatures in the animal kingdom consider sex or libidinous lust to be wrong. Augustine was alone, both in seeing wickedness in sex and in judging living things before they have had an opportunity to commit an immoral act. Augustine had an abnormal hang-up about sex, and for 1,600 years his ideas have misled Christians in the west to believe that sex is bad and something to be ashamed of. Not only is safe, consensual sex enjoyable, it is beneficial for mental and physical health, it harms no one and fosters a wonderfully intimate bond between lovers. Without Augustine's intervention, Christians in the West would believe that sex is good and exactly the way their God designed it, like adherents of its antecedent Judaism. In Jewish law, sex is not considered to be shameful, sinful or obscene. Instead, it is seen as an urge similar to hunger and thirst, and should be dealt with similarly at an appropriate time and in a proper place.[68] After all, the Bible tells that Adam and Eve were unmarried when God commanded them to 'be fruitful and multiply' (Genesis 1:28).

The Augustinian version of original sin dates from a time far removed from our world. Apart from being exploited, by today's standards children lived under poor conditions and generally experienced a lack of respect from adults. Infant mortality was relatively high and sickness was commonplace. Without effective birth control, children were often regarded as an encumbrance. Since ancient times the family unit has changed, children are protected from abuse, health care has improved and attitudes have shifted. The Latin Church's preoccupation with infant guilt remains an absurd hangover from Augustinian antiquity. The church still clings to its long-standing control of education in Britain, but it is hard to see how the government can continue to justify that position, given the growing recognition of Augustine's true nature.

Recent surveys of the adult population generally support the findings of Eurostat's Eurobarometer survey conducted in May 2019. While 50% of UK adults indicated Christian affiliation, just 6% actually take religion on board.[69] Young people are less religious still.

As we noted in the introduction, only 1% of 18 – 24-year-olds identify as Christian. The YouGov pollsters asked if they believe in God, and just 25% said they did. A further 19% believe in some non-God-like 'spiritual greater power' and 30% believe in no God or spiritual power whatsoever. After enduring RE in school, more young people say religion is a force for evil than a force for good. When asked which figures have influence on their lives, religious leaders came out bottom: only 12% felt influenced by them.[70] In another poll, around two thirds of teachers (65%) revealed that they were raised in a religious household but 61% of them reported belonging to no religion.[9] These apostate teachers are forced to mask their beliefs in order to indoctrinate others in a faith they have rejected, and we will return to this topic later.

Religious polls show some surprising inconsistencies. As Wikipedia points out, the wording of the question affects the outcome of polls on religious affiliation.[71] This is apparent when comparing the results of the Scottish census with those of the English and Welsh census. An ICM poll for The Guardian in 2006 asked the question 'Which religion do you yourself belong to?' with a response of 64% stating 'Christian' and 26% stating 'None'. In the same survey, 63% claimed they were not religious with just 33% claiming they were. Those who are committed to religious belief will consistently indicate their religiosity, but for many others religion is extraneous to their lives. They might casually tick the 'Christian' box on the census because, for example, their parents are Christian, or they went to a Christian school. I was reared a Christian and I still belong to my local church choir, engage in socials and contribute tithes. Like other youngsters I unburdened myself of religion as soon as I was free to do so, but I often identify as C of E in polls, although I am a disbeliever.

# 3

# HOW BRITONS ARE HARD-WIRED WITH AUGUSTINIAN GUILT

The mental affliction known as **Catholic guilt** refers to the experience, frequently reported by Christians, of feeling remorse for knowing or thinking they have done something sinful (bad or wrong).[72] Sometimes the meaning is widened to include feeling guilty about not being able to meet all the demands of one's religion.[73] Many studies of Catholic guilt have been published. Some are insufficiently rigorous or inconclusive, but there seems to be a consensus that religious affiliation is related to maladaptive interpersonal guilt.[74,75] Academic literature has specifically identified religiously imposed guilt in Christian communities.[76] A 2013 YouGov poll found that religious people in general feel more guilt than others do (but Catholics do not feel especially guilty about sexual sins, apparently).[77] Why are feelings of guilt so deeply ingrained among Christians?

From age six my siblings and I attended church service each morning, every day of the year. The Christian hymns and prayers I remember from childhood were primarily about my sinfulness, and the need for penitence and atonement together with pleas for mercy from an all-powerful God. My childhood experience was rather fervent compared to the experience of most children today, but otherwise nothing has changed much, and church services continue to focus on the same negative concepts that can be traced back to Augustine. The extant RC Holy Mass contains 18 references to **sin** and 25 pleas for **mercy** or **forgiveness**; **grace** and **love** are each mentioned once.[78] The current C of E Common Worship Eucharist for every Sunday service cites **sin** 24 times, and calls for **mercy** or **forgiveness** 26 times, while **grace** and **love** (from God) get just two mentions.[12] In schools and in churches, similar prayers are repeated over and over, week after week. The prospect of self-improvement is unrecognised here. Augustine denied that humans have free will, so there is no prospect of betterment and no credit is given in his theology for any good that his followers might be capable of.

Most Christian prayers involve an admission of culpability or sin and an appeal for forgiveness and mercy. My mother would quote 'The family that prays together stays together', and we recited the rosary prayers on our knees every evening. One of the most popular prayers in the RC tradition, the rosary is a succession of devotions to the Virgin Mary, mother of God.[79] It takes followers about half an hour to recite. Named after the string of beads used to keep count of the constituent elements of 53 reprises of the **Hail Mary** prayer, it is punctuated after each decade by the **Lord's Prayer** and **Glory Be**, finishing with the **Confiteor** (prayer of penitence) for our sinfulness. Altogether **sinning** or **trespassing** is admitted 60 times in the space of 30 minutes. From the time I could speak, I repeated daily:

> *I confess to Almighty God, to blessed Mary ever Virgin, to blessed Michael the Archangel, to blessed John the Baptist, to the holy Apostles Peter and Paul, to all the Saints, that I have sinned exceedingly, in thought, word and deed, through my fault, through my fault, through my own grievous fault.* [Here we would strike our breasts three times to emphasise our culpability.] *Therefore I beseech the blessed Mary, ever Virgin, blessed Michael the Archangel, blessed John the Baptist, the holy Apostles Peter and Paul, all the Saints, to pray to the Lord our God for me. Amen.'* [80]

In acts of worship, Christian faith schools and churches all over Britain urge children to recite the above Confiteor, or a similar chant, 'Forgive me, I have sinned... through my own fault.'[12]

The term faith school is commonly applied to a state-funded school in the UK that has a particular religious character or formal links with a religious body. Faith schools enjoy concessions regarding selection in admissions. Although they have to follow the national curriculum in other subjects, in RE they are free to only teach children about their own religion. All schools are supposed to cover other religions, but later we will see the law is often ignored and these lessons can be sectarian in practice. Commercial media producers, such as Fertile Heart, Youth for Christ and others, specialise in providing daily prayers and teaching resources for schools. Ten:Ten Resources produce slick PowerPoint presentations to add visual impact to school indoctrination, helping to drum in Augustine's guilt-ridden mentality with a version of the Confiteor reproduced above (in the Anglican Communion a similar version of the Confiteor is used, called The Penitential Act).[11] These professionals charge schools £588 for an annual subscription, funded by the taxpayer. In faith schools, prayers are often led by an authoritatively robed clergyman. Of course, schools do not deliberately set out to sexualise their pupils, but according to the NSPCC, an authority figure or a dominant and persistent person causing a child to feel guilt and shame is a familiar method of child sexual grooming.[81]

St Philip's RC Home for Boys, where I spent many of my schooldays, was established by the Sisters of Charity of St Vincent de Paul in the late 19th century, when a local benefactor bequeathed the building to them. (Fig. 2.) The nuns, distinctive for their winged headdress of starched cotton (the cornette), governed the home. Most of the boys were, like me, from broken homes or they were orphaned.[82] We attended classes at St Philip's Oratory School, about a mile distant and we trooped in line with one of the sisters. Apart from prayers at assembly, religious instruction occupied one lesson every day, and my memory is of reading about and reflecting upon **transgression**,

**culpability** and **punishment**. **Grace** was something we received, when God could be persuaded to give it to us, to neutralise our inherent sinfulness. Teachings about **redemption** and **life everlasting** were part of our religious lessons of course, but these concepts are hollow to a young person. We learned we were intrinsically bad because of the Fall (of Adam and Eve) and we must ask for mercy, not of God directly, since sinful humans are unworthy, but by intercession through Mary, the mother of God or by way of various saints. Every morning at assembly, the entire school recited the Confiteor, with its mortifying **mea culpa** (through my fault) self-affirmation of culpability.

**Figure 2.  St Philip's RC Home for Boys, Edgbaston, Birmingham**

Nowadays most children in Christian primary schools recite a shortened version of the Confiteor, but the penitential prayer still contains the elements of penitence, deference and misplaced reckoning. It requires children to pick over their misdeeds and plead for forgiveness and mercy, withdrawn from and ignoring any harm resulting from wrongdoing. I believe that repeating self-abusive prayers throughout my childhood implanted enduring notions of discredit that ultimately dismantled my sense of self-respect and self-worth.

The power of self-affirmation, or autosuggestion (Méthode Coué), is documented. Apothecary Émile Coué pioneered this self-administered mind training method more than 100 years ago and it has since been widely adopted in business, sports and personal development. The technique, which is thought to be related to the placebo effect,[83] is a means of influencing the subconscious mind by verbal and/or visual self-affirmations, to change one's own beliefs or modes of behaviour. The most famous example is Émile's own: 'Every day, in every way, I'm getting better and better.' Dr Joe Kiff, a consultant clinical psychologist at Dudley and Walsall Mental Health Partnership NHS Trust, describes the process thus:

> *Autosuggestion (or autogenous training) is a process by which an individual trains the subconscious mind to believe something, or systematically schematises the person's own mental associations, usually for a given purpose. This is accomplished through self-hypnosis methods or repetitive, constant self-affirmations, and may be seen as a form of self-induced brainwashing. The acceptance of autosuggestion may be quickened through mental visualization of that which the individual would like to believe. Its success is typically correlated with the consistency of its use and the length of time over which it is used. Autosuggestion can be seen as an aspect of prayer.*[84]

For obvious reasons, research has tended to concentrate on positive affirmations, but if a positive affirmation has a positive effect, it follows that a negative affirmation will have a negative effect. Repeatedly affirming one's own culpability is a mind-training practice, analogous to autosuggestion, that is liable to inculcate feelings of personal guilt or at least exacerbate any guilty emotions. From personal experience

I can say that the ritual of raking over every minor failing, apologising for dubious wrongdoings (often unrecognised as harmful) and expressing contrition and regret, followed by begging for forgiveness and mercy, contributed to feelings of guilt and shame.

A detailed guide to reciting prayers for children is provided by the Canterbury Diocesan Board of Education, to primary school heads. The instruction guide, titled *Doing prayer – meditation and imagery*, seems to confirm Dr Kiff's description. The board of education advises teachers to arrange their charges. 'The legs are uncrossed. Feet are flat on the floor. Hands are resting on the lap and, most importantly, the back is straight.' The technique the teachers are following is described as 'evoking and seeing pictures in the mind.' It 'provides the chance to control that ability to imagine and to use the imagination to some purpose.' The New Statesman carried an article by Nick Cohen detailing how the ritual is applied in practice, making a convincing comparison with self-hypnosis.[85] Ecclesiastics understand perfectly well how the method works: they talk of how schools 'subliminally proselytise children.'[86]

Research supports an association between unhealthy internalisation and religion.[87] People who blame themselves for the results of their behaviour have an internal locus of control (LOC), according to Julian Rotter who coined the expression over half a century ago. That is to say, they internalise outcomes in contrast to those who have an external LOC. Externals are more inclined to see outcomes as being determined by luck, fate, chance or more powerful others. Guilt evokes in us a focus on our behaviour and our interaction with the world outside ourselves, whereas shame evokes an internal focus on our defective, inadequate selves. Those inclined to internalise outcomes will tend to feel shame. Persisting with self-abasing prayers is likely, over time, to cast a shadow over a child's self-worth. Feelings of shame can be corrosive and debilitating, affecting one's core sense of self and we will expand later on how this burden plays out.[88]

The distinguished anthropologist Ruth Benedict categorised differences between a shame culture, which she identified in Japan, compared with the guilt culture she saw in Western societies.[89] Shame cultures are concerned with how one's behaviour appears to outsiders. Shame cultures rely on personal embarrassment and dishonour to promote socially acceptable behaviour and discourage conduct thought to be undesirable. Guilt cultures, in contrast, focus on an internalised conviction of what constitutes bad behaviour, to encourage good behaviour. Guilt cultures rely on atonement and repentance, confession and forgiveness for social control. Guilt cultures are thought to be healthier because in a guilt culture people are liable to feel their behaviour is bad, whereas in a shame culture personal disgrace is liable to make people feel they are intrinsically bad. Western societies, following Augustine, straddle these cultures, taking the worst from each of them. Augustine taught that humans are fundamentally bad and inclined to wickedness. His doctrine on original sin elicits feelings of personal blame and shame. In addition, emotions of guilt as a consequence of bad behaviour are not triggered by what a believer's conscience tells them, but by what religious leaders say. Christian guilt culture removes the individual will to conscience, which might initiate feelings of healthy guilt, and instead passes power to priests and bishops who manipulate the conditions of guilt and the forgiveness of guilt. Thus, interpersonal guilt remains and can never be satisfactorily remediated.

With its auxiliary breast-beating ritual, the **through my fault** incantation takes the form of another mind-transforming technique, the mantra. Mantras exist in many disciplines and cultures, but the earliest forms originated in India. **Mantra** in Sanskrit means **tool** or **instrument of the mind**, and there is scientific evidence to suggest that chanting is a brain-changing exercise. Neuroscientist Dr James Hartzell, researcher at Spain's Basque Centre on Cognition, Brain and Language, who studied 21 Hindu scholars, coined the term the **Sanskrit Effect**. He discovered that memorising mantras increases the size of brain regions associated with cognitive function.[90] In a pilot study in 2017, scientists at Linköping University, Sweden, analysed mantra meditation using a control group tasked with finger tapping.[91] The scientists concluded that training in mantra meditation suppresses activity within parts of the brain known to be the neurological basis for the self, and significantly, the finger tapping exercise was crucial in suppression. In fact, the researchers report a positive outcome because that is what they were looking for, but they concluded that chanting does produce a measurable physical change in the human brain.

Cutting edge research in biology shows our early life experiences have a profound and long-lasting effect on physical and mental health throughout life. Emerging results from Behavioural Epigenetics suggests that mind-transforming techniques might permanently influence behaviour, personality, health and even appearance.[92] The epigenome, a dynamic layer of information associated with DNA that differs between individuals, can be altered through various experiences and environments. Epigenetics in psychology provides a framework for understanding how the expression of genes is influenced by experiences and the environment to produce individual differences in behaviour, cognition, personality and mental health. In time this research might help explain how Augustine's unhelpful tenets have wormed their way into Western mores.

I have explained how, in my schooldays, Christian indoctrination was based around self-castigating prayers, and infants in many Christian primary schools regularly practise similar prayers today. But some schools are using more sophisticated techniques to evangelise their pupils. As we noted earlier, mass media producers are in on the act, offering compelling PowerPoint presentations for ritual school prayers that include a version of the Penitential Act, inflicting self-censure and guilt and asking for forgiveness and mercy.[12] Psychologists generally agree that negative self-talk is damaging. Stress management specialist Elizabeth Scott comments: 'Negative self-talk is any inner dialogue you have with yourself that may be limiting your ability to believe in yourself and your own abilities, and to reach your potential. It is any thought that diminishes your ability to make positive changes in your life or your confidence in yourself to do so. So negative self-talk can not only be stressful, but it can really stunt your success.'[93]

Research has established that certain personality types are innately predisposed to feelings of guilt and self-blame.[94] Bright, imaginative young people often suffer from self-doubt and insecurity and requiring such children to recite a mantra of culpability is liable to exacerbate distress, which seems especially cruel. Guilt-proneness (the tendency to feel bad about a specific behaviour) is more likely to result from nurturing, whereas shame-proneness (the tendency to feel bad about oneself) relates to a variety of life problems.[95] Other factors in one's upbringing can contribute to feelings of self-doubt and insecurity of course, and it seems heartless to demand self-abusive prayers of a child who is already insecure. Constantly making infants focus on their weakness and faults is at best unhelpful, even for well-adjusted children. To inflict feelings of guilt on a child for non-faults, such as thinking about sex, seems pathetic.

I believe my persistent self-affirmation of guilt and pleading for forgiveness and mercy implanted a lifelong feeling of blameworthiness in my mind. For much of my life, I retained a bizarre sense of personal blame whenever anything went wrong around me. Given a self-blame mental schema, it is possible to find oneself culpable in almost any circumstance and I diligently personalised events in my life, taking responsibility for adversity and creating a wretched cycle of guilt, remorse and self-denigration. When a problem occurred around me, even if I was not to blame, if I had neglected to foresee it and so arrange things as to prevent it then I could not help feeling myself to be blameworthy by default. Recognising how these thought patterns became ingrained was the first step in helping me break the cycle of negative thinking. This is why I make a point of explaining the experience in detail here.

I feel aggrieved about the sectarian drilling I received from teachers involved in my schooling. I should have been able to rely on state-funded schools to provide me with a balanced education, free from religious interference. Instead, the state collaborated with the

Church to sacrifice hours of my lesson time punishing me with self-effacing prayers and widely discredited exemplars from antiquity that I found unhelpful and later rejected.

Britain is one of the least religious countries in the world. Recent studies suggest that about 89% of Britons identify as non-religious or notionally Christian and many will be unaware of the church's influence in infant education.[96] Notional Christians are said to be those who believe in God but who never attend church and do not necessarily make any effort to follow the Christian ethic (perhaps because they confuse **Christianity** with **Britishness**). There are over 500 private fee-paying primary schools (pre-prep and prep schools) in the UK and most of these institutes are Christian in character.[97] All other primary schools are state-funded (maintained) and Christian in that their pupils are obliged to undergo daily acts of collective worship to comply with The Education Act of 1944. Despite several amendments since 1944, schools are still required to teach a programme of RE to 'reflect the fact that the religious traditions in Great Britain are in the main Christian'.[8] To accurately reflect the reality of religious belief in Britain, RE would need to be pluralistic and the curriculum should support non-religious viewpoints. Some schools simply flout the law, but 90% of primary faith schools comply.[9] Although schools without a religious character can apply for exemption from Christian RE, nearly one half of non-faith schools in the UK also choose to have some form of Christian collective worship. (Note that legislation varies between the countries of the United Kingdom since education is a devolved matter.)

'Faith schools', known as denominational schools in Scotland and Northern Ireland, comprise one third of state-funded schools in England and Wales. They are also mostly Christian in character.[98] This number has grown in recent years as religious groups have persuaded successive governments to expand the church's influence in the state-funded education system. Faith schools follow an agreed syllabus drawn up by local committees known as SACREs (Standing Advisory Council on Religious Education) made up of teachers, local churches, faith groups and the local authority. SACREs are not obliged to involve secular members, but if they choose to do so, any non-religious members are denied voting rights. Thus, any attempt to introduce a guilt-free, non-Augustinian viewpoint can be blocked.

The Education Act 1944 mentions religious instruction, but that was later replaced by the term religious education. Education implies impartiality and objectivity. Instead, state-funded faith schools can meet their legal obligation by providing religious instruction from an exclusive or confessional faith perspective. Instruction suggests teaching how to do something, for example, driving instructions are instructions that teach one how to drive. Denying children a pluralist, non-partisan education and requiring them to recite self-mortifying prayers as depicted above seems better described as indoctrination. That is why I use the term indoctrination where it is applicable throughout this book.

Ignoring all-through schools and independent schools (which are mostly Christian in character), in state-funded primary schools alone over one million of our UK young undergo indoctrination.[99] In many of these schools, pupils recite St Augustine's Confiteor or a version of it, making affirmations of self-blame, dwelling upon their wrongdoings, expressing sorrow and pleading for forgiveness and mercy. If Augustine's potentially harmful chants and mantras are recited just once a week, these infants will abase themselves less often than I did, but still hundreds of times through the duration of their primary school life. Constant repetition of self-castigating school prayers is liable to compound the mind-set of guilt and disgrace implanted in these infants' minds at birth with the stigma from Augustine's concept of original sin. The banning of this harmful archaic practice in schools seems long overdue.

Various editions of the Confiteor have appeared since Augustine's time, but the form widely recited today was inaugurated in the medieval liturgical treatise *Micrologus de ecclesiasticis observationibus*, as part of the introduction to the Mass by Bernold of Constance (1054 - 1100).

The British state continues to insist 1000 years later that her children, children below the age of criminal responsibility, should be marked sinful and should spend their lesson time chastising themselves. Civilised society has progressed from the brutal times when Bernold of Constance laid down the Confiteor. Our understanding of a child's brain has advanced, and the values we respect have been refined and humanised, yet the government persists in sponsoring this mental punishment, contrary to the terms we signed up to in international agreements and directives.[100]

In the widely respected journal *Psychology Today*, Peg Streep declares, 'The adult habit of self-blame is often an internalization of childhood experience'. Reviewing academic literature, her article attributes responsibility for the habit to parents, siblings, work colleagues and relationships.[101] The possible effect that the infliction of original sin, or their childhood years of ritually admitting gratuitous guilt, apologising and asking forgiveness might have on those suffering with this habit of self-blame is lamentably disregarded. Writing in the online magazine *PsychCentral*, Darius Cikanavicius lists ways childhood experiences lead to self-blame in adulthood. These include: experience of trauma, disapproval of emotional expression, overt criticism, unjust blame, being held to unrealistic standards, etc. Although self-blame is mentioned, the connection with Augustinian indoctrination is ignored in this article.[102] In their book *Sex, Priests, and Secret Codes: The Catholic Church's 2,000 Year Paper Trail of Sexual Abuse*, the three distinguished authors report that child abuse by clerics is a deep-seated problem that spans the Church's history. Yet these experts, who served as consultants in over 1,000 cases of cCSA, fail to note the possible link between this extraordinary chronicle of abuse and indoctrination in Augustine's teaching about infant sexuality.

In her book *Sexual Abuse and the Culture of Catholicism: How Priests and Nuns Become Perpetrators*, abuse survivor and mental health practitioner Myra Hidalgo compares the prevalence and characteristics of sexual abuse by Catholic priests and nuns to sex offenders in the general population. She cannot explain why Catholic priests and nuns in positions of trust abuse children, but she agrees that existing theories regarding causation are not supported by research. Myra discusses credible causes and contributory factors, but ignores what influence repetitive confessions of guilt and blame by infants might be having upon the attitudes and expectations of sexual abuse victims and perpetrators.[103]

Christian theology, inviolable by statute in the UK, is so woven into Western culture, even specialists are apt to overlook or disregard the subtle influence of early indoctrination on long-term mental health. Another factor that helps to account for these omissions is the absence of good evidence. There is a remarkable deficiency of rigorous research in this field, the reason for which is examined in the next chapter.

# 4

# THE 'RELIGIOSITY GAP' IN MENTAL HEALTH PROVISION

Richard Dawkins was disparaged for repeating the aphorism 'Give me the child for the first seven years and I will give you the man'[104] (attributed to the Jesuits, but also to Aristotle). In the introduction to this book, you will have read that the founder of my old school, now canonised St Newman, put the idea another way. Aged nine, he wrote in his notebook, 'Train up a child in the way he should go, and, when he is old, he will not depart from it.' Because an infant's brain is especially susceptible to religious ideas, indoctrination in Augustine's ideas can mark vulnerable children. Piaget's celebrated theory of cognitive development explains that before age seven a child lacks abstract reasoning. [105] Thinking is binary, basic and incohesive. Much of their brain development happens after birth, which makes infants particularly responsive to external influences in their early years when neural connections are being made. Numerous respected studies confirm that 'Early experiences affect the development of brain architecture, which provides the foundation for all future learning, behaviour, and health. Just as a weak foundation compromises the quality and strength of a house, adverse experiences early in life can impair brain architecture, with negative effects lasting into adulthood.'[14]

I have described the feelings of blame and culpability that I used to experience and which I believe were caused, or at least exacerbated, by my childhood religious indoctrination. Surprisingly mental health problems resulting from indoctrination are yet to be properly documented. The only relevant diagnosis in the handbook used by mental health professionals, *Diagnostic and Statistical Manual of Mental Disorders 5th edition* (DSM-5), is 'Religious or Spiritual Problem'. Informally, 'scrupulosity', is used to describe the symptoms resulting from indoctrination, such as guilt, depression, anxiety, grief, anger, shame and relationship issues. There is no recognition of the disturbing feelings of blameworthiness, inadequacy and disgrace that can assault the minds of followers and apostates. Little wonder politicians, teachers and even mental health professionals often perceive Augustinian indoctrination to be a benign influence. Lack of awareness by those who could intervene is sustained by a dearth of good quality research and want of rigor in existing studies that we will consider later in this chapter.

The consequences of indoctrination are starting to be acknowledged and documented. In 2009, Kansas psychologist Darrel Ray set up an online community called Recovering from Religion (RfR) to support apostates suffering from religious trauma or other effects of indoctrination. The need proved so great that support was soon extended to a 24/7 hotline, a professional therapy resource, a blog, Zoom meetings and podcasts. Today RfR has a presence in most parts of the world, including the UK.[106] Religious Trauma Syndrome (RTS) is a term coined by psychologist Dr Marlene Winell, who specialises in counselling men and women in recovery from religion. RTS classifies a recognisable set of symptoms experienced as a result of prolonged exposure to a toxic religious environment and/ or the trauma of leaving a religion. Although related to other kinds of chronic trauma, religious trauma is uniquely complex. This is because sufferers are themselves blamed for the psychological difficulties they exhibit. Victims of indoctrination did not pray enough, or did not believe unconditionally, or they were unstable in the first place. Thus, anything they say is automatically suspect and builds the case against them. By discrediting sufferers in this way, symptoms of depression, anxiety or panic attacks are written off with a peculiarly religious circular logic. Victims cannot disagree or object because the louder they protest, the more easily they can be dismissed with a smug smile, saying, 'See, I told you so.'

Another reason religious harm goes unrecognised is that the established Christian tradition provides a cultural backdrop for Augustinian world views. Although Britain is a mainly secular society, Augustine's ideas are embedded in our customs and traditions, partly because of a long history of indoctrination of infants. Later we will examine why these circumstances came about in the UK and how they are perpetuated. Britons point jingoistically to the perceived iniquities of other religions and we deceive ourselves that Augustine's ideas are wholesome and virtuous. This makes religious trauma difficult to recognise since Augustine masquerades under a Christian cloak of unmerited respectability.

Raised until aged 16 in the Exclusive Brethren, psychologist Jill Mytton speaks of 'deprivation' and claims the use of fear and a judgmental environment (like the concept of hell) to control a child can be traumatic.[16] Ms Mytton now specialises in treating victims of religious abuse and those suffering from RTS. The Exclusive Brethren defines itself as a Christian fellowship, and I identify with much of the mental trauma Ms Mytton describes. Ingraining ideas of blameworthiness and punishment in a receptive young mind is liable to be unsettling. Dr Winell says, 'Emotional and mental treatment in authoritarian religious groups also can be damaging because of: toxic teachings like eternal damnation or original sin, religious practices or mind-set such as punishment or guilt, and neglect that prevents a person from having the information or opportunities to develop normally.' (Quoted by Valerie Tarico.) [107]

My personal experience of guilt in adulthood amounts to a feeling of fundamental blameworthiness, which is a largely undocumented mental health handicap. There is a reason for the dearth of rigorous academic literature on religious abuse and mental punishment and it may have something to do with an apparent mismatch in religiosity between professionals and consumers (clinicians and patients).[108]

In Western countries, mental health professionals tend to be less religious than their patients are. This results in a belief systems incongruity between clinicians and patients in a clinical setting, the so-called religiosity gap, which can lead to misunderstanding and misinterpretation. Patients have reported perceiving disrespect and having a lack of confidence in their clinician. Consequently, professionals in secular mental health care are inclined to avoid religion and spirituality. Clinicians should provide an opportunity for patients to discuss their religious and spiritual beliefs and tailor their evaluation and treatment to meet their specific needs, but instead they tend to neutralise religious and spiritual differences and be reticent about self-disclosure in such matters.[109] A 2007 survey of US psychiatrists found that 56% never, rarely, or only sometimes inquired about religious/spiritual issues in patients with depression or anxiety.[110]

Religion has been associated with harmful outcomes in some academic studies, including higher rates of depression and lower quality of life.[111] Indoctrination can engender a range of negative feelings such as guilt, shame and powerlessness.[112] Confusingly, other research links religious belief with fewer symptoms of anxiety, reduced suicide rates, alcoholism and drug use and an increase in self-control and general well-being. Multiple studies claim religion gives people something to believe in, provides a sense of structure and typically offers a community of like-minded others. These factors can have a positive influence on mental health. However, not one of the papers that I examined reporting benefits to the mental and physical health of subjects had attempted to investigate potential for the collateral damage we have discussed resulting from indoctrination in Augustine's unsound ideology. This lapse might be explained when we realise that studies that have yielded findings favouring religious belief tend to have been conducted by supportive theologians, or were underwritten by religious institutions. Given the religiosity gap between the practitioner and consumer discussed earlier, that is perhaps understandable and getting at the truth, particularly in matters of belief, is not straightforward. The old adage comes to mind: 'Lies, damned lies, and statistics.' The studies discussed below are undermined by the researchers' failure to rigorously audit and classify participants. Deficiencies in research design and methodology suggest researchers might have been affected by implicit bias against sceptical participants.[113] Several prominent studies claiming benefits for religious belief are ignored here because they have already been discredited elsewhere.

A meta-study of religiosity and spirituality by Dr Harold Koenig cites 93 research papers endorsing religious belief. These papers record the health of unbelievers against those of the faithful, to show that believers are mentally and physically healthier, and Dr Koenig claims they 'underscore the need to integrate spirituality into patient care'.[114] However, in each of these papers, participants who identified variously as 'unbelievers', 'sceptics' or 'non-believers' were not interrogated, so any troubled apostates will have been misrepresented and placed on the wrong side of the balance sheet. Earlier we noted that Christian education of minors is compulsory in the UK. At least half of primary schoolchildren receive Christian instruction or indoctrination. Most adults recant, so many of those classified by Dr Koenig as 'unbelievers' will be apostates and religious indoctrination often inflicts emotional and psychological scars, as we have seen. The cause of unbelievers' distress might truly be religion, due to childhood evangelisation and the stress often associated with apostasy. Moreover, the benefits that Dr Koenig attributes to religion might ride on sociocultural values. According to one study of almost 200,000 people in 11 European countries, religious people only have higher self-esteem and better psychological adjustment than the non-religious do in countries where belief in religion is common. In more secular societies, the religious and the non-religious are equally well off.[115] It should be noted that Dr Koenig's study was funded by the pro-religious John Templeton Foundation.[116]

The studies cited do not appear to have taken the obvious step of interrogating non-believers to filter indoctrinated apostates from green unbelievers. Each comparative study segments participants differently depending upon the hypotheses being explored, but apostates suffering distress after having repudiated religion are unrepresented as a negative component in any research that I have been able to access comparing the positive with the adverse effects of religion. For a proper study of the effects of religious indoctrination on developing young people, it would be necessary to identify all the subjects who have been indoctrinated and later recanted, and classify them separately. Joseph Baker, a sociologist of religion at East Tennessee State University points out that nonreligious Americans should not be treated as a monolith. He argues atheists, agnostics and the nones should be treated as separate groups by researchers. There is a case for apostates to be treated as another separate group.[117]

Research literature abounds on the macrocosmic consequences of religion, but I can find little research covering the lifelong effect on individuals of a religious schooling in Augustinian values, and much research ignores the potential for inflicting lasting harm on infants, as other researchers have remarked.[118] None of the studies I have mentioned attempts to classify the mental state of apostates from religion discretely, as would be needed in order to ascertain the effects of proselytisation on children. Academic papers testing the psychological effects of religion are generally based upon self-classifying questionnaires, posing screening questions about religious affiliation. QuestionPro[119] offers a bank of 22 typical survey questions, but none is designed to identify those who have renounced the religion they were raised in. Suggested questions divide believers from non-believers by asking, 'Do you consider yourself to be religious? How often do you attend religious services? How often do you pray alone?' etc. Studies using these questions take no account of non-believers who, having been indoctrinated, have rejected religion. Research on the benefits of religion that relies upon similar interrogation is unlikely to recognise the fallout suffered by apostates. I and other sceptics would be categorised simply as **non-believers** and consequently any issues resulting from our struggle to throw off the psychological chains cast about us by indoctrination in our formative years would be mistakenly dissociated from religion.

About the same proportion of the UK population as are currently joining in collective worship in primary schools have also undergone a Christian baptism. 45% of Britons have been baptised in the C of E, 9% have been baptised in the Catholic faith and an unknown number in other denominations.[120] As we have seen, most reject or discard religion in adulthood. But in studies of religiosity and health, any mental health problems that apostates might have is likely to be wrongly categorised as due to unbelief, and so the cycle of misplaced approval accorded to Augustine's teaching persists. A small number of serious sufferers (perhaps the proverbial tip of the iceberg) eventually came to the attention of one of the few professional psychologists, such as Jill Mytton, specialising in RTS.[121] Otherwise, like many quietly endured mental health disorders, the psychological consequences of indoctrination generally remain hidden and neglected.

We have examined the 'religiosity gap' phenomenon in mental health provision and noted how sensitive religious people are to criticism. Blasphemy was a crime in Britain until recently, but blasphemy refers specifically to disrespect for God or religion. It has never been illegal to disrespect a non-believer for his or her reasonable doubts. The common law offences of blasphemy and blasphemous libel were formally abolished in England and Wales in 2008, yet there is still a general reluctance to ridicule followers for holding ridiculous beliefs. I chose to write this book under an assumed name because I anticipate an abusive reaction from some of the small but vocal minority of the British population that still clings to religious faith. Are atheist academics being browbeaten into shunning research in this area?

In his book *Is Religion Dangerous?* Prof. Keith Ward (a Christian cleric) cites research papers supporting his claim that religiosity is not a major causal factor in psychosis,[122] and in her book *Guilt and Children,* Jane Bybee alludes to empirical evidence indicating that intrinsic religiosity is associated with good mental and physical health.[123] The studies referred to compare mental health amongst the faithful with the mental health of non-believers, but non-believers were not scrutinised. Any mental torments, suffered by apostates such as Jill Mytton and myself because of religion, will have been perversely categorised as resulting from our unbelief in these research studies. We established earlier that most adults in the UK have received RE as minors and a majority of these individuals later relapse or cast off their teaching. Accordingly, the reason for any mental distress or ill-health found amongst unbelieving adults might be related to any number of causes and quite possibly attributable to early proselytisation and not due to unbelief.

In the previous chapter we looked at guilt, which can result from or be exacerbated by indoctrination. However, guilt is not inherently harmful. Guilt is constructive when it gives us an appropriate sense of power and agency. It is healthy for children to feel guilty for having acted in a way that violates their own standards of right and wrong: it inspires them to modify their behaviour and improve. They are motivated to take action and remove the distressing feelings associated with guilt. Guilt is toxic when it is tied to something over which we have no power or agency, such as the stain of original sin or some innocuous act that we believe to be inoffensive but we have been told is wrong and sinful. It can damage our sense of integrity when we are marked guilty by others, yet we believe we have conscientiously lived up to the values we claim to uphold. Getting infants to feel bad about an explicit wrongdoing can motivate them in a good way. Getting them to persistently repeat their culpability when they believe themselves to be blameless is liable to make them super sensitive to feelings of toxic guilt later in life.[124]

In an ABC News interview, researcher Kathleen Vohs talked of **healthy guilt**, claiming that inculcating guilt in children is good. 'Parents need to instil guilt in children, because kids are not born with it. Guilt is a wonderful thing for our society, because it keeps people in check.'[125] Jane Bybee justifies inculcating guilt by pointing out that, 'One of the markers of a psychopath is that the person doesn't experience guilt at all'. How guilt can be instilled in a child with a psychopathic personality disorder, or what the negative effect might be on a healthy child, is not discussed by these researchers. Other academics suggest that the labels **healthy guilt** differentiated from **maladaptive guilt** are too binary and unfocused to describe the subtle effect of inculcated guilt on a child's life chances. Scholars such as Fischer and Richards argue for more refined definitions, and measurement of both religion and guilt to address the sparsity of research.[15] Others argue that mixed and sometimes contradictory results can be traced to the lack of standardised measures, poor sampling, failure to control for threats to validity or experimenter bias.[126]

The acclaimed book *Guilt and Children* by Jane Bybee, referenced above, contains a fascinating discussion on the interrelationship of guilt and religion in childhood, but unfortunately the author does not say enough about how guilt develops in these individual children as they mature into adulthood. An entire chapter is devoted to religion and guilt in childhood and we learn the difference between extrinsic religious motivation (what is in it for me) and intrinsic motivation (what is required of me). Jane distinguishes two forms of guilt: chronic guilt (an ongoing feeling of guiltiness) and predispositional guilt (a tendency to feel guilty in reaction to events). Alas, none of these challenging ideas link into how they relate to the long-term emotional well-being of indoctrinated children. Jane acknowledges 'the important role that religious faith, texts and leaders play in inculcating guilt' concluding that 'the research literature on guilt and religion is quite sparse.' This is regrettable, but there is hope. Downing Street ordered a review to investigate racial disparities in the UK in response to the *Black Lives Matter* protests in the summer of 2020. The Commission on Race and Ethnic Disparities published their report the following year, acknowledging that racism is still a real force which has the power to deny opportunity and painfully disrupt lives. However, the researchers claimed other factors, such as religion, have a more 'significant impact' on life chances than the existence of racism.[127] The annual *Good Childhood Report* produced by the Children's Society found that of 24 countries surveyed, UK teenagers have the lowest levels of life satisfaction. The charity's chief executive cited increasing child poverty and fear of failure.[128] However, there has not been a rise in child poverty in the UK and our children are better off than many others in Europe. There is a single factor that differentiates British minors from all others. One of the least religious countries in Europe, the UK is the only one that requires all children to join in Collective Worship. It should be no surprise that many of our teenagers have a low level of life satisfaction. Having undertaken daily doses of collective worship, they leave school into a world where religion is irrelevant to 85% of the population. The opportunity that these pupils should have had to explore and develop a sense of purpose in their lives will have been denied to them. Instead, many of them will have suffered hours of self-abasing prayers, as I did. Religious indoctrination can destroy a young person's confidence in their own abilities so they become disengaged with school. Yet the same youngsters often show real potential once they are involved in inspiring, engaging activities and given positive role models, away from the influence of Augustine's negative creed.[129] Religious saints of past millennia are doubtful role models for today's children.

A good quality longitudinal study revealing the effect, if any, on the life chances of proselytised infants might make an important contribution to literature supporting adult mental health. Meanwhile we have to accept that the question of whether religious indoctrination is generally beneficial or harmful to the individual is open, in spite of personal experiences like mine. I have explained how, in troubled situations that objectively were not my responsibility, I sought to attribute what went wrong to something I had done, triggering a sense of unwarranted guilt. Persistently accepting blame, expressing regret and begging forgiveness in my childhood blurred the lines of responsibility for most of my life. Inflicted punishment, including mental punishment, often leads to self-punishment. We try to ease our feelings of guilt and free our conscience by punishing our-selves. Self-punishment first presents as a stern inner voice. People who typically feel bad about themselves can acquire an unconscious internal critic demanding punishment as self-retribution for some untoward action in the past. Most Westerners will have suffered mild examples of self-punishment. Having made a silly blunder, we might punish ourselves with a reproving self-admonishment such as 'You idiot!', 'Why do I keep making these stupid mistakes?' or 'I am hopeless!' Unrecognised and unchecked, this inner dialogue can become toxic.[130] In extreme cases, some individuals develop unhelpful defences to counter toxic guilt, which can include self-harm. Sensitive young people can be extraordinarily impressionable.

The youngest of three sisters, Molly Russell, seemed well adjusted and happy. A keen rider and a sailor, she had just won a lead part in her school play in 2017 when she took her own life. She was 14. Her parents described her as a 'caring soul' and they blamed, in part, the social media content she viewed about self-harm.[131] The suicide prevention charity Papyrus disclosed it was aware of 30 other cases similar to Molly's. Christian belief encourages self-harm, from penance and atonement to stigmata. Few believe today that stigmata appear miraculously, and the wounds are an example of self-inflicted violence prompted by sadistic Christian media, which we will explore in detail later. Unfortunately, there is little prospect of ending indoctrination by schools while the church is allowed to retain power in government.

In 2018, the Commission on Religious Education (CoRE) pub-lished a widely acclaimed report emphasising the central importance of learning about religious and non-religious worldviews for all pupils, regardless of their background, personal beliefs or the type of school they attend. The authors were from backgrounds inside and outside religion and they spent two years consulting and interview-ing thousands of concerned individuals and organisations including students, teachers, lecturers, advisers, parents and faith and belief communities, to produce a balanced and insightful report. The

Way Forward, a national plan for RE, stressed again and again how 'Knowledge of religious and non-religious worldviews is an essential part of all young people's entitlement to education.'[132] Because this report advocated the discussion and dissemination of non-religious views it was immediately buried by the Secretary of State for Education at the time, Damian Hinds. Mr Hinds is a Roman Catholic: he was educated at St Ambrose College, a Roman Catholic Grammar school in Greater Manchester. Mr Hinds stated that 'some stakeholders have concerns that making statutory the inclusion of "worldviews" risks diluting the teaching of RE'. Instead, towards the end of 2020, the government appointed Colin Bloom as the Faith Engagement Adviser at the Ministry of Housing, Communities and Local Government (MHCLG) to conduct yet another review into how best the government should engage with faith groups in England. This time the parameters have been fixed in advance to ensure that any non-religious views will be excluded.

Mr Bloom's review is described as 'limited in scope.' The government circulated a call for evidence, explaining 'Because the review is specifically about faith and religion, priority will be given to responses that fit within those parameters.' In other words, any non-religious views will be relegated. Although the review is labelled **Independent**, Mr Bloom's previous roles have included Executive Director of the Conservative Christian Fellowship and Director of Christians in Politics. Before he started his review he declared his bias: '…the recommendations may well come to strengthen how government engages with faith groups during the COVID-19 recovery phase and beyond.'[133] The call for evidence showed appalling prejudice. The questionnaire implied that only faith organisations or members of religious communities have supported their neighbourhoods during the COVID pandemic. Mr Bloom marginalises the contribution made throughout the pandemic by the vast majority of NHS staff, other key workers and mutual support groups who are non-religious. His failure to acknowledge the contribution made by others typifies the closeted ingroup dynamics one often finds in religious institutions. Like the CoRE report, this book shows the urgent need for an independent and inclusive assessment, but most of the content fits outside the parameters of Mr Bloom's limited review.

In 2010 The Rt Hon Nick Gibb MP, Minister of State for School Standards and 'a supporter of faith schools - and Catholic schools in particular',[134] proclaimed 'Could an atheist or a member of another faith successfully run a [Christian faith] school? Of course not.' [135]Nick Gibb's assertion that only a Christian teacher could successfully run a Christian faith school implies support for using schools to proselytise children. This contradicts the government's own advice to teach about religions objectively. Nick Gibb credits the work of American educationalist ED Hirsch as being the main influence on him in advocating Christian teaching.[136] Yet Hirsch is critical of the 'knowledge deficit' that hinders comprehension, describing the Christianity-focussed education system in American as being hostile to research-based findings and dissenting ideas.[137] Against this background of contrary evidence, and despite the UN Committee on the Rights of the Child requiring the British government to repeal its regulations on collective worship in schools, Nick Gibb is unmoved. In 2018 he announced that any breach of the requirement for collective worship will be investigated and the government 'has the powers to enforce compliance'.[138]

Even the National Census is biased to artificially inflate the extent of religious belief in the UK. The wording of the census question on religion is likely to exaggerate the number of religious people in the population, and under-represent the non-religious by as much as 50% compared with other surveys.[139] This discriminatory attitude of government is a product of the unhealthy mindset that I believe has become entrenched in the UK establishment through the unwarranted influence of 26 unelected bishops having the automatic right to sit, speak with unique privilege and vote in our Parliament. Other than the Islamic Republic of Iran, the UK is the only sovereign state in the world to allow clerics voting rights in the legislature. In March 2021, a YouGov poll found that more than half the country, 53% of respondents, want the bishops removed, with just 16% favouring keeping them.[140]

# 5

# SPIRITUAL WELL-BEING AND AUGUSTINE'S UNSOUND MORES

Christianity's moral values are distorted by Augustine's preoccupation with sexual lust. In her amusing book recounting her schooldays, Germaine Greer comments 'The nuns wanted us to know that sex was something very powerful that you fooled with at your peril. They convinced us that our bodies were just charged with this amazing stuff and if we did so much as bare the top part of our arms, we could be an occasion of sin.'[141] Such moral training usually proves counterproductive. Children who are excessively controlled tend to binge when they grow up and gain freedom.[142] In my teenage years, ex-convent schoolgirls were famed for their wanton behaviour, so promiscuity is not discouraged with the threat of Augustinian sin.

The Convent of the Immaculate Heart, USA was devastated in the early 1960s when the nuns underwent psychoanalysis and started thinking for themselves. In an attempt to keep pace with the rapidly changing social order outside, the sister superior had recklessly arranged weekend psychoanalysis retreats. The nuns were encouraged to open up, reveal their hidden feelings and emotions and just be themselves. Soon the nuns discarded their habits for ordinary clothes, and within a year over 300 of them had petitioned the Vatican to release them from their vows. Most of the remaining nuns abandoned their Augustinian teaching and turned to lesbianism.[143] When they were encouraged to think for themselves, the nuns discarded their imposed moral values and discovered their true personal values.

According to some moral sceptics, there is no objective moral truth: only one's own judgement is valid in any given circumstance for that individual.[144] Looking to Augustine, or any outsider, to define what we should do or who we should become is a root cause of low self-esteem.[145] If it becomes a habit, this pattern feeds insecurities because we do not trust ourselves to determine what we want in life. Besides, Christianity's rigid doctrines encourage bad casuistry and moral subterfuge.

If my mother wanted to avoid revealing a confidence, she would reply to a query with a forlorn shrug and say 'I'm sorry, I couldn't tell you,' and the listener assumed she did not know. Later she would turn to me and claim, 'I didn't tell a lie.' Lying contravenes Christianity's moral commandments, it is sinful and my mother wanted me to know she would never commit a sin by telling a lie, but deceit is not sinful according to Catholic doctrine. Incidentally, we will see in chapter 7 that even if she did lie, she could account for it to a priest in the ritual of confession (penance and reconciliation). The priest would be compelled to bestow forgiveness and absolution without my mother having to admit deception to the victim, who would be excluded from the entire process. To be clear, reconciliation refers to reconciling with God, not with the wronged victim who is conveniently disregarded.

The modern understanding of casuistry is 'Specious, deceptive, or over-subtle reasoning, especially in questions of morality; fallacious or dishonest application of general principles; sophistry.'[146] As society evolves, attitudes and mores change and novel situations are thrown up that were unanticipated in past millennia when Augustine's moralities were laid down. One example already considered is the upswing in the age of consent. Applying 2,000 years old doctrines to today's situations leaves many open questions and much room to manoeuvre. From time-to-time church doctrine demands unpalatable sacrifices of Christians as they go about their daily lives, earning a living and enjoying leisure. Believers find themselves drawn to use contorted reasoning in an attempt to reconcile archaic church doctrine with a contravening activity in modern day living.

Edward Hartnett, Catholic Professor of Law at New York University, offers workarounds to judges dealing with reasoning moral dilemmas and he gives examples as follows. The use of contraceptives is a sin according to Catholic teaching, but shop-workers can adopt the following moral fudge: 'Clerks in a drug store may never advise customers in the purchase of contraceptives, but to keep their employment and their income they may sell these things to those who ask for them.'[147] Here is a related example: A shopkeeper may sell an item that can only be used in sin, so long as the seller disassociates his intention with that of the sinner, and 'the purchaser can easily get the article elsewhere'. Finally, another example: Although immoral dances and shows promote sin, the owner of the theatre, the staff and the musicians can all work in connection with the shows, because 'these are income-generating positions and people need to make a living'.[148]

In each of these cases, giving up an activity that is sinful according to Church teaching will inflict a financial sacrifice. However, Catholic casuistry allows the believer to perform that activity without committing a sin and violating the moral teachings of the Church. This is how Professor Hartnett advises Christian judges to square their outdated religious convictions with progressive principles.

Home grown UK judges who have suffered a Christian upbringing can also struggle with moral dilemmas when their innate moral judgement conflicts with religious teaching. National newspapers reported that Lord Sumption, who was raised a Roman Catholic, appeared in a televised discussion show, *The Big Questions*, broadcast on BBC One in January 2021. He claimed that he did not accept 'all lives are of equal value'. He said 'Some lives are worth more than others.'[149] He also said that a stage four cancer patient's life was 'less valuable'. The former supreme court justice expressed a different view in 2014. Addressing the Tony Nicklinson case in a decision that upheld a ban on doctors helping patients to end their lives, he called the sanctity of life a 'fundamental moral value'. Parroting a classic Christian viewpoint, he continued his supreme court judgement 'A reverence for human life for its own sake is probably the most fundamental of all human social values. It is common to all civilised societies, all developed legal systems and all internationally recognised statements of human rights.' Either point of view has its merits no doubt, but the moral muddle that Lord Sumption appears to suffer from is typical of the confusion that I used to experience and have encountered time and again in the Christian community.

From Paine's *Age of Reason* to Dawkins' *The God Delusion*, the moral template that is Christian doctrine is shown to be misguided, dishonest and unethical. As we noted earlier, when they encounter a clash with religious ideals and values, many Christians apply their own instinctive moral code to decide which parts to follow and which to ignore. This is especially true of Augustine's irrational tenets on sex. We have noted that many Catholics ignore Christian doctrine on sexual sins.[76] Frederic Martel spent years investigating the Catholic Church, conducting interviews with senior figures and speaking to Vatican rent boys for his book *In the Closet of the Vatican*. He claims that homosexuals, 'most of them secretly practising', dominate the Vatican.[150] Yet active homosexuality is a sin in Catholic doctrine. One Bible study group interprets scripture to claim that '… our sexuality is at the very heart of who we are and thus it not only informs our spirituality but is the impulse of our desire to be in relationship with God.'[151] We can only imagine what Augustine would have had to say about that.

Christianity makes much of tradition in its teachings, but moral values change over time and today, nearly 1,600 years later, Augustine's ideas are invalid, inappropriate or simply wrong. Laws have to be updated to keep pace with progress in the values societies hold to. We noted in chapter 1 that most civilised societies have advanced and people's lives have improved. Capital punishment has been abolished, as has slavery, and it is no longer acceptable to bugger children, all of which were normal in Augustine's time. The Church has always been a late adopter of moral advances, and even now the Christian community is being dragged kicking and screaming towards progressive ethical practice in instituting reform on child abuse, restorative justice,[152] women's rights and equality issues[153] etc. as we have noted in these pages. Science shows that there are far better explanations for why human morality exists and how it developed—including biological, psychological, cultural, and social explanations. The simplistic assertion that good and bad acts are objectively decreed from an invisible supernatural entity is no longer valid, as we will see in chapter 8. The briefest study of history is enough to show that morality evolves, and has evolved far ahead of the brutality found in scripture.

The most violent and immoral societies in the world, also the most unequal, are in Latin America where 90% of the population is Christian (mostly Roman Catholic) whereas some of the most peaceful and humanitarian societies, Denmark and Sweden for example, are also the least religious.[154] Of course, additional factors are in play in these comparisons, and another example might show it is possible for societies to be both religious and virtuous. The point is, with regard to setting moral standards in society, religion is at best irrelevant. When photographer Chris Johnson asked 100 atheists about their moral values or what gives their lives joy and meaning, their answers emphasised spiritual qualities of love and connection, compassion and service, environment and sustainability, beauty and morality, etc.[155] These values cross religious and cultural boundaries and jurisdictions, and in chapter 8 we will explore the latest research that explains the mechanism behind this intellectual congruence.

Many of the studies I have mentioned conflate morals and religiosity with spirituality, which seems to me outdated and inappropriate. Modern religious historian and theologian Philip Sheldrake encapsulates my understanding when he says 'Spirituality refers to the deepest values and meanings by which people seek to live. In other words, "spirituality" implies some kind of vision of the human spirit and of what will assist it to achieve full potential.'[156] **Spirit** comes from the Latin **spīritus**, whose original meaning was 'breath, breathing.' Blind faith stifles inquiry and suffocates thinking. It seems to me we each have a spiritual dimension to our being which we gradually uncover and develop. Religion involves accepting absolutes in faith, whereas spiritual growth requires challenging the status quo and questioning given beliefs. Religious belief is a form of **adoptive spirituality**, a sort of spiritual template that satisfies many people, but it can interfere with one's personal development as we noted with the nuns who submitted to psychoanalysis. Briefly summarising approaches that chime with me, spirituality can be described as a character-building process of formulating a personal set of standards and values to give one's life a sense of order and purpose. For me, spirituality has nothing to do with the **sacred** or **transcendent**, as some apologists argue. It is a lifelong process of growing up which is likely to be subverted by worshipful submission to a rigid transcendent overseer. Part of the process of growing up involves developing one's understanding. The natural world has a spiritual dimension which is enhanced by an understanding of biology. That understanding is likely to be confused by inserting an omnipotent deity into the equation. I believe I was disadvantaged, as many children are today, by starting out believing that life was created and is influenced by a divine being. My religious instruction had to be undone before I could begin to appreciate the world.

Augustine's negative influence is an iron maiden of the mind, liable to crush the spirit. It is the antithesis of spirituality. His ideas impose a moral strongbox of dubious or discredited tenets and doctrines which disallow advancement for personal development and growth. There is nothing spiritual about Augustine, or anyone else, dictating to us what we should think. My experience in a devout Christian community persuades me that the ethical and intellectual shackles imposed by Christian doctrine hinder compassionate, rational thinking. It is easy to show that sound morality is built on facts, not faith. Rational thinkers look to science for answers, while accepting their understanding may be incomplete. Intuitive thinkers can be open to treating insanity as a possessive demon rather than an illness. Societies based upon science refer sick children to the doctor and not to the exorcist.

Several studies confirm that people who show a greater inclination towards the use of intuitive thinking tend to endorse belief in God and the afterlife, whereas those who tend to think analytically or rationally are likely to reject religion.[157] I do not claim a clear dichotomy in which intuitive and analytical thinking are by nature opposed to each other, but people who are inclined to think intuitively are generally more likely to feel comforted by religious belief and thus less likely to suffer mental distress from indoctrination.[158,159]

In his book *Is Religion Dangerous?* Prof. Ward argues that unlike the sciences, God is unknowable to the senses. Religion is like mathematics, he says, '...an appropriate form of intellectual imagination that gives access to a reality that cannot be known'. I can see that it is possible to sense, and even to know, that I have the right answer when I add one and two together to make three. An intuitive thinker like Prof. Ward has the extra ability to add together the sum of scripture to make Christianity. Rational thinkers like me find this idea incomprehensible: to me, maths is as far removed from religion as one can get. As a result, we rational thinkers seem more liable to suffer psychological distress due to our early proselytisation.

One cannot doubt his sincerity in promoting religion, but in common with many well-meaning Christian academics, Prof. Ward seems susceptible to the 'earned dogmatism effect', blind to the punishment religion inflicts on certain individuals.[160] Unfortunately, or perhaps happily, his education in Hexham Grammar School and beyond is unlikely to have exposed him to the harmful effects of indoctrination on the minds of some children. Prof. Ward flaunts evidence of the joy people get from religious belief, and there is no doubt that religion pleases some people. Whatever the mechanism, it is clear that some children thrive as a result of religious instruction, but it is equally clear that other children suffer. It must be said that many faith schools have a balanced RE curriculum, but others do not. For me, and for countless unseen rational thinkers like me, religious ideas delivered a punishing experience that caused lifelong distress.

I grew up believing that pride in oneself is sinful. Pride is the original and most deadly of Pope Gregory I's 'seven deadly sins'.[161] Lucifer and the angels were thrown out of heaven and Adam and Eve were expelled from Paradise due to pride: they got too big for their boots. Showing humility before clerics, who are standing in for an omnipotent God, is paramount for church leaders as we have noted from the prayers infants recite in primary faith schools. As a result of my indoctrination, I had difficulty simply acknowledging my own strengths, goodness and virtues. The fun and education I was entitled to receive in my formative years were lost, in my view, to hours and hours of inane worship and futile prayers to someone else's God.

I was into my teenage years before I was free to discover my own heroes. The childhood interactions I should have had with unbelievers, sceptics and rational thinkers like myself were prohibited. Religious sectarianism alienated my parents and estranged my father. My siblings and I missed the natural benefits of family life and the advantage of a positive relationship with my dad. My parents in their turn were denied the happiness they deserved. By the time I reached adolescence I had been scrupulously indoctrinated with what I consider to be wrongful ideas on ethics and victimhood. I refrain from using the word because it has baleful connotations, but note that the dictionary definition of **brainwashed** accords with my childhood experience of 'making someone believe something [Augustinian doctrine] by repeatedly telling them that it is true and preventing any other information from reaching them'.[162] Many of today's faith schools perpetuate my childhood experience at the behest of the state. 99.8% of places at Catholic state supported secondary schools are subject to religious selection in admissions criteria. For Church of England schools the figure is 49.7% but for those C of E schools fully in control of their own admissions policies with no legal or regulatory limitations it is 68%.[163] Many schools provide a pluralistic study of religion and worldviews. But few primary schools defend the non-religious viewpoint that I espouse and some of the pupils attending faith schools will be repeatedly told that Christian beliefs are true and any other information will be prevented from reaching them.

In chapter 3 we looked briefly at SACREs, the body that sets an RE syllabus for schools with the diocese called the Local Agreed Syllabus. It is important to note that the local bishop determines the content of religious indoctrination in faith schools. Schools are supposed to teach about other religions as part of the RE curriculum, but it is up to the bishop to decide the extent to which this requirement is applied. By means of religious selection, faith schools specifically deny pupils the opportunity to mix with diverse friends and hear other opinions. There is no legal requirement for the schools to offer a balance of ideas and viewpoints. A faith school might teach that abortion is wrong, although it has been legal for 50 years in Britain. A Catholic school might advance Pope Francis's teaching that nuclear disarmament is a moral imperative, contrary to the values espoused by Britain.

Apart from the potential for political bias, Christian tradition offers damaging lessons in flawed ethical reasoning. In the Christian ritual of penance, otherwise called confession, the celebrant forgives wrongdoings without reference to, and hidden from, the person wronged. Seeking forgiveness for interpersonal transgressions from a third, unconnected party (a celebrant, standing in place of God) is morally objectionable. If I harm someone, the right course of action is to ask that person for forgiveness, directly. It is for me to resolve my wrongdoings honourably face to face with my victim. Going behind the back of the victim to ask forgiveness of a third party is craven. Furthermore, this gutless ritual adds insult to injury. Not only do the confessor and the penitent agree between them to forgive and forget without considering disclosure or restitution to the injured party, but they conspire to keep both the confession and absolution strictly secret between them forever. Penance is a dishonourable lesson in cowardice and deceit that is wrongly held up to schoolchildren as decent. Ironically, confessions to a third party also harm the perpetrator, as we shall see in the next chapter.

The British criminal justice system aims to 'deliver justice for all, by convicting and punishing the guilty and helping them to stop offending, while protecting the innocent'.[164] Modern practice attempts to bring closure to victims and help rehabilitate offenders by getting them to understand the harm they have done. The restorative justice approach goes further and recognises the flaw in administering justice disengaged from the victims of crime, by confronting criminals with their victims. Restorative justice gives victims the chance to meet or communicate with their offenders to explain the real impact of the crime, and it empowers victims by giving them a voice. It also holds offenders to account for what they have done and helps them to take responsibility and make amends.[165] The government's own research demonstrates that restorative justice provides an 85% victim satisfaction rate and a 14% reduction in the frequency of reoffending.[166]

Deliberately shielding perpetrators from the victims of their crimes points in the wrong direction and hails from a bygone age. The concepts of Creative Restitution and Restorative Practices were unknown in the western hemisphere until hundreds of years after Augustine's ancient philosophy. Psychologist Albert Eglash developed the concept of creative restitution in the 1950s. Working with adults and youths involved in the criminal justice system, Eglash found Augustine's retributive ideas to be lacking in humanity and effectiveness. He proposed an alternative process, creative restitution, where an offender is helped by the system to make amends to the person or people harmed by their offence. Eglash went on to identify three different approaches to justice: 'retributive justice', imposing punishment; 'distributive justice', involving therapeutic treatment of offenders and 'restorative justice', based on restitution with input from victims and offenders.[167] Despite these proven developments in the administration of justice, UK schools are compelled by the state to confuse pupils with Augustine's outdated and unsound philosophy which ignores the victim and places the administration of justice in the hands of a nebulous monitor.

Recovering my stability and ridding myself of the moral disorientation inflicted by Christian indoctrination has been a lifetime's effort. From the earliest time I remember, my natural sense of right and wrong was eclipsed by the confusing Christian tenets around guilt and accountability explained above. I am ashamed to admit now that in my late school years, before I developed my own moral framework, I embarked on a period of petty criminality: shoplifting and vandalism. In addition, as a result of my indoctrination I have felt a deep sense of anxiety, guilt and culpability throughout most of my life, and today, 50 years later, I still fight my tendency to assume false blame. Although not seriously sexually abused, I believe my indoctrination punished me. It is shocking to note that in modern Britain the state continues to sponsor the mental punishment imposed by Christian drilling, both legislatively and financially, especially in light of evidence of the cost to society in the longer term.[168] Today child exploitation is a crime, yet the UK government continues to fund potentially harmful, faith-focused schooling.

Let us be clear that Christians do much good for children around the world. Typical is the charity Stand by Me, which was founded by Good Samaritan David Spurdle. Since 1995 the charity has provided valuable food, medicines and schooling to thousands of children.[169] Help that is generously provided to children, often desperately in need, is commendable, whoever or whatever the source. That said, Mr Spurdle is a Christian and the children being helped are simultaneously being proselytised, as I was, with all the attendant risk of causing distress that I have described. Although the charity claims never to coerce a child to change their beliefs, children do not have any religious beliefs until they are indoctrinated. The efforts of numerous non-religious children's aid charities, helping in similar ways, dwarf that of Stand by Me without attempting to proselytise their charges.

# 6

# A RIGHTEOUS PUNISHMENT, BLESSED BY ST AUGUSTINE

'Turn around boy…'

'Now, walk to the stool and don't look back.'

Choked with dread, I turned my gaze where Father had directed. The carpeted, sparsely furnished priest's study looked vast to my 12-year-old eyes, and the stubby kneeling stool seemed needlessly distant at the far end of the room. Once a stately suburban mansion, St Philip's Home for Boys had impressed my mother, with its high ceilings and grand proportions, but for us boys it was grim.[170] I trudged across the floor and stopped when I arrived in front of the stool. 'Pull down your breeches and bend over.' I undid my fly buttons, lowered my short trousers and leaned forward to kneel. 'And your underpants!' demanded Father firmly. I duly obeyed and dropping onto my knees, bent across the stool, exposing my naked, defenceless bottom. However, that was not enough for the priest.

'Right down, past your knees!' The instruction was cross now and I quickly rose, dropped my clothes to my ankles as I was bid, and resumed my stoop. My ears strained against the beat of my pulse throbbing in my ears as I tried to pick up Father's footfall treading the thin pile. I felt my buttocks stiffen in anticipation – but minutes passed and the room remained eerily still and silent.

This ominous delay was unexpected. I fretted pointlessly upon the choice of weapon with which I was about to be beaten. No one knew for sure how our punishments were delivered: there were many guesses of course, but we were instructed not to look. One boy, whom Father had repeatedly beaten, proposed a gym slipper; another said he had seen a lavatory brush. We will never know the truth, but everyone agreed on the bitter sting. As time painlessly slipped by, I relaxed, wondering if Father had been called away and left the room, forgetting me. Should I call out? He might have been taken ill; dare I turn around? No. Father had told me specifically NOT to look back.

Perhaps I had been excused, or a reprieve had been arranged. Yes, that was it! After all, I recalled, my transgression had been a minor lapse. I was up to play tennis, but when I went to my locker to collect my racquet, one of the strings was broken. It had been perfectly sound when I put it away and on impulse, I swapped it for another boy's racquet, without saying a word, so I could play my game. He blabbed to the nuns, who conducted a search. It was a very fine piece of kit, easily identifiable – and soon found in my locker. The nuns returned it to the other boy, but I had lied; I denied any wrongdoing and this is why Sister Superior sent me to the priest for spanking. I had committed a slight sin, a venial sin perhaps, but to my mind not a serious sin deserving a beating.

My puerile deliberations were made sharply redundant as I felt a bracing whack delivered to each cheek in quick succession. I remember being astonished that such a spindly looking priest could muster such vigour, but my punishment was light. Some boys got up to six. I winced; now my bottom was sore and uncomfortable. I stirred to shift my weight, preparing to rise, but Father barked, 'Wait!' and I endured another interminable delay while he drooled over his handiwork.

An age later, after I had imagined all possible reasons my ingenuous mind could invent to explain this distressing wait: 'Pull up your breeches, boy.' His voice whistled abruptly. 'You have taken your punishment well; put it out of your mind and don't talk about it to anyone. You may go back to your dormitory.' I thanked the good Father, as instructed by my house prefect, and quickly left.

My beating had been preceded by a brief review. Seated with his hand around my waist, Father had seemed unexpectedly mellow then.

'You know you have been a bad boy?' he had purred mellifluously.

'Yes, Father.'

'And do you deserve to be punished?'

'Yes, Father.'

'Turn around boy…'

Although he only visited occasionally, mostly to deliver St Philip's degrading punishments, the parish priest made a lifelong impression on me. After nearly 60 years I cannot recall his name, but his influence continues to unsettle me, and the image I have of him is so fresh it comes to mind effortlessly. Still unnerving, scary even, and not only due to his role as the schoolboys' torturer; as Father Confessor he was God's broker of forgiveness or eternal damnation.

The nuns in St Philip's knew that a priest was performing the beatings I have described on boys' naked buttocks, and they were compliant. The sisters appeared to act robotically for the priest; his judgement in all things was final, and given that mindset it is not surprising that the priest felt uninhibited in pursuing his rude punishment of boys entrusted to his care. With the acquiescence of all around him, this clergyman and those before him must have thrashed hundreds of unclothed boys, the tradition having been established for at least 50 years before my spanking.[171] At the time corporal punishment was relatively common, but today the science is clear. The physical punishment of children '…is ineffective over time, and is associated with increased aggression and decreased moral internalisation of appropriate behaviour.'[172] Multiple good quality studies have shown that corporal punishment does not work and can lead to mental health problems for children. The point made in many studies is that the experience can be more damaging for some children than for others.

Despite the science, it seems unlikely that a bill ending the beating of children could get passed any time soon by the UK Parliament, because of resistance by bishops and senior Christians sitting in the House of Lords. Peter Forster, the 55-year-old Lord Bishop of Chester, spoke in May 2004 in favour of the amendment allowing the beating of children as 'reasonable chastisement'. He voiced the following caveat: 'If there is no possibility of physical punishment, the temptation will be for a society to engage in forms of mental and non-physical punishments, which themselves can be demeaning and very oppressive.'[173] The 66-year-old Baroness Richardson of Calow responded: 'I, too, support the amendment. In speaking to it I represent the views of a great many Christians across a wide range of Churches, particularly those which have come out in support in official statements, such as the Methodist Church, the United Reform Church, the Roman Catholic Church and many children's charities.' St Augustine's unsound tenets are so entrenched in the Western psyche that, alone in the civilised world, Christian nation states continue to permit children to be physically disciplined. That the UK, a mostly non-Christian population, still permits damaging physical punishment to children is testament to the unwarranted power the church continues to hold over the rights of citizens.

Physical discipline of minors, including spanking, hitting and other means of causing pain, is now outlawed in Scotland and Wales and in 52 countries around the world, in all settings including in the home (2017).[174] All 52 countries are non-[Augustinian] Christian, whereas in England, also predominantly non-Christian, and Northern Ireland parents are allowed to smack their children, provided it is a 'reasonable punishment'. Physical punishment is also permitted in certain alternative care settings and in penal institutions.[175]

St Philip's left mostly unpleasant memories of the three terms I boarded, but I was only partly to blame for being sent there. I had been a miserable student. A creative and spirited child, dry lessons bored me and I was easily distracted. However, my mother's determination to secure isolation from my father's influence was a more pressing reason for her to separate me than concern to reduce opportunities for distraction from my studies and improve my progress.

Steeped in folk tales of Black and Tan[176] atrocities, my mother applied postage stamps upside down as a protest against the British Crown. Born into a reverent RC community in a southern Ireland hamlet (baile), her family farm was, ironically, one of Gladstone's beneficial smallholdings with a sturdy, slate-roofed cottage.[177] Investment in mechanisation was unrealistic for these small farm plots, usually little more than an acre, and their viability rested upon the availability of cheap labour, i.e. child labour. The farm passed down to the eldest son on her father's death and Mum and her 12 siblings contemplated a bleak future in Ireland as farm labourers. The world beyond beckoned and in 1935 aged 22, Mum immigrated to the UK to train as a nurse, having a brother already employed in a London hospital.

Only 14 years old when WW1 broke out, Dad falsified his age to enlist and 'see the world' as his father had done before him. He was soon dispatched to France with the British Expeditionary Force, and he found himself on the Western Front witnessing the horrors of trench warfare. He spoke little of the Great War, but once told me, 'The allies were assured God is on our side, while German soldiers had inscribed on their belt buckles "Gott mit uns" [God with us].' (Fig. 3.) After one long bombardment, he and his best friend were whistled out of the trenches and over the top. As they charged across no man's land, shells were still exploding around them. One shell landed close by and he saw his pal obliterated. Having witnessed the perfidy of power and grim manifestations of man's mortality, Dad deemed religion phoney, impotent and irrelevant.

**Figure 3. German Army belt buckle from WW1**

My parents' unlikely coupling sprang from the chaotic circumstances of their time, amid the turbulence of the Second World War. Dad proposed marriage, but the RC Church's Code of Canon Law forbade Catholics marrying non-Catholics.[178] Dad impetuously agreed to convert and was required to promise to rear his children in the RC faith.

At the war's end, Dad retrained and took up teaching at a local state school. Life for my two brothers, my sister and me was unremarkable but contented. The family was close knit, caring and cheerful. Our local park was a stone's throw away and we played together happily there for hours, but such delights came to an abrupt end when I was about six years old. One frosty winter Sunday morning Dad refused to venture out to church. Any Catholic missing Sunday Mass without good reason commits a mortal sin in the canon of the RC Church.[179] My parents had a blistering row and the upshot was that Dad renounced the RC faith. From that moment, a parental feud began and heated quarrels became a daily occurrence.

Several years later, my mother arranged for the local parish priest to visit and talk with Dad in an attempt to heal the rift. Mum hoped that the priest would restore Dad's faith; contrarily Dad thought to trap the priest with a paradox by pointing out that the pope leads Christ's church, yet he claims the title **Pontifex Maximus,** given to Caesar who ordered Christ's execution.[180]

I was not privy to the discussion and cannot say how the priest argued his corner, but on leaving the meeting with Dad, the priest took my mum to one side. He pronounced my father to be 'possessed by the devil' and instructed her that we children must be protected from his influence. The devil is the trump card of the cornered Christian; the pope branded his critics as 'friends of the devil.' The priest recommended that Mum should take us away as far as possible to avoid any contact with my dad. Sydney Macartney, in his 1999 film *A Love Divided*, an exposition of the Fethard-on-Sea affair, accurately depicts the power of the RC Church of the 1950s and the commanding grip that the parish priest had over the Church's followers. Tony Doyle, who plays Father Stafford, perfectly conveys the conviction of authority, rectitude and sagacity that prevailed at the time. The RC parish priest was, and is today, doctrinally and purportedly Christ in person on earth. Believers continue to refer to themselves as sheep, and the flock are disposed to follow wherever the priest or pastor leads.[181]

Having fought in close combat through two world wars and survived victorious against all odds, my dad was laid low by a priest. Dad never attempted to stand in the way of our religious practice, but shortly afterwards my mother secured a formal separation, divorce being forbidden by the Church that had divided them. Homesick now, and yearning for the security and solidarity of her birthplace, Mum arranged for herself and us four children to move in with her older brother and his wife and daughter in their two-bedroom cottage in Dublin. My siblings and I attended the local RC school. The family returned to England several times and I was boarded at various RC schools and colleges to shelter me against any influence from my father.

I spent several terms in St Kieran's College, Kilkenny, accommodated in a magnificent neo-Gothic building dating from the 1780s. In addition to boarding students, St Kieran's was also a seminary, and hundreds of priests were trained there. The school was run by the Christian Brothers who were ruthless teachers. One poor boy in my class was mercilessly thrashed lesson after lesson because he failed to recite his Latin perfectly. The lad was not capable, and he shook with fear before each lecture, knowing he would be beaten. One of the priests seemed to take particular delight in discussing the evils of masturbation. Hardly a lesson passed when he was unable to find an opportunity to discuss the topic and highlight the dangers for us. Augustine, we were gravely reminded, condemns all sexual activities that are not procreational, including masturbation. We students kept reverent silence when being told that the intentional stimulation of the genitals in order to derive sexual pleasure was a mortal sin, deserving of punishment in hell. 'It is an act of loneliness;

it turns us away from the love of God and inward towards a love of ourselves.' Just thinking about masturbation is a sin, he insisted. We were to strive to overcome the temptations of the devil that distract our minds to dwelling on our lower organs. The deliberate use of the sexual faculty, for whatever reason outside marriage, is contrary to God's purpose. Most gravely, ejaculation was a loathsome destruction of God's sacred gift of the seed of life.

St Kieran's College closed down in 1994 due to a fall in the numbers of novitiates putting themselves forward for priesthood. Thankfully, priests no longer enjoy the authority they once held, yet religious differences still cause relationships to fail. In the past the UK's strange divorce laws required couples to give one of five reasons why their marriage had irretrievably broken down. I know of at least one case where religion caused a marriage to fail, but religion was not one of the five listed reasons and never got cited. The Divorce, Dissolution and Separation Act 2020 requires no reason to be given why a relationship has permanently broken down and there are no statistics of religious grounds for separation or divorce. However, the malign power the church retains over children's education in the UK is extensively documented, and that continues unabated.

# 7

# 'IN PERSONA CHRISTI' – THE DISGRACE OF INSTANT FORGIVENESS

Confirmation is a sacrament in the Catholic tradition; Anglican and Orthodox Churches have a simpler service, sometimes called Chrismation. In the Roman Catholic Church, the Code of Canon Law specifies that the sacrament of confirmation is to be conferred when a child reaches 'the age of discretion' which is generally accepted to be about seven years of age. The C of E admits any time of life, from 10 years of age. In all denominations, confirmation is held to be necessary for the completion of baptismal grace and it is deemed to be a sign of full membership of the Christian community. Usually the bishop celebrates, and the child confirms the promises made on his or her behalf at baptism. I was confirmed by Rev. Cyril Cowdery, Bishop of Southwark at St Thomas the Apostle in London; I still have my confirmation certificate. I was six years old, entirely dependent upon my parents and not, in any meaningful way, at liberty to exercise my own free will. My confirmation served to reinforce the sense of awe and deference for Church leaders that I was required to exhibit. According to my prayer book I was imbued with, amongst other things, 'the Spirit of holy fear in God's presence'.[182]

At seven I was old enough to start induction training as an altar boy, learning to assist in the solemn ceremonies of the church. Having attended Mass daily for several years, I already knew most of the Latin liturgy by heart.[183] Now I repeated the Confiteor in Latin, 'Mea culpa, mea culpa, mea maxima culpa,' – 'through my fault, through my fault, through my own grievous fault,' striking my breast three times. I had a good singing voice and served as choirboy and altar boy in churches, oratories and cathedrals in Birmingham and London. As altar boy and chorister, I regularly witnessed caresses from clergymen, mostly casual but occasionally intimate. Drawing a line between what is sexual and what is friendly and harmless is not straightforward as we noted in the introduction.

Certain clerics were disposed to touch their charges in a way that would be considered inappropriate today, with a careless hand on a boy's shoulder or an arm around his waist. Such behaviour was not widespread, but it was tolerated, no eyebrows were raised, and out of the spotlight abuse could be more sinister. At the Birmingham Oratory, the reception office was staffed by a secular administrator and I was drafted to stand in for him at break times, by myself. Whenever the sacristan saw me and there was no one around, he would ask, 'Are you a good boy?'

In my naïveté, I replied, 'Yes, I'm a good boy,' and he approached and felt my genitals with one hand and stroked the cheeks of my bottom with the other. On reflection, whatever reply I gave would probably have been considered an invitation. I felt embarrassed and dismayed, but most of all I was confused. There were perhaps half a dozen such encounters; each episode took several seconds in total and went no further than I have described. I mouthed a rebuff and pulled away, but I did not feel that I could be assertive with the cassocked sacristan and I was too docile, too reverential to escalate the issue. To whom would I make a formal complaint? I was doubtful who might be receptive and responsive. Now I see that my entire school experience – inculcating deference, subjugation and submission to the priest – could not have been better arranged had it been expressly designed to make me vulnerable to a cleric's advances. Not having made enough of a fuss engendered a feeling of having consented, which provoked within me a distressing sense that I was somehow to blame.

I was taught that priests are Jesus Christ personified on earth, **in Persona Christi**. [184] An explanation from the Catholic Seminary of St John clarifies the status of priests in the eyes of believers: 'By virtue of the sacramental consecration which the priest receives, he is ontologically changed. He is configured to the Person of Jesus Christ, Head and Shepherd, in a new way in his very being.'[185] As recently as 24th June 2009, Pope Benedict XVI confirmed the status of RC priests: 'The priest is an alter Christus [Latin for **another Christ**]'. Priests are trained to stand up in front of an audience and bestow blessings, all the while imagining themselves to be God Almighty. The ordination of a Catholic priest is solemnised in an arena of theatrical pomp and circumstance. If 'unlimited power is apt to corrupt the minds of those who possess it', we might expect a corruption of morals to arise from a man being assured, in a grand manner, that he is truly Christ reincarnated on earth with the unlimited power of Almighty God.[186] The Canadian Royal Commission of Inquiry, known as the Hughes Inquiry, portrayed priests as assuming their priesthood sanctioned child abuse, and reported that the abusive clerics demanded (and received) special treatment from the Christian community, the attorney general, social workers and police.[187]

In the previous chapter we looked at the extraordinary deference accorded to the priest by nuns. In the opening statement to his report, Peter Davies, Director of The National Crime Agency declared, 'The sexual exploitation and abuse of children is most likely when vulnerability meets power.'[188] The head of the Centre for Child Protection in Rome, Karlijn Demasure, agrees. 'In all cases [of cCSA] it concerns someone who abuses his position of power.'[189] In other Christian traditions, priests, presbyters or vicars are said to be disciples of Jesus Christ and do not claim to stand in the place of Christ, but they do claim divine authority. In 2016, the C of E was dealing with 3,300 complaints of cCSA.[190] Since this figure was released, many more cases have come to light and the total will be higher now.

Only RC priests are licensed to perform the divine miracle of transubstantiation where they change the host of leavened bread and the chalice of wine into the actual body and blood of Our Lord Jesus Christ.[191] I was penitent, dutifully compliant and imbued with dread and deference for the priest, whom I accepted as equivalent to God himself. Children are taught that when the priest is acting **in Persona Christi,** a miraculous physical change in the substance of bread and wine takes place, notwithstanding that humans cannot see the transformation with their frail senses. Adults might well harbour reservations, but children are suggestible and I accepted that the priest performed miracles, as grown-ups told me. Numerous studies confirm that young children are especially trusting of things they are told by adults. Research author Vikram K. Jaswal, of the University of Virginia comments, 'Children have developed a specific bias to believe what they're told, it's sort of a short cut to keep them from having to evaluate what people say. It's useful because most of the time parents and caregivers tell children things that they believe to be true.'[192]

RC dogma proclaims the pope to be infallible when decreeing matters of faith or morals: he cannot make a mistake when deciding between what is right and what is wrong.[193] Since the priest is a delegate of the pope, my fledgling mind accepted the priest's judgement, when pronouncing upon right and wrong, as indisputable. Thus, I did not shout or scream when the robed sacristan abused me, although I felt uncomfortable about it. An instruction from a priest could not be wrong. As I remarked earlier, my innate ability to differentiate right from wrong was clouded by Christian indoctrination and I was made dependent upon the priest for leadership.

Impressionable children are likely to be susceptible to suggestions made to them in private by a priest who is held out to be Christ himself, present in person and capable of performing miracles. I empathise with the sexually abused boy who told the Pennsylvania Grand Jury that he revered priests and the RC Church and 'did not know how to say no to a priest or nun.'[194] Formal investigations into cCSA tell repeatedly of victims' statements that no one would believe their accounts of abuse.[195] Researchers point out how societal structures are established in favour of perpetrating clerics, and in Britain bishops even retain the privilege of a reserved place in government.[102] The religious influence and status enjoyed by clergy **in Persona Christi** gives credibility and authority, undermining the stories of victims. My mother would have been unlikely to believe a story of abuse against a RC priest had I spoken about my assault, and I consider myself fortunate to have escaped more serious harm. Most RC boys are never sexually molested of course, and nothing that I witnessed amounted to serious abuse as reported from other RC institutions, yet my childhood experiences denote an unseemly permissiveness accorded to abuse, even for the liberal 1960s. We noted in the introduction that clergy of all denominations claim the power to forgive sins. In Catholic theology, the priest, acting **in Persona Christi**, receives from the Church the power of jurisdiction to give absolution and free the penitent from sin caused by any wrongdoing against an unnamed and disregarded third party.

Confession is mentioned in the New Testament.[196] It was not made a sacrament until the 11th century and in the meantime the ritual was developed and refined, but the idea of making a detailed confession to a bishop or priest first appeared in Augustine's time.[197] After the Roman Empire turned to Christianity, bishops became judges at episcopal courts, engaged to hear confessions of sins by the faithful. Augustine, as bishop of Hippo and the local judge and confessor, defined **sin**[198] for the Catholic Church and helped clarify the distinction between **mortal sins** (serious or grave sins) and **venial sins** (mild sins).[199] These bald lines abridge a complex story. The saga of confession, otherwise called penance, could fill this entire book, and has indeed filled several books. History is shoe-horned here to fit in the space available. Suffice to say that Augustine was the most important early influence and if you Google **sin** or **penance** or **confession** you will find his name prominently mentioned in every result.

Once a week, students of St Philip's were marched to the Birmingham Oratory to have our confessions heard. Confession, or to be precise the Sacrament of Penance and Reconciliation, is one of the seven sacred sacraments of the RC Church.[200] The faithful are obliged to admit their misdeeds committed against God and neighbour to a priest in confession at the earliest opportunity and obtain forgiveness to reconcile themselves with Christ. This is where Augustine's unethical moral template is formalised.

We started by kneeling in front of the altar for an examination of conscience, a check-up of sinful actions since last confessing. Sometimes I had difficulty thinking of any bad things I had done. We were told, 'You must have sinned: we are all sinners; only God is perfect; go through each of the ten commandments and your cat-echism and search your conscience for all your misdeeds.'[201] I made up sins so I had something to tell the priest. (Later I discovered my peers were doing the same.) This regular exhortation to focus again and again upon how bad I was reinforced my mounting sense of guilt and blameworthiness. Today, primary school infants are made to go through the same humbling ritual.[11] Sin is everywhere and in everything: even thinking about sinful things is sinful, according to Augustine. It would take 40 years, long after I had discarded religion, for me to recognise these harmful thoughts. Then I could start to remedy my negative self-image by learning to reflect upon the good things I had done and rationalise my sense of guilt.

Having established an inventory of past wrongdoings, the penitent must express sorrow for having sinned, and I was truly sorry for my wrongdoings. I said a prayer expressing my regret and resolving not to commit the same sins again. Entering the confessional box,[202] I knelt, blessed myself with the sign of the cross and recited, 'Bless me Father, for I have sinned; it is one week since my last confession.' The confessional box was unlighted, but peering through a grille in the partition, I could just make out the silhouette of Father Confessor in the dimness.

I duly confessed that I had taken the racquet and I was repentant. Father Confessor did not ask about the victim, but told me that I had done wrong and I must say ten Hail Marys and try to be better in the future. The priest did not question the circumstances, nor did he ask if I had returned the racquet I took or if I had made recompense. Some confessors asked if I had examined my conscience properly, or if I had any other sins to confess. In one confession, the priest asked if I had masturbated since my last confession. I said the Act of Contrition and received forgiveness from God, which freed me from all my sins, including any that I had honestly forgotten to name. I was in no doubt that had I died that minute my soul would have gone straight to heaven to sit beside God in the company of all the angels and saints.

In the Christian tradition, the penitent is at once the accuser, the person accused, and the witness, while the confessor pronounces judgment and sentence. No prosecutor is present, no independent witnesses and no victims. The priest and the penitent communicate in secret[203] and the priest's power to confer forgiveness is detached from, and independent of, the injured party. Dogma requires the confessor to forgive the penitent of all sins, regardless of the circumstances of the transgression or level of wickedness or corruption of the perpetrator.[204] This power of a cleric to forgive any transgression, which might be rape, child sexual abuse or even murder, is unlimited.[205] No distinction is made between venial (minor) or mortal (grave) sin, or between one class of sinner and all the rest. The Church has merely three prerequisites for forgiveness and absolution: contrition, confession (to the priest) and penance:[206] usually prayers to the saints. Note that the penitent is accountable only to the confessor for wrongdoing: any loss or suffering that might have been inflicted upon the victim of sinning is disregarded. In my experience of church penance, the victim was never considered, and not once did any priest mention restitution or compensation to the victim in the hundreds of confessions I made.

Failing to encourage reconciliation with the victim of wrongdoing rules out healthy closure and can contribute to the perpetrator's sense of unresolved guilt. Everyone will be familiar with that warm glow of decency after resolving differences with someone whom we feel we have wronged. Clinician Will Friedman points to the sense of release experienced on resolving conflict with a harmed party. 'With repair complete in the eyes of the one harmed, this episode is now done; say, "Is this now over and complete for you? If so, then great! We both can completely let this go starting immediately".'[207] Having obtained forgiveness and absolution from a priest as the appointed arbiter, the incentive to resolve guilty feelings by also connecting with the one harmed becomes avoidable and thus more challenging.

In a BBC Podcast interview, Stephen Mulhall, fellow and tutor in philosophy at New College, Oxford has this to say: 'Guilt drives you to atone, to alleviate the harm that you have done so you focus on the victim. If you have an ethical culture that's built around the notion of guilt, you're building into it an idea of autonomy, emancipation (from social expectations), and a genuine concern for the harm you did to others. This is the core of any genuine morality.' [208] So, Augustine's penitential code offers an immoral resolution to guilt, focussing the wrongdoer away from the victim and onto a third party, the confessor. Augustine's idea of needing only God's grace for forgiveness stifles Mr Mulhall's 'healthy concern for the harm done to others.' It denies the perpetrator a proper resolution of guilty feelings, allowing the Catholic guilt we explored in chapter 3 to grow and fester.

Clergy are often in contact with vulnerable or distressed children who are required to confide deeply personal failings. The ritual of confession provides an opportunity for a priest to question a child in secrecy, on intimate or humiliating topics, but ordination is no assurance of a priest having had professional training in counselling. In the past, the power inequities of the sacrament of penance have led to sexually exploitative relationships.[209] The confession box gives priests 'easy, intimate access to children without anyone else being present'.[210] There is no intimidation or sexual experience that is out of bounds for discussion in the privacy of the confessional box. In 1919, American Cardinal Theodore McCarrick was one of the few clerics defrocked for soliciting sex while hearing confessions. The Church found him guilty of sexually abusing children over several decades.[211]

The concerns raised here focus on the harm being done to children, but they are not new. The Nolan report, published in 2001, noted that the Christian rite of penance inhibits reporting abuse and assists in silencing the victims.[212] Several scholars have gone further, arguing canon law operates as a parallel legal system.[213] In the eyes of the Christian Church, cCSA is a sin rather than a crime and the abusing priest is accountable only to God, not the victim or the state.[214] The ecclesiastical authorities have been accused of applying the doctrine of forgiveness as an institutional strategy to protect abusing clerics.[215]

Although more commonly associated with Catholicism, all Western denominations offer to forgive transgressions without reference or restitution to the wronged victim. As St Augustine's dogma on Adam and Eve's legacy of infantile guilt was endorsed, so the penitential doctrine was recognised and ratified by the C of E. During the Reformation the C of E resisted attempts to have references to private confession (e.g., with a priest or confessor) and absolution removed from the prayer book. Anglican priests will meet penitents on request to hear confessions face to face and offer absolution for sins, without such trappings as confessional booths. As in the Catholic tradition, the power to confer forgiveness is detached from, and independent of, the injured party. In the 19th century the Oxford Movement encouraged a revival of private confession, and it was accepted by some Anglo-Catholics. Many Anglicans, however, favour the general confession and absolution of the Holy Eucharist, when the priest pronounces general absolution for the sins of all those present. Absolution is given without reparation and without knowing what sins have been committed or what harm or grievance those sins might have caused. Infants learn that the identity and suffering of the victim are immaterial in the eyes of Christian Churches: clerics have power to forgive regardless.

Assured of confidentiality and forgiveness, a clergyman who has sexually abused many children multiple times can be confident in advance of obtaining absolution for each and every occurrence from one of his peers without reference to any of the victims, who might be unaware that the perpetrator has confessed, let alone that they have been forgiven. There is currently no independent, regulated process for reporting cCSA to the police. Indeed, until 2019, the canon law of pontifical secrecy prohibited bishops from informing anyone, including the statutory authorities. I am not the first to point out that this failing could be a factor aiding and perpetuating cCSA.

Christian Churches, of all denominations, have made insufficient progress in resolving these grievances and they continue to resist attempts to implement the progressive restorative practices discussed in the previous chapter.[145,216] Ampleforth College, one of the country's leading RC public schools, staffed by clerics and lay teachers, experienced a series of sexual abuse scandals in recent years. An independent inquiry in August 2018 published a highly critical report describing 'appalling sexual abuse inflicted over decades on children as young as seven', but the school's response was considered 'slow and insufficient'. Two years later, in December 2020, the government had no option but to bar the school from taking in new pupils pending improvements in safeguarding and leadership requirements.[217] Other reports confirm that regulatory compliance is half-hearted, documentation and reporting incomplete and supervision and monitoring casual. Crucial safeguarding measures agreed and put in place following moral panics in earlier years have since been blunted or quietly dropped by the Catholic Church.[218] Meanwhile, convicted priests who should have been defrocked continue to enjoy clerical perks and privileges.

The Australian government's Royal Commission into Institutional Responses to Child Sexual Abuse recommended that priests should be forced to report cCSA disclosed during confession, but in 2018 the RC Church formally rejected the inquiry's recommendation. The five-year inquiry found tens of thousands of children had suffered abuse in Australian institutions. Not only did the RC Church have the most cases, but 'The most notorious cases of sexual abuse in the Australian church occurred in institutional settings in the 1940s – 60s by men (and sometimes women) who were thoroughly trained in the strict morality and meticulous piety of the pre-Vatican II church.'[219] (Before the second Vatican Council devotions were more autocratic. For example, services were in Latin, not in the vernacular, and the priest faced away from the congregation who prayed in silence.) In 2017, a hearing of the UK child abuse inquiry backed up this latter point. Christopher Jamison, abbot primate of the English Benedictine Congregation, told the inquiry that the reason monk-priests had perpetrated abuse was because their training focused too much on doctrine.[220] In chapter 2 we noted how priesthood training concentrates rigorously on doctrine and how this narrow training affects the conduct of clergy. This seminarian training and its apparent consequences are discussed in chapter 11.

There is another morally reprehensible doctrine associated with the rite of penance and it is known as the penitential system of indulgences. If the soul is in a state of divine grace at the time of death (i.e. completely without stain of sin), Roman Catholics believe they will be allowed immediate access into the Kingdom of Heaven. In practice, sin is so prevalent that a state of divine grace is possessed only by saints and so the sinful soul is sent to a place called purgatory where it is made to atone for sins and so become cleansed before entering heaven. Purgatory is an unpleasant place of incarceration: not as horrible as hell, but not so heavenly as heaven.

The Church provides a simple solution to the problem of purgatory, and again the victim of sinning is excluded. Roman Catholics can mitigate the wages of sin by earning an indulgence, which will take time off one's stretch otherwise spent making reparation in the custodial void of purgatory. Nowadays no money changes hands: the sale of indulgences was outlawed in 1567 and the entire system was discontinued in the 1960s by the Second Vatican Council. But in 2000, as part of the celebration of the church's third millennium, Pope John Paul II reintroduced the system. Indulgences are bestowed by the Church and given secretly to the follower, in return for 'benefits in kind'. Some indulgences are granted on behalf of the living only, while others may be applied for on behalf of souls departed. Partial indulgences are available in multiples of days or years, like penal prepayments on account. Unfortunately, there is no way of knowing in advance the tariff to be exacted per sin, so to speak, so no way of knowing if one has overpaid or is in debt. Again, the Church has a solution. A plenary indulgence offers the blessed prospect of instant and total eradication of all one's punishment due to sins, venial or mortal, cCSA or murder, committed up to the time of gaining the indulgence.

My mother's pious aspiration was to cultivate in me, her eldest son, a priestly vocation, so she could receive a special plenary indulgence, which was spontaneously granted to the mother of a Catholic priest upon his ordination. A special plenary indulgence was the ultimate prize for a follower. Held on account to take effect at the exact moment of death, a special plenary indulgence granted the bearer instant access into heaven, bypassing purgatory. The attendant to the priest in celebration of the Holy Mass, as I was in my choirboy and altar boy roles, is a novitiate to ordination. Had I progressed, my ordination into priesthood would have conferred upon my mother the maximum benefit that Catholicism can offer – and the Church would gain a new priest.

# 8

# ARE WE BORN EVIL?
# SCIENCE AND AUGUSTINIAN GUILT

A core belief of most religions is that children need to be taught the difference between right and wrong. Augustine argued passionately that humans were born predisposed to wickedness and evil. Most parents will relate interactions with their children that might challenge both these claims. From the time my daughter was about two years old, she seemed to have an inkling of right and wrong. She would do something unkind, like pinch me purposely. I would react, perhaps with a yelp or just a frown, and she would kiss me better. I think she was exploring right and wrong and even making amends for a wrong she understood she had done. However, until recently, the orthodox theory on human development was that human beings start their lives with a 'moral blank slate'. Swiss psychologist Jean Piaget is famous for his pioneering work in child development. He concluded that for the first four years of life, children were in a pre-moral stage, but new research contradicts this view.

In 1897 Darwin suggested (in *The Descent of Man*) that morality is rooted in human nature: he considered it part of our evolutionary heritage. The latest science supports this view. Recent studies have found babies as young as six months old already make moral judgments, and perhaps we are born with a moral code hard-wired into our brains. In 2010 experiments were conducted with babies between six and ten months old. The tots were shown a toy dog puppet attempting to open a box, with a friendly teddy bear helping the dog, and an unfriendly teddy thwarting his efforts by sitting on him. After watching at least half a dozen times, the babies were given the opportunity to choose one of the teddy bears. A significant majority chose the helpful teddy. Another experiment used a puppet cat playing with a ball with a helpful rabbit puppet on one side and an unhelpful rabbit on the other. The helpful rabbit returned the ball if the cat lost it, while the unhelpful rabbit stole the ball and ran off with it. In this test, five-month-old babies were allowed to choose one of the rabbits, and most of them chose the helpful one. When the test was repeated with 21-month-old babies they were asked to take a treat from one of the rabbits. Most took the treat from the unhelpful rabbit, and one baby even gave the rabbit a smack on the head as well. The study was led by Paul Bloom, professor of psychology at the Infant Cognition Center at Yale University in Connecticut in the US, and used the ability to differentiate between unhelpful and helpful behaviour as its indicator of moral judgement. Bloom said there is mounting scientific evidence that the theories of Piaget, Freud and others might not be true and that 'some sense of good and evil seems to be bred in the bone'.[221]

Experts caution that adult assumptions can affect how a 21-month-old's behaviour is interpreted, and other factors could be influencing babies' reactions. However, another study in 2012 seems to confirm that infants know the difference between right and wrong before they reach the age of two. Researchers say babies will watch a scene for longer if they think it contains something unfair. In two experiments, 19-month-olds were timed on how long they watched a live scenario about fairness. In the first, the babies saw two giraffe puppets given either a toy each or both toys to one of the giraffes. In this experiment, three quarters of the infants looked longer when one giraffe got both toys. Psychologist Stephanie Sloane, who led the study at Illinois University, said 'We found that 19 and 21-month-old infants have a general expectation of fairness, and they can apply it appropriately to different situations.'[222] Aside from fairness, research has shown that small children expect people not to harm others and to help those in distress. Today, most psychologists accept that a child's moral development begins at birth as part of social and emotional growth. That foundation for ethical behaviour with others builds over the first five years, as a child's sense of justice and understanding the concept of right and wrong grows.

Some scientists believe that, rather than religion being the source of moral values, it is this inherent human moral awareness that created religious belief in the first place. Pascal Boyer, an anthropologist turned psychologist at Washington University in St Louis, Missouri, suggests that religion is a by-product of other cognitive capacities we evolved which had advantages. Psychological tests Boyer has run on children go some way to proving our natural tendency to believe. 'If you look at three- to five-year-olds, when they do something naughty, they have an intuition that everyone knows they've been naughty, regardless of whether they have seen or heard what they've done. It's a false belief, but it's good preparation for belief in an entity that is moral and knows everything,' he claims. 'The idea of invisible agents with a moral dimension who are watching you is highly attention-grabbing to us.'[223]

Science has made great strides in recent years in unpicking the source of human morality. Humans are innately disposed to be cooperative because we are an extremely social species. According to anthropologist Susanne Shults of the University of Oxford, ancestors of modern humans started living in social groups around 52 million years ago, and cooperative relationships have been essential for survival and prosperity ever since.[224] Being cooperative with others is the best way of establishing and maintaining relationships so it is little wonder people are cooperative with their families, friends, spouses, community members and even strangers. This tendency to be cooperative and kind comes in many forms – including love, loyalty, camaraderie, compassion, reciprocity, respect, generosity, gratitude, fairness, forgiveness, heroism and humility.

These expressions of morality appear to be evolutionarily ancient, psychologically distinct and cross-culturally universal. The same tendency to cooperative behaviour and kindness is present in societies throughout the world, regardless of religion or any other belief system. British scientists have discovered that the choice of moral values recognised within a community reflects the value of cooperation within that community. It is easy to see why we find investing in our relationships rewarding, and why helping others makes us happy. Just as Darwin predicted over 100 years ago, cooperation and kindness are indeed heritable. Humans have 'genes for kindness' and in societies like ours, about 33% of the difference in kindness (empathy, prosociality) between people is due to differences in genes.[225] In his book, *Good Natured*, Frans de Waal argues convincingly that our tendency to be kind towards others might not be uniquely human, but shared with the wider animal kingdom.[226] (This idea will not have surprised many of Britain's dog owners.)

Aware of this new science, in hindsight it seems self-evident that the world has an abundance of good-natured people. There is plenty of anecdotal evidence to suggest that most people are inherently good, regardless of beliefs. By far the majority of people we meet day to day are kindly and willing to cooperate. Of the hundreds of people I got to know well in my life, there are two or three that I might class as wicked, but even they had redeeming traits. If people were not inclined to cooperate with one another and be helpful to each other, the human race would not have survived for long. As David Allen points out in *The Wisdom Project*, the vast majority of people, when faced with clear ethical alternatives, will choose good over bad and even good over neutral options. If we saw a stranger's baby about to fall off a chair next to us, we would instinctively reach out to catch it. Almost everyone would do the same. We understand what actions are good and those that are bad, detached from any teaching by religion. When followers perceive that church teaching is wrong, when the rules of their religion conflict with their inner sense of what is right, believers ignore their teaching and act in accordance with the innately sound moral code they were born with.[76] That said, under circumstances of illness, fear, desperation or hate, we are all capable of doing harm to others. The cycle of evil is broken by understanding and compassion, as demonstrated by our historic heroes, such as Mohandas Gandhi and Nelson Mandela.

Thus, it turns out Augustine was mistaken and the British monk Pelagius was right. Humans are not naturally predisposed to evil. On the contrary we are naturally disposed to be cooperative and kind. These research findings by our own British scientists lead to the conclusion that man's innate sense of right and wrong predates Augustine by thousands of years. Far from religion offering a lead, religion was probably conceived to satisfy a human need to explain our evolved sense of morality. Ironically, Augustine's ideas threaten our capacity to cooperate and be kind. When we brand everyone with Augustine's dark label of fundamental wickedness, we lose the opportunity to address the causes of evil actions by ourselves and others. 'If the soul is left in darkness, sins will be committed,' Victor Hugo wrote in *Les Misérables*. 'The guilty one is not he who commits the sin, but the one who causes the darkness.'[227]

A churchgoer and chorister, I know lots of lovely, kind and cooperative Christians. They are decent people despite their Augustinian indoctrination telling them they are inherently wicked and evil, not because of it. People might be good or bad, but if someone is good you can be sure their good nature has nothing to do with religion. I give credit to myself and my fellow countrymen for having gained moral stability despite our wayward Christian indoctrination in infancy. So why did Augustine think we are all born evil? He is not alone. Great philosophers of the past have disagreed about whether humans are inherently kind or evil; Hobbes and Rousseau took opposite views on this long-standing question of human nature. We are concerned here with the effect on infants who have assimilated Augustine's ideas, but I am curious to understand how these, and other great thinkers of the past, could have got it so wrong. Although most humans are cooperative and kind, it is a matter of clinical record that some humans are innately wicked, and science can often explain the mental disorders that make them so.[228] Now, I am not a clinician and I do not have St Augustine in front of me anyway, but we can consult experts who have studied and analysed Augustine's writings. It is fascinating to speculate, in a light-hearted spirit, on why Augustine managed to misjudge human nature so badly.

In chapter 1 we noted that several academic researchers studying Augustine have identified multiple narcissistic traits. If we strip away the gilded prose in Augustine's writing, his character and his underlying behaviour do seem to bear the hallmarks of narcissism. Narcissistic personality disorder is a psychiatric illness and defined in DSM-5 as comprising a pervasive pattern of grandiosity (in fantasy or behaviour), a constant need for admiration, and a lack of empathy.[229] It would be preposterous to suggest that Augustine was mentally ill, but we can observe that certain of the traits he exhibits seem to match those generally associated with narcissism. The classic attribute is grandiosity, expressed in charisma and charm, well matched to a career in rhetoric. Such individuals often present as superhuman, however narcissists typically lack the ability to empathise. This is because they are incapable of imagining themselves standing in another person's shoes. Far from being superhuman, people deprived of empathy perform in a subhuman way in their interpersonal relationships, and these individuals wreak havoc in positions of power.[230] We noted earlier that Homo sapiens have survived and thrived because we are inherently cooperative. If we all lacked empathy, we would be disinclined to help one another and society would descend into chaos.

In our brief look at his life, we noted the way Augustine treated his concubine. People who exhibit narcissistic attributes are often capable of expressing love eloquently, vocally or in prose, but they have a reduced capacity for human emotions like sympathy, compassion or genuine affection. Without the ability to see things from another person's standpoint and share another's feelings and emotions, there is no desire to cooperate and be kind. If Augustine was marked by traits associated with narcissism, he would have lacked the human qualities of sensitivity and compassion that bond partners. Certain narcissistic individuals believe the world to be hostile and antagonistic, and if that was Augustine's mental state it would explain why he considered all humans to be inherently wicked.[231] It would also explain his aberrant view of sex. As Fredriksen puts it in *Augustine and his Analysts*: 'He cannot truly love; his assessment of the nature of sexual love is shaped by his experience of only enjoying a narcissistic gratification from the person loving him. His sexuality is "a torture to the will".'[232]

Whatever the nature of Augustine's mental demons, his assertion of the lust and wickedness he imagined to be inherent in infants was abhorrent and it was wrong. Babies are born pure and innocent and capable of developing a socially responsible moral framework entirely of their own free will.

Within a few months of my birth, long before I could understand the significance, I was taken to church to be christened. Water was poured over my head three times while the celebrant of the sacrament pronounced, 'Michael, I baptise you in the name of the Father, and of the Son, and of the Holy Ghost.' Apparently I bawled my head off throughout. Of course, I knew nothing of this until afterwards when my mother told me I had been baptised and sketchily explained the concept of original sin. I did not think much about it until I was older, but subconsciously I believe it added to a vague sense of me being culpable, particularly because the reason for blame was unclear to me. In my schooldays I was taught the Bible story of Adam and Eve, supported by the drawing with sexual allegories that I mentioned earlier. Infants see the world in black and white terms; a misdeed is simply a wrongful act. It was confusing to be told the morally misleading concept of taking blame for someone else, but I was naïve and trusted what grown-ups told me. Later I became aware that original sin was associated with sexual lust, and that was more confusing still.

About half of the present population of Britain have had a church christening, but the proportion of babies being baptised into the C of E has fallen from a high of 70% in 1930 to 12% in 2011. Nearly all Catholics, about 9% of the population, still get their babies baptised. In modern times original sin and its sexual connotations have been dimmed and most Christians get baptised for ethnic or familial reasons. Conformance with cultural norms might be one reason, but there are other reasons why parents might want to get their babies baptised. A recent opinion poll in Catholic Ireland found that one in five parents baptised their child just to get them enrolled in school.[233] Although the percentage of Catholic schools is lower in the UK, faith schools in Britain are legally entitled to discriminate in favour of children on the basis of religion in their admission. It seems likely that a similar percentage applies to British parents, because faith schools have an undeserved reputation for performing better than other schools. Faith schools appear to get good results, but Church schools and other faith schools in the state sector are selective and any selective school can easily achieve better than average results.[234]

Interestingly, the above survey shows that even in Catholic Ireland, a majority of parents think RE should be scrapped and a new subject including ethics and the facts on all religions should be taught, not just instruction in Christianity. Speaking in 2008, the general secretary of the Association of Teachers and Lecturers, Dr Mary Bousted, said, 'In our increasingly multi-faith and secular society it is hard to see why our taxes should be used to fund schools which discriminate against the majority of children and potential staff because they are not of the same faith.'[235]

The school management setup shows the influence exercised by the C of E. Of the state-funded schools in England and Wales, about 30% are Christian faith schools and most are Voluntary Aided (VA schools). A foundation or trust (usually a religious organisation) inputs a small proportion of the capital costs for the school and forms a majority on the VA school's governing body. The governing body employs the staff, decides the religious agenda and sets admissions criteria. The land and buildings are usually owned by the religious organisation. Voluntary Controlled schools (VC schools) are like VA schools, but are run by the local authority. The local authority employs the staff, decides the religious agenda and sets admissions. Once again, the foundation or trust (usually a religious organisation) owns the land and buildings, and commonly forms a quarter of the governing body. This situation favours religion and ensures the UK population continues to be indoctrinated in flawed Augustinian values, despite the majority being non-religious and a significant and growing minority being anti-religious.

Because faith schools choose their pupils, they decrease choice for the majority of parents who are not prepared to join, or pretend to join, a religion. Parents sometimes have no choice but to allow their offspring to be indoctrinated. Despite requesting secular education, 20,000 schoolchildren were forced to attend faith schools in 2019 because there was no alternative locally.[236] Parents have been able to withdraw their children from RE and from collective worship since the 1944 Education Act and no legislation since has affected this right. It is most recently confirmed in Section 71 of the School Standards and Framework Act 1998, but the option to withdraw a child does not offer a solution. In practice fewer than 6% of schools report any children having been withdrawn from RE or collective worship.[237] Dr Lundie, Senior Lecturer in Education at Liverpool Hope University, lists confusion regarding parents' rights, embarrassment, fear of isolation and concerns about disruption to explain why so few children are withdrawn. Schools are discouraged from easing withdrawal, since they have no access to funding to support the supervision of children withdrawn from an assembly the law requires them to provide.

An argument often put forward in favour of faith schools is that religious organisations build the schools which would not otherwise exist. Campaign group the **Accord Coalition** reported in 2019 that the funding contributed by faith schools towards opening and maintaining their own buildings has fallen sharply over the past decade. Today the Church makes a relatively minor contribution of 10% to the funding of its schools. An analysis of the Department for Education shows £643,240,000 of capital funding was given to Voluntary Aided (VA) faith schools in 2009 – 2010 and these schools contributed just £67,290,000 towards their costs.[238] Furthermore, capital values are enhanced with state funds when buildings are improved. Since the Church trust often retains ownership of the land and buildings, the trust is likely to make a net gain over the life of the average school. Ignoring unsalable artifacts, the Catholic Church is already the wealthiest organisation in the world and the C of E is far from being impoverished as we will see in chapter 9. Housed for free, often in grand accommodation, the C of E's 42 diocesan bishops are each paid over £46,000 a year, plus expenses.[239] Assuming an average spend on rent in the UK of 34% of income, that equates to more than £62,000 compared with average UK earnings of £31,461 (2020).[240] Note that in addition to their salary, bishops often enjoy significant earnings from outside interests, providing what seems to be a princely income for their role.

From a communal perspective, and from my own experience, religion can be shown to be tribal and divisive, at least some of the time. Even within belief systems there are multiple denominations, so the doctrines themselves are divisive.[241] Having been raised in a Catholic household and having attended only Catholic schools, by the time I started work I had developed an instinctive disdain for anyone who admitted to being a non-Catholic. I was convinced my beliefs were right and proper; thus, anyone who was not Christian was necessarily stupid, or ignorant or wilfully bad. This attitude of arrogant religious oblivion, implanted by factional indoctrination, persists today.[242] Recent reports conclude that 'faith schools, to the extent that they are segregated, deprive young people of the opportunity to mix across ethnic and religious lines.'[243] It is obvious that intergroup contact in a diverse school setting is more likely to cultivate attitudes favourable to social cohesion. In an increasingly divided society, the ability to understand the views of others is essential. It behoves schools to equip children with these skills by fostering an environment that is inclusive and respectful of everyone's belief or non-belief. Yet the government refuses to change its pro-religious position despite having lost a court case in 2015 defending a claim that it did not treat religious and non-religious views equally. When it published the new GCSE, AS and A level criteria in 2014, the government 'decided not to include the optional systematic study of non-religious beliefs alongside religious beliefs.'[244] Since the largest slice of the UK population is non-religious and a significant propor-tion is hostile to religion, Mr Justice Warby ruled that this decision by the government was unlawful.[245]

Unsuccessful attempts have been made to establish schools with-out a Christian ethos in the UK. In September 2007, Dr Paul Kelley, head of Monkseaton High School in Tyneside, proposed to eliminate the daily act of Christian worship in his school. The plan was blocked because it would cause 'a fundamental change in the relationship with the school and the established religion of the country'. A senior figure at the then Department for Education and Skills told Dr Kelley that bishops in the House of Lords and ministers would block his plans. Religion, they admitted, was 'technically embedded' in many aspects of education.[246]

Despite supporting religious indoctrination in schools, the government refuses to support other pseudo sciences. One could arguably compare Christianity dealing in redemption with, say homeopathy, dealing in health. Both work with alchemy and accu-mulate wealth in the process. A House of Commons Science and Technology Committee review on homeopathy in 2010 reported that homeopathic remedies perform no better than placebos (dummy treatments). NHS England recommended that GPs and other pre-scribers should stop providing it. The review concluded that the principles on which homeopathy is based are 'scientifically implau-sible'.[247] The government agrees that Christian ideas are scientifically implausible (teaching creationism is barred in state-funded schools) [248] but it continues its financial and legislative support of Augustine's equally implausible theories and views despite evidence of the harm indoctrination has done to people like me.

The UN Convention on the Rights of the Child (Article 14) envisions a child being free to express their religious beliefs, not necessarily the beliefs of their parents.[99] In Britain only pupils in sixth form education or over the compulsory school age of 18 may withdraw themselves from collective worship.[249,250] Even then, faith schools often make withdrawal nigh on impossible, but regardless, by age 16 it will be too late.[251] As we have seen, brain architecture is moulded in infancy, so by adolescence the Augustinian ideas that have burdened me will have already taken root in a child's brain. Long before age 16 the school's punishment will already have been administered with all the long-lasting consequences for the individual.

Parents are given the right to control their own children's religious upbringing, no matter how unsound their beliefs. That privilege of parents is wise and unassailable, but it is unreasonable to place the cost of proselytising children onto taxpayers. For the benefit of the child and for the sake of society, schools should open an objective window on the world to all pupils. Currently, regulation and supervision of religious education is inconsistent as we have seen, and this situation is bound to punish some children, through no fault of their own. The increasingly chaotic state of RE in schools threatens the safety and unity of the UK.

# 9

# AUGUSTINE'S TORMENT EMBEDDED IN WESTERN MORES

We looked briefly at attitudes towards children in antiquity; let us bring this discussion up to date. Until the early twentieth century, there were no standards of protection for children, even as Europe started to industrialise. As soon as they were old enough, children were expected to pull their weight, working alongside adults. In the countryside this meant working outside in gruelling conditions, in all weathers. In towns and cities working situations in factories and shops were often unsanitary and unsafe. The earliest known schools in England were established by cathedrals and monasteries in the late sixth century. Their role was not to educate, but to prepare boys for monastic life and the priesthood. Education was mostly conducted within the family until the 19th century. Even then, only wealthy parents had real access to education, provided almost exclusively by the Church. Universities were mostly aimed at training priests; Oxford and Cambridge were only open to members of the C of E. It was not until the Elementary Education Act of 1870 that the possibility of a broader education became available to the few children in England and Wales lucky enough to benefit. The Voluntary Schools Act of 1897 provided grants to public elementary schools not funded by school boards, which were principally church schools teaching the Bible, song schools teaching church music or grammar schools teaching Latin. The study of temporal subjects was limited or absent from the curricula; these schools were set up to proselytise students. Most schools at the time were owned by the C of E and the 1897 bill changed little, apart from subsidising C of E schools with taxpayers' money.[252]

Major changes were introduced with the Education Act of 1944, purging the education system of fragmentation and introducing a new examination, the 11-plus. This controversial exam included psychological intelligence tests to grade children suitable for academic, technical or general education: this was known as the tripartite system.[253] The C of E took advantage of the opportunity to extend the reach of its grip on children's education. Before WWII, roughly half of all schools were church schools, and the church used its land ownership to gain control of religious education in all UK state-supported schools. The disturbing details are contained in the document ED 138/22 filed away in the National Archives. Collective Worship and instruction in Christian beliefs became a legal requirement in all supported schools, and in return the government gained a share of control over church schools to carry out refurbishments and desperately needed reforms.[254] Year by year public demand for separation of state and religion has grown. Yet the Church continues to maintain a stranglehold on education in Britain, notwithstanding the damage done to the lives of people like me, and in spite of declining contributions made by religious bodies.[231] In 1924 the League of Nations adopted the Geneva Declaration on the Rights of the Child, drafted by Eglantyne Jebb, founder of the Save the Children Fund. Despite the entitlement of children to decide their own beliefs being defined by international convention, children's right to an education free from sectarian religious indoctrination is not properly protected in any part of Britain, even 100 years later.

As we have seen, nearly all children reject religion when they leave school and a majority believe religion is more a force for evil than a force for good. In the wider community, even the core tenets of Christian belief are generally doubted. For instance, a 2013 YouGov survey found that just 27% of the population believed that Jesus Christ was the son of God, and just 33% believed in the essential Christian doctrine of life after death. The scientifically discredited view that 'People need religious teachings in order to understand what is right and wrong' was accepted by 27% of respondents.[255] More work needs to be done in educating young people openly and honestly, yet all schools in Britain are supposed to teach some version of Augustine's unsound values. Many Christian faith schools still apply the disturbing self-abusive practices described in chapter 3. The UK is the only country in the world that requires all her children (other than those enrolled in a specifically different faith school such as an Islamic one) to be instructed in Christian values through daily acts of collective worship, whatever their beliefs.

Returning to the science discussed in the previous chapter, confirming the genetic proclivity that humans have towards being kind and cooperative, the point I wish to make is this. Since children are born with a positive and socially valuable sense of morality and fair play, it seems perverse for government to insist upon indoctrinating them with Augustine's unsound mores of Christian faith that we have been discussing. Even basic Christian teaching is feudalistic, sexist or associated with other discredited moral principles.[256] Blanket commandments deny the subtleties of real-life situations that children need to experience in order to learn, and Christian dogma invites the unhelpful casuistry we discussed in chapter 5. Casuistry is an example of how the natural inclination of humans to be cooperative and fair-minded shines through Christian indoctrination. Legislation would be ineffective if citizens were unwilling to respect the spirit of the law, but the indoctrination we have examined seems likely to encourage followers to look for any technicality and loophole to exploit.

Section 78 of the Education Act (2002) requires all schools in England and Wales to promote the spiritual, moral, cultural, mental and physical development of pupils in accordance with societal norms and to prepare pupils at the school for the opportunities, responsibilities and experiences of later life. It is hard to see how any faith school can meet this requirement while promoting Christian beliefs. For example, the doctrine of original sin fosters unmerited guilt and contradicts a child's innate sense of justice and reason, while the doctrines of penance and blood sacrifice are primeval and contrary to society's fundamental understanding of fair play. These teachings hampered my ability to thrive and prosper, and I submit that they are liable to disadvantage many children.

We have seen that around a third of schools are faith schools and in chapter 3 we looked fleetingly at the role of SACREs in these schools. Although a statutory subject, RE is treated differently from all others. There is no nationally agreed curriculum to specify the topics to be covered: instead there are more than 100 diverse syllabuses (LASs) agreed locally throughout the UK by individual SACREs. Religious belief in the UK population is concentrated in the senior age range, according to multiple surveys referenced in this book. The typical age demographic of these controversial SACRE bodies tends to preordain an approach to religious belief that conflicts with the views and needs of the youngsters they aim to educate. Lax regulation has led to a situation where Christian oriented professionals have been able to seize control of the subject, paid for by the state through school funding. Some local authority SACREs are able to circulate syllabuses promoting values espoused by specific faiths rather than those of the pluralistic and predominantly non-religious society that Britain has become. This allows sexist, misogynistic and even extreme views, contrary to British values, to be presented as normal.[257,258] Everyone seems to agree that education in ethics and religion is important, yet many schoolchildren are denied access to a full and proper study of the subject. A child, raised in a Christian household as I was, might have no opportunity to hear and scrutinise a wide religious perspective. In order for the state to meet its own declared obligations, and to comply with international law, schools should be compelled to provide children with a rounded education in ethics and religion from an objective, critical and pluralistic viewpoint.

Religious leaders demand that children of parents following their faith are kept in ignorance of information about topics like same-sex marriage, LGBT relationships and transgenderism.[259],[260] Churches object to children learning about subjects that conflict with their doctrines. Education is the nemesis of religion and the struggle to provide open and questioning education for young British pupils has always been challenging. We noted earlier in this chapter that faith schools follow a long line of church school institutions for proselytising young people. Schools owned by the Church have never been committed to general education and it is understandable that the Church wants to preserve their traditional function. However, depriving children of information on religious grounds disadvantages those who happen to be born of parents following a particular faith. That is contrary to the international agreements that Britain signed up to as we noted in chapter 2, yet denying children access to education in state-funded faith schools is not unlawful in Britain. All sides agree that the current system of religious education is divisive and unworkable: it is not fit for purpose. SACREs should be reformed to ensure the nation's children do not continue to be unfairly punished as I was.

In faith schools, moral values and basic human and civic principles such as compassion, truthfulness, tolerance, respect, responsibility, forgiveness, generosity and justice are often promoted as 'Christian values' unique to religion. Not only is this untruthful but it is socially divisive. It creates prejudice and distorts children's religious outlook to paint Christians as morally superior and all others as morally second-rate. On abortion, birth control, medical research and other moral issues, Christianity is out of step with society and often even with its own followers.[13] Yet reports by the C of E scrutinising body, Statutory Inspections of Anglican and Methodist Schools (SIAMS),[261] often criticise schools that promote values such as compassion if teachers have not misled children by presenting them as being distinctively Christian.

Thornier still is the requirement for all schools to actively promote the values of 'democracy, the rule of law, individual liberty and mutual respect and tolerance for those with different faiths and beliefs'. Since most religious people deny the righteousness of all other faiths, it seems impossible for teachers to adhere to the demands of the law while inculcating one specific religious belief. In chapter 13 we see that in practice, respect and tolerance is absent from many syllabuses. Indoctrinating partition and bigotry towards other faiths encourages the racism, misogyny and homophobia identified within the ranks of ecclesiastics themselves.[262] From personal experience I can say that my Catholic background made me spontaneously scornful of non-Catholics for years after I left school.

Modern schools are places where one would expect children to be educated, not places where pressure is applied for them to be proselytised. Evangelising is a role for churches, not for classes of impressionable infants. My school experience could, and in my view should, have helped to broaden my mind – instead it confined me. Among many other distortions, I was taught at school that Luther was an evil heretic and that Queen Mary was a hero who upheld the faith. No doubt my peers in a Protestant school would have been told the opposite. Only later did I learn about Bloody Queen Mary and the corruption surrounding the church's system of priced indulgences.

In his plenary lecture to Amnesty International in 1997, Cambridge neuropsychologist Nicholas Humphrey criticised religious indoctrination, pointing out:

> *If children have a right to be protected from false ideas, they have too a right to be succoured by the truth, and we as a society have a duty to provide it. Therefore, we should feel as much obliged to pass*

*on to our children the best scientific and philosophical understanding
of the natural world – to teach, for example, the truths of evolution
and cosmology, or the methods of rational analysis – as we already
feel obliged to feed and shelter them.*

I admire the criterion that Humphrey proposed to judge false
ideas. Here it is:

*If it is ever the case that teaching this system to children will mean
that later in life they come to hold beliefs that, were they in fact to
have had access to alternatives, they would most likely not have
chosen for themselves, then it is morally wrong of whoever presumes
to impose this system and to choose for them to do so. No one has
the right to choose badly for anyone else.*

At the start of this book we noted evidence that when they leave
school, 99% of juveniles will reject the religion the state imposed
upon them. The support currently provided to faith schools by the
state is immoral, using the standard set by Humphrey.

We have taken note of the slick Christian presentations vended by
the commercial publicists Ten:Ten Resources. Over a third of RE
syllabuses are written by another commercial resource provider that
is funded by a Christian trust working closely with the C of E to promote its approach to instruction in Christianity. This is binding many
community schools to what is, in effect, an exclusively Christian
syllabus. Over 10% of authorities have adopted a syllabus that relies
largely on the C of E resource *Understanding Christianity* for teaching
that faith. Any lesson plans drawn from this resource will disseminate
views far from the aim of an impartial, objective and pluralistic study
of religion and worldviews encompassing a wide range of disciplinary
approaches, as recommended by CoRE, examined in chapter 4.

Chris Selway of the NSS who undertook an entire one full day
and two half-day sessions of the *Understanding Christianity* teaching
course, remarked:

*At first glance just some of the titles that are leading questions are an early warning of bias: 'Who Made the World?' and 'What is the Good News Jesus Brings?' are leading questions that feature in Key Stage 1, whilst 'What Did Jesus do to Save Human Beings?'; 'What Would Jesus Do?' and 'What Kind of King is Jesus?' are features of Key Stage 2. Key Stage 1 follows the common tendency in RE to start younger children off with an uncritical pattern of telling stories that are important to Christians, much as you might do in a Sunday school.*

Bible stories such as the creation and Noah's ark are taught to infants who are not yet able to appreciate the differences between history, fact, fiction, myth etc. In an introduction to this resource, Nigel Genders, Chief Education Officer at the C of E says: 'We wanted this resource to be available not just for Church of England schools but for all schools across the country as part of the Church of England's offer of education for the common good.' Genders' evangelical common good does not chime with my idea of common good; his offer is more in line with the portrayals of Christian indoctrination laid out in these pages. Quite apart from failing to provide a truly impartial, critical and pluralistic study of religion and worldviews, pupils in faith schools suffer an unacceptable loss of lesson time engaging in ideas that nearly all of them are liable to discard the moment they leave.

Mr Selway goes on to demonstrate numerous misleading claims and blinkered portrayals of religious ideas contained in the teaching course.

*This serves the purposes of the Church of England and other evangelicals, but ... The wider study of socio-historical aspects of Christianity as a world religion have been neglected, resulting in an unrealistic representation that invites low-level confessionalism, particularly in the primary school phase. Controversial and negative manifestations of Christianity in the wider world have also been glossed over by both making texts central to the study of the religion and selecting only benign extracts from the Bible.*[263]

RE Today Services, the publishers of *Understanding Christianity* and over a third of locally agreed syllabuses, have restricted public access to what schools are legally bound to teach. This denies parents the opportunity to understand what will be taught to their young and is contrary to government guidance that they are statutory documents agreed by a public body and paid for out of public funding budgets. Costs to the state of implementing the resource are significant. Each teacher taking the course will spend two full days on the lessons, plus further time studying and planning for using the resource. This time could be better spent preparing coursework that encompasses wider cultural, political, religious and societal diversity and how they interact. These learning modules are essential to meet the needs of pupils who are growing up in an increasingly pluralistic and mainly non-religious society.

Instead of valuable open-mindedness, many children will carry a burden of unhelpful images with them from their childhood prose-lytisation. Let me say that I found many RE images disturbing. The idea of a powerful, evil devil is not a positive thought for a child. I was told that this dangerous demon was intent on dragging me into a horrible place of everlasting fire called hell. Not that hell and the devil upset me deeply. Perhaps the image was inconceivable. A good God sending people to be burned alive for ever and ever because they did something wrong was unimaginable. The tangible religious icons I encountered made a more profound impression. In the Catholic tradition, the passion of Christ is followed by contemplating 14 pictures, called *Stations of the Cross*, each depicting an episode in the suffering and death of Christ. Our local church had these pictures arranged on the walls and the detailed contents of every picture were impressed on me from infancy.

In the first picture Christ is condemned to death. He is shown crowned with a band of thorny stems which soldiers had forced down onto his head. Blood is trickling down his face while the soldiers look on, laughing. We had wild blackberries at the bottom of our garden and I was well aware that brambles scratch painfully.

I could feel Christ's sharp thorns piercing my flesh and everyone pointing and laughing at me. The following picture shows Christ being scourged by the soldiers and his back is raw and bleeding. My school prayer book said the soldiers lashed him 39 times and one more would have killed him. The teacher explained that scourges were made of leather strips knotted at the ends to inflict severe pain. Next Christ is forced to carry the huge cross upon which he will later be crucified. I remember thinking how heavy the cross must be if it had been made strong enough to carry someone's weight. Further along Christ is shown having fallen from exhaustion. Several pictures showed Christ having collapsed and each time he is being beaten by soldiers to make him get up. A later picture showed a man with a big hammer bashing huge nails into Christ's hands while a soldier watched on. Our teacher said that the nails probably were not put though Christ's hands because they would have pulled through the flesh. They must have been nailed through the wrist. Checking my own small hands, I could feel the fleshy gap between my bones (metacarpals). It was obvious even to my junior mind that the bony wrists offered better holding and I shuddered at the pain a nail hammered through the wrist would cause. One of the final pictures showed a soldier stabbing a sword into Christ's chest. Reading my prayer book I learned that all blood had left Christ's body, and water flowed out proving that Christ had died for us. My prayer book said that the suffering and sacrificial death of Christ shown in the *Stations of the Cross* was required to atone for my sins and reconcile me with God.

Nothing has changed, and today infants in faith schools are put to work drawing pictures of Christ being brutally put to death. In at least one primary school, infants' gory pictures are put on show and even posted on Twitter by a diocesan adviser. Christianity's cruel images are likely to be the first pictures of brutality a child will see. It is appalling to find primary schools taking risks with infants' mental health, when there are strong indications that some children exposed to violent scenes can become antisocial and emotionally distressed.[264] Crucially, the long-term effects are greater for young children.[265] A recent film presented on BBC TV was heralded by a warning 'Scenes that may distress younger viewers'. In fact the film was tame compared with the images I have described. Society tries to protect infants from violent images, but today Christianity's distressing pictures and effigies of ancient torture and brutal death are recklessly presented to younger viewers, and even to infants as described in chapter 13.

I had learned about original sin and how Adam and Eve were disobedient and how that act of naughtiness makes everyone guilty, not for doing wrong but just for being born. Now my prayer book told me that God sacrificed his only son to make up for Adam and Eve's disobedience and for all our wickedness. That was confusing. God tortured and killed his own child to let everyone else off the hook for their wickedness. If I hurt someone, how does another person being hurt make up for the hurt I caused? Only I can make up for my own wrongdoings and harmful actions. If I offend another person and I want to earn their forgiveness, I need to say sorry to that person. Another's actions cannot make amends for my wrongdoing. The story of Christ 'dying for our sins' puzzled me. It seemed to echo Christianity's blame-blurring message of confession, where the perpetrator gets absolved in secret and the victim is disregarded. It was another confusing and disturbing lesson in Christian morality and a further turn of the screw in the Augustinian mind-vice of dread and deference. Not only is religion unsound in its provision of moral guidance, the lessons of blood sacrifice that Augustine teaches seem to hail from a bygone age of ignorance. The ideas that are embedded in a child's mind at this tender age get accepted and can imprint for a lifetime. Even decades later, former believers who intellectually reject these ideas can feel involuntary anxiety or shame when some minor happening triggers their unconscious learning. Moral confusion can be dangerous for society, as we noted when we looked at Christian judges in chapter 5.

It might be no coincidence that nearly half the population of the United States supported one-time American president Donald Trump, and swallowed his falsehoods. That is roughly the same proportion of Americans who say they believe the myth of creation rather than the observable evidence of natural selection.[266] When Trump's supporters stormed the senate on 6th January 2021, one man mounted the podium and shouted, 'Jesus Christ, we invoke your name.' The insurgents carried Bibles, crosses and 'Make America Godly Again' flags. (Fig. 4.) Augustine's followers were easy prey for Trump's deceits and misrepresentations delivered from an evangelical platform. Said to be the most untruthful leader in modern times, Donald Trump is what you get when you encourage young people to ignore facts and rely on faith.[267] The warning given by conservative Republican senator Barry Goldwater in 1986 (quoted by John Dean) seems prescient:

> *Mark my word ... if and when these preachers get control of the [Republican] party, and they're sure trying to do so, it's going to be a terrible damn problem. Frankly these people frighten me. Politics and governing demand compromise. The government won't work without it. But Christians [politicians] believe they are acting in the name of God, so they can't and won't compromise. I know, I've tried to deal with them.*[268]

Educating our young people to be inquiring and critical has never been more important. With today's knowledge of climate change it is clear that science deniers in positions of power can threaten the health of the planet and the futures of the infants now passing through primary schools. Professor of Education John Elmore (one of my heroes) wrote '...the fragile and fast-dissolving separation of church and state is critically necessary to protect democracy from religion, not the other way around'. [269] Dr Elmore was speaking of USA politics, but the risk to democracy from deficiencies in critical, dialogic education that he identified applies equally to the UK.

**Figure 4. Christian symbols flaunted by
Trump supporters, USA, January 2021**

(Photos by Selcuk Acar-NurPhoto-Getty Images,
Nina Berman and Hope O'Brian/Cronkite News)

To summarise the words of another inspirational lecturer, religious
studies should encourage philosophical thought, decision-making
skills, collaboration and independent working skills and the search

for compromise and conflict resolutions that work. It should create opportunities for young people to develop their skills of dialogue, interpretation and analysis in a coherent context. It should make a unique contribution to understanding British heritage, plurality, values and futures, providing an opportunity for young people to engage with contemporary contentious issues, developing social, cultural, political, philosophical and historical awareness. It should help pupils learn to respect themselves and understand their own identity, to respect others and to understand their own and others' rights and responsibilities.[270] To replace all these ideas with confessional indoctrination in one religion short changes our young people. As Chris Selway points out, RE has to become a secular subject taught from an objective, critical and pluralistic viewpoint.[227] The recommendations contained in Mr Selway's report provide a balanced and sensible basis for progress but while churches hold ownership of school land and buildings, little progress will be made.

We have noted that Britain is a country with a non-religious population and a commendable tradition of tolerance towards communities of diverse faiths. Yet some parts of the UK are divided by religious sectarianism. State education provides the opportunity to reduce intolerance and improve social cohesion. Instead, faith schools are liable to exacerbate intolerance and division. Again, Dr Elmore, makes the point well. In his insightful analysis he advocates 'critical, dialogic education against dogmatic training.' The requisite absolutism inherent in religious training (as opposed to religious education) inevitably invites sectarianism, threatening our characteristic British tolerance.[271]

A housing commission set up by the archbishop of Canterbury suggested land owned by the C of E could be used to build affordable homes in the next few years.[272] Property values and equities have soared over the past decade, swelling church coffers, and this proposed grant of land is a welcome initiative.[273] Since the Church Commissioners, the C of E's main property arm, owns 105,000 acres of land and 'earns more money than McDonald's' from around £8 billion in assets, the C of E could go further.[274] Releasing Church holdings of school land and buildings would detach religion from education and allow RE to be free and unfettered. The Catholic Church is wealthier still, one of the richest institutions in the world, and the churches income from capital gains is earned free from taxation. Given independent, unfettered control of all schools, a common syllabus for RE could be agreed covering ethics and religion from an objective, critical and pluralistic viewpoint, agreed and incorporated into the national curriculum, which all schools, state-funded or otherwise, should be required to follow. The current approach which imposes Christianity on children, under threat of statutory violation, is not working. Statistics show religious leaders are mistrusted; only 12% of young people feel influenced by them.[69] Religious studies should inspire rectitude and should not encourage recourse to bad casuistry.[275] In today's interconnected world, religion would stand a better chance of being accepted if all schools presented the subject in a more open and questioning way. Liberating their school buildings could provide an opportunity for the churches to show conviction and leadership. A common syllabus on neutral school ground would avoid disagreement and all pupils would gain the benefit of an open and rounded education.

# 10

# CHILD SEXUAL ABUSE AND THE AUGUSTINIAN FACTOR

What evidence is there that Augustine's view on infant concupiscence influences those indoctrinated in his beliefs in childhood? In the late 1970s and early 1980s, a number of like-minded individuals formed a group calling itself the Paedophile Information Exchange (PIE). It campaigned for 'children's sexuality', and lobbied the government to axe or lower the age of consent. The real aim was to normalise sex with children. It offered support to adults 'in legal difficulties concerning sexual acts with consenting "under age" partners'. Although not explicitly a Christian group, it was founded, managed, enabled and supported by Christians, or individuals that led lives characteristic of the Christian faithful. The BBC wrote up the story of how Christian paedophiles attempted to go mainstream in the 1970s with this headline 'How did the pro-paedophile group PIE exist openly for 10 years?'[276]

Ian Campbell Dunn (1st May 1943 – 10th March 1998) and Michael Hanson were co-founders of the group. Ian was schooled at RC Hillhead High, Glasgow (which became comprehensive in 1972) and his funeral was held in 1998 at the Catholic Apostolic Church, Mansfield Place, Edinburgh. Hanson went to the Anglo-Catholic

Ardingly College in West Sussex. The financial backer to PIE was former Anglican vicar and millionaire Michael Studdert. Among the members was Father Barry Ingram, a Catholic priest, and Richard Travell, a Sunday school teacher. John Stamford, a former church minister, published international guides for child molesters. After 40 years it has proved impossible to trace all the members of PIE and check their religious identity. What can be said from my research is that I did not find any identifying as non-believers, and those members whom I have been able to identify led lives that implied belief in one or other Christian denomination. According to the BBC report referenced above, it was not difficult to join PIE. 'There was no need for subterfuge, just an application and a cheque for £4', which makes it all the more noteworthy that the membership seems to have been wholly or substantially Christian.

The group achieved recognition on a freedom of speech and freedom of association platform. By 1978, PIE had become affiliated to long-standing and well-respected civil advocacy groups such as the National Council for Civil Liberties (NCCL, later rebranded Liberty) and the Albany Trust (a specialist counselling and psychotherapy charity). At the time the Albany Trust tied up with PIE, Sir Harold Haywood OBE and Raymond Clarke were in the driving seat. Clarke was a Methodist and later a member of the United Reformed Church while Haywood was an accredited Methodist preacher.[277] There is no suggestion that either Clarke or Haywood supported paedophilia; these gentlemen are undoubtedly opposed to infant sex. However, it is extraordinary that both these respectable individuals, heading up a distinguished charitable trust, could have aligned themselves with a group openly advocating the sexual exploitation of children. It seems at least possible that their Christian indoctrination in Augustine's teaching on infant sexuality unconsciously numbed them to the physical and mental cruelty of sex between adults and children.

Another supporter of PIE was NCCL, headed by Patricia Hewitt, a one-time cabinet minister, who was educated at Canberra Church of England Girls' Grammar School. Catholic Harriet Harman, who has served in various cabinet and shadow cabinet positions, and her partner MP Jack Dromey, both worked for the NCCL: Harriet as legal officer from 1978 to 1982. They sent their son Joseph to the grant-maintained Roman Catholic London Oratory School. NCCL campaigned blatantly against newspapers' treatment of the paedophile activist groups. The Guardian reported that in an NCCL briefing note dated 1978, Harman urged amendments to a 1978 Child Protection Bill, declaring that 'images of children should only be considered pornographic if it could be proven the subject suffered'. Harman claimed later that this was an argument intended to protect from 'unintended consequences' such as parents being prosecuted for taking pictures of their children on the beach or in the bath.[278] Several national newspapers claimed that Jack Dromey MP and Patricia Hewitt had offered support to apologists for the sexual abuse of children while they were working for NCCL. The Daily Mail published a submission by NCCL to Parliament claiming that 'childhood sexual experiences, willingly engaged in, with an adult, result in no identifiable damage'.[279] Dromey denied supporting PIE or its aims, stating that he in fact actively opposed the links between the two groups. Harman said the Mail was trying to make her 'guilty by way of association' and the Daily Mail responded by accusing Ms Harman and Mr Dromey of issuing statements 'full of pedantry and obfuscation' which failed to answer central allegations and denied others it had not made. I do not believe for a moment that any of the members of NCCL consciously wished to condone or support paedophilia and there is no evidence of a structured conspiracy. That leads me to suggest the possibility that Christian indoctrination of the leaders, in Augustinian infantile lust, inured them to the obvious falsehood in the claim that 'childhood sexual experiences, willingly engaged in, with an adult, result in no identifiable damage'.

St Pauls is a London public school that espouses the humanist ethos of its founder, John Colet, who reviled the church. In 1976 Philip McGuinness, a housemaster at St Pauls, wrote to Hewitt expressing his disgust at an NCCL press release and accusing the organisation of having 'some very twisted minds' behind it. Hewitt's name had appeared on a press release a month earlier proposing a cut in the age of consent to 14, and in some circumstances to 10 years old. In her reply to McGuinness, Hewitt wrote: 'Our proposal that the age of consent be reduced is based on the belief that neither the police nor the criminal courts should have the power to intervene in a consenting sexual activity between two young people. It is clearly the case that a number of young people are capable of consenting to sexual activity and already do so.'[280] Harman's name appears on a March 1976 NCCL press release which states: 'NCCL proposes that the age of consent should be lowered to 14, with special provision for situations where the partners are close in age, or where consent of a child over ten can be proved.'

It should be said that there was significant hostility to PIE, and some opponents were Christian. Campaigner Mary Whitehouse (who opposed liberalising anything associated with the Augustinian expletive 'sex') and evangelical MP Geoffrey Dickens railed in Parliament against PIE. More opposition came from universities and the secular community. The famous atheist philosopher Roger Scruton declared that freedom of speech must be forfeited when it came to groups like PIE. In an item in the Times of September 1983 he wrote: 'Paedophiles must be prevented from "coming out". Every attempt to display their vice as a legitimate "alternative" to conventional morality must be, not refuted, but silenced.' Scruton returned to church music in his later years and Christians have tried to claim him for their own after his sad death. It is clear from his later writing that, like me and many other church choristers, his organ playing was part of a quest for his cultural roots and had nothing to do with his beliefs.

After a decade of continuous success and growth, PIE was betrayed by one of its own Christian members, Charles Oxley. His report appeared in the Daily Star newspaper under the headline 'Child Sex Spy Tells All'. That the leaders in the organisations that supported

PIE lacked an instant sense of abhorrence at the idea of legitimising sex with minors is astonishing, even taking account of the 1960s eruption of libertarian causes. One would expect any morally sensitive person to suffer a crisis of conscience for having been involved in providing any level of comfort or support for the sexual abuse of children, but such has not been apparent from Christian members of the network said to have aided and abetted PIE – quite the contrary.[281] The UK Independent Inquiry into Child Sexual Abuse (IICSA) commented, 'Given the awareness now of the extent of child sexual abuse and the damage caused to victims and survivors, it is extraordinary that such an organisation could have attracted support for such a long period of time.'[282] Perhaps it is not so extraordinary, considering the Augustinian belief system of those who joined PIE and those who supported the group's rise. If Augustine's theology was not embedded in the British establishment, it seems unlikely PIE would have enjoyed institutional support.

Despite all the above-mentioned exposure, only after bad publicity had made clear that there was no support for PIE in the wider community did anyone in the Anglican community or in the Catholic Church condemn PIE. After a series of articles in the Daily Mail, 30 years after the dissolution of PIE, the Christian community tried to distance itself by belatedly criticising Harman.[283] Without denying that other factors are also involved, it is worth noting that intolerance of paedophilia has intensified as Christianity has become less influential. In 2021 PIE would struggle to survive within Britain's largely non-religious population. In 1970s Britain well over three quarters of citizens identified as Christian, but 50 years later that number has halved. Christian belief today is mostly confined to the older population; 60% of those in the age bracket 18 – 24 say they have no religion.[284] This emergent scepticism threatens to amplify the disconnection between government and electorate in the years ahead.

The attitude of Christian PIE members to children was not confined to the UK. At about the same time PIE was becoming established, a version surfaced briefly in the USA. In 1978 a group of USA self-identified Christians formed a paedophile group calling itself the North American Man/Boy Love Association (NAMBLA). Aiming to re-establish the ancient custom of pederasty, the group claimed: 'NAMBLA is strongly opposed to age-of-consent laws and all other restrictions which deny men and boys the full enjoyment of their bodies and control over their own lives.' The group was hounded out of public view and has since gone underground, but the organisers still maintain a website.[285]

In the twentieth century, more than 100,000 children, mostly orphans, were sent to live in foster homes and institutions in Canada, Australia and Rhodesia (now Zimbabwe). The government wanted to relieve the state of the costs of caring for destitute children and the British colonies were desperately short of labour. The last cohort of 3,000 children left for Australia in 1970. The Archbishop of Perth welcomed British child migrants with the words: 'If we do not supply from our own stock, we are leaving ourselves all the more exposed to the menace of the teeming millions of our neighbouring Asiatic races.'[286] Most of these children were sent by C of E or Catholic groups and hundreds of them have reported being abused. The worst cases that have so far come to light were in homes run by the Christian Brothers. A 1998 House of Commons Health Select Committee report found that sexual abuse was widespread, systematic and exceptionally depraved.[287] One of the children, Michael O'Donoghue, described how his mother placed him, aged three, in the care of Nazareth House in Romsey, Hampshire, run by nuns. He was badly beaten by the nuns, repeatedly raped and on one occasion thrown downstairs and seriously injured. When he was 11, he was taken by a priest to Clontarf, an orphanage in Perth, Australia, operated by the Christian Brothers. O'Donoghue reported that, 'On the second day they called us all up and told us that if any child complained they would be given a severe beating.' He recalled that the animals were better fed than the children, who resorted to getting scraps out of the bins. Five violent paedophiles worked at Clontarf and O'Donoghue says he was abused so often and by so many of the Christian Brothers that he lost count of the number.[288] Another boy, Clifford Walsh, ended up at a place called Bindoon Boys Town. Within two days of arriving, he says he received his first punishment at the hands of one of the Christian Brothers. 'He punched us, he kicked us, smashed us in the face, back-handed us and everything, and he then sat us on his knee to tell us that he doesn't like to hurt children, but we had been bad boys. I was sobbing uncontrollably for hours.' He described one brother luring him into his room with the promise that he could have some sweet molasses – normally fed not to the boys, but the cows. The man sexually abused him. He claims another brother raped him, and a third beat him mercilessly after falsely accusing him of having sex with another boy.[289]

Lagarie House, built in 1901, was taken over by the Christian seafarers' charity, The British Sailors' Society, as it was then called, in the late 1940s and was opened as a home for orphans of sea-farers.[81] In 1972, the Rev. William Barrie and his wife Mary were appointed to care for the children. Mr Barrie, a one-time minister of the Congregational Church, lived on the grounds in a cottage with his wife. The Barries' approach to child care involved controlling by fear and violence, cane in one hand, Bible in the other. More than a dozen former residents and staff claimed Mrs Barrie was a cruel, violent tyrant who spared few her wrath. At night time Mr Barrie would go into the home to abuse the girls. One resident, Mary, who is now 57 and living in the US, says the abuse she endured began soon after Mr Barrie arrived. 'It started with a kiss goodnight. Then it progressed with him taking me out of my room and into his office. He used to make excuses to his wife to take me places in his carava-nette and he'd stop on the quiet roads. I was never safe from him.' Mary claimed Mr Barrie must have raped her 'hundreds of times'. 'He told me that if I didn't let him, he'd take my younger sisters. I suffered so my siblings wouldn't have to. But in the end, I couldn't stop him. He moved on to them anyway.'[290]

Several Christian sects have supported paedophilic relationships. One such cult, known as Children of God, in Renfrewshire, Scotland, actively encouraged sexual activities among minors as young as two or three years old. Member Alexander Watt was convicted in February 2018 after admitting four charges of sexually abusing his daughter from the age of four, and another child in the 1980s. The cult was founded in the USA by David Berg, who claimed to have 10,000 full-time members in 130 communities around the world. The cult now goes by the name of The Family International.[291]

Sir James Wilson Vincent 'Jimmy' Savile, OBE, KCSG, branded by police as 'probably Britain's most prolific child sexual abuser' was a Roman Catholic.[292] He was honoured with a papal knighthood by being made a Knight Commander of the Pontifical Equestrian Order of Saint Gregory the Great (KCSG) by Pope John Paul II in 1990.[293] In 2012 Scotland Yard launched a criminal investigation into allegations of child sex abuse by Savile, spanning six decades, describing him as a 'predatory sex offender'. In January 2013, a joint report by the NSPCC and Metropolitan Police, *Giving Victims a Voice*, stated that 28 children aged under 10 had made complaints against Savile, with 10 boys aged as young as eight. A further 63 were girls aged between 13 and 16. Savile's knighthood has never been rescinded or revoked or withdrawn.

Michael Jackson, who was raised a Jehovah's Witness (he reportedly dropped out in 1987) was credibly accused of persistent child abuse. In Dan Reed's documentary *Leaving Neverland* Jackson's victims describe in heart-breaking detail how he sexually abused them for years.[294] Like other Christian denominations, Jehovah's Witnesses have been implicated in multiple cases of flagrant child sexual abuse.[295]

Matthew Falder, whom the press dubbed 'one of Britain's most prolific paedophiles' (jailed for 25 years in 2018), attended The King's School, Church of England in Macclesfield.[296] Richard William Huckle (given 22 life sentences in 2016), described in print media as 'Britain's worst ever paedophile', was convicted of 71 counts of serious sexual assaults against children while working as a Christian teacher in Malaysia.[297]

Brian Mitchell, a religious fanatic, snatched Elizabeth Smart from her bed at knifepoint in her home in Salt Lake City in 2002. Just 14 years old, she was kept tied to a tree like an animal for nine months and raped repeatedly. Mitchell, a self-proclaimed prophet who called himself Emmanuel and ministered to the homeless, was confirmed to be of sound mind and sentenced to two life terms for the abduction and rapes. He was aided and abetted by his similarly Christian wife, Wanda Barzee, who is serving a 15-year sentence for her part in the kidnapping and abuse.[298]

The most notorious ringleaders in online paedophilia were likewise instructed in Augustinian beliefs. Australian paedophile Peter Gerard Scully, labelled by the media one of the world's most depraved child traffickers and rapists (sentenced to life imprisonment in 2018), was raised a Catholic and claimed that he was sexually abused by a priest when he was growing up in Victoria.[299] Scully produced a notorious video titled *Daisy's Destruction*, so extreme it was regarded as an urban legend at the time. Made in 2012, the multi-part film features the torture and brutal rape of a number of girls, one as young as 18 months.

Another infamous online paedophile was Matthew Graham (jailed for 15 years in 2016). Known online as 'Lux', he ran an empire of hidden websites specialising in the torture, rape and sexual abuse of children. Graham, who attended Greensborough Denominational Primary School in Australia, was described by the FBI as 'the dark net paedophile kingpin and one of the most prolific child sex offenders ever.' [300]

A handful of observations do not demonstrate that all Christians sexually abuse children and there is no evidence to suggest that all child abusers are Christian. However, these criminals were all indoctrinated in St Augustine's unwholesome moral values and it seems possible that the ideas they were imbued with may have influenced their behaviour. It can be said with certainty that Augustine's teaching did not convince these criminals of the sacrosanctity of infants. Perhaps their indoctrination instilled an attitude toward children that diminished the sense of instant disgust most of us feel when contemplating child sexual abuse. The unhealthy Augustinian ideas that take root from a Christian upbringing might trigger abusive behaviour in an individual with an innate tendency to abuse children that might otherwise be supressed. Literature concerning the effect childhood experiences have on behaviour and personality into adulthood has been discussed in chapter 3. However, the personality traits we are born with also have enduring effects on well-being.[301] This is the other half of the nature/nurture interaction that shapes us all.

Research on deviancy suggests that criminal tendencies are triggered by a combination of inherited (i.e. genetic) or acquired (i.e. learned) influences, including environmental factors and upbringing. For example, offenders often have low empathy, but only about half of young people with low empathy grow up to offend.[302] It is not far-fetched to speculate that an individual with a proclivity towards paedophilia might have his weakness triggered by a Christian upbringing inculcating Augustinian ideas of infantile lust and wickedness. Another individual with an upbringing untouched by Augustine's ideas might be more inclined to repress these tendencies. We have noted flaws in studies claiming benefits for followers in terms of physical health, mental health, and overall happiness and well-being. Research overwhelmingly looks at the consequences for the individual and not at the consequences of religious indoctrination with respect to society. If the benefits are doubtful, might there be detrimental outcomes for society resulting from religious indoctrination?

To gauge the effect of Augustinian indoctrination, if any, on the world audience is tricky. In the introduction we looked at various terms used in defining the different forms of CSE. The complexity we encountered is magnified when we try to compare statistics between populations around the globe. In addition to international and cultural inconsistencies in defining child abuse, there is no international agreement on a definition of child pornography. Legal definitions of both **child** and **child pornography** differ globally and may differ even among legal jurisdictions within the same country. Possession of child pornography is not a crime in most countries. The magnitude and distribution of child pornography is difficult to determine, but it is clear that the problem has exploded with the advent of the internet. The National Center for Missing and Exploited Children (NCMEC) received an increase of reports to its CyberTipline from more than 24,400 in 2001 to more than 340,000 by the beginning of 2006.

In 2012 the hacker collective Anonymous organised a sting operation called *OpDarknetV2* as part of its ongoing anti-paedophile campaign. They hosted a honeypot IP address to trick those attempting to browse clandestine sites hosting child pornography into accessing a service that would identify them and their location. According to a statement attributed to the loosely-banded group, a custom Firefox button was developed and links placed to it – along with a fake Tor (a browser) update message – on the 'Hard Candy' and 'Lolita City' sites offering the illegal content. Those who clicked on it 'would then be forwarded to our special forensics server and log the incoming IP and destination'. The method, which Anonymous named 'Paw Printing' in a reference to the 'pedo bear' character, collected data for 24 hours, grabbing 190 user entries in that period. The map reproduced here shows the rough location of each entry indicating activity. (Fig. 5.)

**Figure 5. OpDarknet sting map showing
distribution of child abuse images**

(Courtesy of Chris Davies/SlashGear)

The United States had the world's largest number of requests for access and the largest number of Christians (more than 247 million Christians according to Pew Research Center [2010]), followed by Brazil and Mexico. More than a third of Christians worldwide (37%) live in the Americas, where nearly nine in ten people (86%) are Christian.[303] Given that the website addresses were in English, it might be no coincidence that those English-speaking areas with a high concentration of Christians also have the largest traffic for sick child pornography. I should point out that the pins in the map also correspond with concentrations of populations having access to the internet. This was a relatively small sample and other studies of internet distribution of child sexual images have reported unclear results.[304] Nonetheless, the closeness of the correlation in the *OpDarknetV2* sting is remarkable. Later, the hacker collective posted the following: 'There was a large amount of resistance from the paedophile community … with messages such as "It is our God-given right that we can choose to have our sexual preferences for youth".'[305]

In chapter 1, I recounted how the nuns in my boarding school seemed accommodating to the abuse of boys. Not only do men and women in religious orders seem more yielding to cCSA, but they are generally more flaccid in their attitude towards the exploitation and maltreatment of children. This mindset is epitomised in the series of Magdalene Laundries scandals operating up to the 1990s, where young mothers-to-be and their babies were mistreated and oppressed by nuns.[306] Roman Catholicism teaches that sex outside marriage is shameful and a grave sin and the girls and their newborns were vilified.

In the small Irish town of Tuam in County Galway, a Catholic religious community of the Sisters of Bon Secours ran a home for unmarried mothers. Over several decades, the nuns took in thousands of pregnant girls who were denied basic medical care and refused painkillers for even the most difficult birth because the pain was 'God's punishment for your sin'. Their babies were crowded into communal nurseries where infection and disease ran unchecked. The result was an appallingly high death rate, with measles and dysentery killing hundreds. Infant mortality was often five or six times worse in the Church's homes than in the rest of Ireland. The nuns buried nearly 800 babies unceremoniously in a disused sewage tank. On discovering the mass burial, BBC author and radio/television presenter Martin Sixsmith commented, 'A Church that sets such store by the sanctity of human life shows very little respect for young souls in its care.'[307] Although exploitation and abuse by nuns has harmed thousands of young girls and their babies,[308] it receives less publicity and scrutiny than abuse committed by priests.[309]

I recount these stories here, against the backdrop of evil criminals, because I have an important point to make. The nuns were not monsters. These nuns were not inherently evil. Their aspirations were commendable; as young women they set their lives on a path of generosity and goodness. The name of the order they joined is French for 'good help'. Their motto is 'Good help to those in need' and the order is committed to the highest values of caring for the sick and dying. It seems doubtful that the contemptuous and neglectful attitude of the nuns towards their charges had nothing at all to do with their indoctrination in St Augustine's grotesque ideas of filthy sexual lust and infantile wickedness. I suggest these nuns were betrayed and they were misled by Augustine's dark ideas. When they were infants, and later as novitiates, they were indoctrinated to accept his teaching and in consequence their innate sense of right and wrong became muddled. They were trained to believe that unmarried mothers and their babies were evil and sinful. Girls who got pregnant outside marriage were not pitiable or vulnerable, they were simply **wicked**.

Having experienced indoctrination personally, I believe I understand how that travesty of righteousness becomes ingrained. The nuns were taught, as I was, that single mothers are filthy for giving way to carnal desires, and they were taught that babies are born stained with original sin, just as I was. Philomena, a book by Martin Sixsmith, later made into a film, tells the true story of one unmarried mother-to-be who was sent to a home for single mothers in Ireland

and forced to give up her son to be sold for adoption. He was sent to America, as most babies were, and the religious order was paid by way of a 'donation'. The nuns told the distraught mother that she deserved to be punished for becoming pregnant outside wedlock. Despite this seemingly cruel comment, in their hearts I believe the nuns were kind, conscientious people, just like my parents were. My dad continued to support the family financially and my mother continued to lavish love and devotion on us children, after they had been divided and alienated. Like the nuns, my parents were punished by the religious bigotry with which my mother had been indoctrinated.

Thankfully the last of these homes was shut down in the 1990s. Britain has become more secular and we no longer tolerate the persecution of unmarried mothers. In chapter 3 we looked at the story of nuns in the convent of the Immaculate Heart, USA where the nuns quickly recovered their natural personas and revelled in sexual freedom when they were encouraged to open up and just be themselves. Yet today in Catholic faith schools, children are still indoctrinated to believe that girls who have babies outside marriage are immoral, and pupils are, paradoxically, given misleading advice such as 'condoms put people at risk'.[310] Girls in Catholic faith schools are taught that unmarried mothers commit a grave or mortal sin and they will burn in hell for eternity if they die before confessing to a priest.[311] In chapters 12 and 13, we will see further evidence of teaching like this being perpetuated in Catholic schools, and we will discover that similar attitudes can easily find their way into C of E schools too, via overly evangelistic teachers. Lest the reader should imagine indoctrination in bigotry and division to be a relic of the past, this book exists to show that it persists today, creating ripples of punishment beyond the churches.

# 11

# CLERICAL CHILD ABUSE AND AUGUSTINE'S INFLUENCE

*The creed that grooms, with carnal stain*
*From St Augustine's sin of blame,*
*Makes Christian children fairer game.*
*Then, self-reproachful prayers ingrain*
*These fledgling minds, with guilt and shame*
*While priests abuse them, in God's name.*

MICHAEL MOLONEY

The term 'paedophile' when used to describe child sexual offenders is potentially misleading. A paedophile is a person who is sexually attracted to children, not necessarily someone who sexually abuses children. Not all sex offenders are paedophiles and not all people with paedophilia commit sexual offences. Another crucial point is that the majority of sex crimes against children are perpetrated by someone known to the victim, such as clerics or family members. According to a widely respected report by the American NCMEC, all sex offenders, not just child abusers, can be placed along a motivational continuum of situational to preferential.[312] (Note: extracts from this

FBI report are regularly misquoted to support the false claim that most child abusers are 'situational offenders' and not paedophiles.)[313] Although a variety of individuals sexually abuse children, preferential-type sex offenders, and especially paedophiles, are the primary acquaintance sexual exploiters of children.

Michael Seto, who produced the clinician's handbook for the American Psychological Association (APS), agrees.[314] The section of his handbook dealing with paedophilia and sexual offending against children was updated in 2018. Seto summarises decades of research across multiple disciplines and he reports that extrafamilial child sexual abusers are more likely to be diagnosed with paedophilia and are often unable to maintain adult relationships.

Exactly what causes someone to be sexually attracted to children is not known. Multiple studies point to specific neurological features that appear to increase the likelihood of an individual being paedophilic.[315] Childhood abuse by adults, co-existing personality disorders and substance abuse are some of the known risk factors that might encourage an individual to act on a compulsion to sexually abuse minors. In the studies that I have examined, religious indoctrination is not listed as a possible contributory factor that can increase the likelihood of a predisposed individual yielding to paedophilic urges. None of the studies I have seen even attempts to question offenders to establish their religious identity. This omission of religious analysis might be due to the reasons we discussed in chapter 4, i.e. the so-called religiosity gap between professionals and subjects. The general approval accorded to Augustine's beliefs by Christian theologians might be an additional factor discouraging good quality research. Despite this failure to analyse offenders' religious affiliation in research studies, theories on the causes of cCSA cram academic literature.[316]

Probably the most detailed study available, a 152-page investigation of cCSA in the Catholic Church, was commissioned by the Church itself. The research was conducted by the John Jay School of Criminology and published in 2011 under the title *The Causes and*

*Context of Sexual Abuse of Minors by Catholic Priests in the United States, 1950-2010.*[317] Researchers went to each diocese in the US and logged the credible accounts of abuse involving clergy who served between 1950 and 2002. From a total of 109,694 priests, they found that 4.2% had been plausibly accused of abuse. The John Jay report is useful for our purposes since it has been validated by the Catholic bishops and it illuminates a blind spot that I perceive, which is referred to repeatedly in this book and is apparent throughout literature on the subject.[318]

The John Jay researchers provide their list of causes of cCSA that we will examine in detail in a moment. Firstly, let us look at some of the commonly alleged causes of cCSA that the report rejected. These were as follows.

**Allegation** Commitment by RC clergy to celibate chastity encourages cCSA.

**Report Quote** '[A]n exclusively male priesthood and the commitment to celibate chastity, were invariant during the increase, peak, and decrease in abuse incidents, and thus not causes of the "crisis" ' (p3).

**Reality Check** Rejection of this oft-repeated allegation is supported by strong evidence. We noted in chapter 4 that there is no foundation in the claim that a commitment to celibacy encourages cCSA. It flies in the face of all scientific psychosexual orthodoxy to equate heterosexual adult attraction with the sexual abuse of boys by grown men. Moreover, the incidence of paedophilia predates the First and Second Lateran councils in 1123 and 1139, before which time priests were allowed to marry and many did so.[319] Celibacy might cause challenges with adult sexual expression that could result in a priest violating their religious vows with other adults, but it does not increase the risk of cCSA.[320] Clerics in other Christian denominations are free to marry and these institutions are also afflicted with thousands of reports of cCSA.

**Allegation** Homosexual clerics are especially motivated to abuse children.

**Report Quote** 'Priests who had same-sex sexual experiences either before or in seminary... were not significantly more likely to abuse minors' (p4). 'The clinical data do not support the hypothesis that priests with a homosexual identity or those who committed same-sex sexual behaviour with adults are significantly more likely to sexually abuse children than those with heterosexual orientation or behaviour' (p119). 'Access to victims played a critical role in victim choice …priests had more access to boys until recently (primarily because parishes permitted girls as altar servers only after 1983)' (p120).

**Reality Check** There is good evidence to support this rejection. There is no reason to suppose that a cleric's sexual orientation is relevant in cases of cCSA, and with the caveat noted earlier, it is widely accepted that access to victims plays a role in cases of abuse.

**Allegation** Post-Vatican II seminary training stimulated cCSA.

**Report Quote** 'The majority of abusers (70%) were ordained prior to the 1970s, and more abusers were educated in seminaries in the 1940s and 1950s than at any other time period' (p118).

**Reality Check** The evidence produced here is persuasive and there is no reason to believe that the seminary training clerics received in this time period is more or less relevant in inciting cCSA. However, although Post-Vatican II seminary training is not specifically relevant, that is not to say that seminary training generally does not stimulate cCSA, and we will examine this possibility in a moment.

**Allegation** The priesthood is infested with paedophiles.

**Report Quote** 'Less than 5 percent of the priests with allegations of abuse exhibited behaviour consistent with a diagnosis of paedophilia (a psychiatric disorder that is characterised by recurrent fantasies, urges, and behaviours about prepubescent children). Thus, it is inaccurate to refer to abusers as "paedophile priests"'(p3). ' "Generalists", or indiscriminate offenders, constituted the majority of abusers and were influenced by social factors' (p119).

**Reality Check** The report's repudiation of this allegation is not robustly supported. The body of the report explains, 'For the purpose of this comparison, a paedophile is defined as a priest who had more than one victim, with all victims being age eleven or younger at the time of the offense' (p34). However, the professionals' diagnostic manual, DSM-5, which is referred to in the reference section (note 164) provides the following definition: 'The diagnostic criteria for paedophilic disorder are intended to apply both to individuals who freely disclose this paraphilia and to individuals who deny any sexual attraction to prepubertal children (generally age 13 years or younger), despite substantial objective evidence to the contrary.' On this measure, up to 73% of victims of predatory clerics fall within the range that would identify the abusers as paedophiles. The John Jay researchers, by declaring a weak distinction between the behaviour of priests and the diagnosis of paedophilia, felt able to conveniently lower the age threshold for ascertaining paedophile abuse to below 11. This reading permitted the claim that a majority of abusing priests are not paedophiles. The report goes on to support the fudge by separating paedophiles from ephebophiles. Ephebophilia, meaning sexual interest in adolescents, is loosely defined in terms of age.

**Allegation** Abuse by clerics is mostly confined to minors.

**Report Quote** 'The majority of priests who were given residential treatment following an allegation of sexual abuse of a minor also reported sexual behaviour with adult partners' (p 3).

**Reality Check** This wording, placed in the executive summary, tends to play down the reality of cCSA, but the data contained in the body of the report is clear. 'Most sexual abuse victims of priests (51%) were between the ages of eleven and fourteen, while 27% were fifteen to seventeen, 16% were eight to ten, and nearly 6% were under age seven. Over 40% of all victims were males between the ages of eleven and fourteen' (p10). Although a slender majority of priests also reported sexual behaviour with adult partners, the proportions reported here indicate a strong tendency towards cCSA over adult sexual abuse by clerics.

**Allegation** Clerics who abuse children are paedophiles.

**Report Quote** 'The most significant conclusion drawn from this data is that no single psychological, developmental, or behavioural characteristic differentiated priests who abused minors from those who did not' (p74).

**Reality Check** This conclusion is weakened by the evidence provided in the body of the report. We noted above that nearly three quarters of victims of predatory clerics fell within the range that would identify the abusers as paedophiles according to DSM-5. Serial abusers (priests with more than 10 allegations against them) were responsible for 27% of the allegations. It could therefore as easily be claimed that a single psychological, developmental and behavioural characteristic that differentiated a significant number of priests who abused minors from those who did not might be paedophilia.

So, what were the factors this report concluded had contributed to clerics sexually abusing children?

**Report Quote** 'The sexual abuse of minors is a pervasive problem in society and... 1950 until 2002 was a time of great social change in the United States' (p25). 'The rise in abuse cases in the 1960s and 1970s was influenced by social factors in American society generally' (p3).

**Reality Check** This conclusion implies that social change is responsible for cCSA, but that claim is weak. Correspondent John Daniel Davidson is well known for blaming cCSA on the sexual revolution and liberalisation of moral values, but his dismissal of cCSA as a product of the hippie culture stretches credibility.[321] Societal notions of what was or was not sexually acceptable behaviour were undeniably realigned during this period, but that fact does not explain or excuse cCSA. Child abuse in the Catholic church predates the rise of moral relativism in the sixties. Besides, there was no bulge in child abuse in the population outside the church, despite the rise of groups like PIE (see chapter 10). Child sexual abuse was considered immoral before, during and after the period reviewed. The significance of the date 2002 is that this is the year Boston Globe reporters broke the story of the full extent of abuse in the United States, uncovering what was already there but had never been revealed. Poland, with a relatively high number of priests, was not exposed to this 'sexual revolution' and recent media exposure has shown the church in Poland is equally afflicted with cases of cCSA.[322] The liberalisation since 1960 is merely a partial return to sexual attitudes previously held, buoyed by the freedom that modern contraception now gives women to avoid the risk of conception and everyone to reduce the risk of infection. It could be argued that the loosening of sexual mores would tend to decrease abuse of minors, as more opportunities for consensual sex outside marriage became possible.

**Report Quote** 'Sexual abuse continues to occur, but 94 percent of the abuse incidents reported to the Catholic Church from 1950 through 2009 took place before 1990' (p118).

**Reality Check** This conclusion is supported by the data, but the implication that the crisis is over might be premature. Sexual abuse by Catholic clergy became the subject of widespread publicity in 1984 with the celebrated case of Father Gilbert Gauthe in Lafayette, Louisiana.[323] This led to numerous revelations of similar cases of abuse around the United States. The diminution in cases coming to light after 1990 is to be expected, following exposure, but that does not necessarily mean cCSA has diminished. Abusers might be more secretive and greater efforts might be being made at concealment. Altar boys and choirboys will be more alert to the risk of abuse. We do not know the true extent of cCSA because the Church's efforts at reporting and safeguarding have been perfunctory and inadequate.[211]

**Report Quote** 'Knowledge of the extent of child sexual abuse increased, as did knowledge about abusers, the harm of victimization, and the dynamics of victim–perpetrator relationships' (p25).

**Reality Check** The report implies that the church 'came clean' and recognised the harm being done to minors of its own volition. That interpretation of the data is misleading. Knowledge of the extent of abuse surfaced in 2002 due to the tenacity of Boston Globe journalists who refused to be intimidated and diverted by the church. The scope of cCSA was unknown only because the church hierarchy covered up cases of abuse until the true magnitude of abuse was exposed by outsiders.[324]

**Report Quote** 'The development of a curriculum of "human formation" as part of seminary education follows the recognition of the problem of sexual abuse by priests. Participation in human formation during seminary distinguishes priests with later abusive behaviour from those who did not abuse. The priests with abusive behaviour were statistically less likely to have participated in human formation training than those who did not have allegations of abuse' (p3).

**Reality Check** This conclusion is revealing. We are told that priests who had participated in a special indoctrination programme, described as 'training in self-understanding and the development of emotional and psychological competence for a life of celibate chastity' were less likely to abuse. This claim points to the possibility that the usual programme of indoctrination that seminarians receive might stimulate cCSA.

**Report Quote** 'When allegations of abuse were made, most diocesan leaders responded. However, the response typically focused on the priest-abusers rather than on the victims. Data indicate that the majority of diocesan leaders took actions to help "rehabilitate" the abusive priests' (p4).

**Reality Check** This admission is corroborated in reports by external authorities, in the United States and elsewhere, and also here in the UK.[324] Diocesan leaders rarely consulted victims directly, and when they did the child was mistrusted. Invariably the victim was blamed instead, and sometimes punished. At best the abusers were moved, but nothing was done about the harm done to the child.[188] The fact that child victims were so often blamed for seducing their priest abusers indicates that the church leaders believed the abused children to be concupiscent.

**Report Quote** 'Priests who were sexually abused as minors themselves were more likely to abuse minors than those without a history of abuse' (p4).

**Reality Check** If abuse was more likely to be perpetrated by priests who were themselves sexually abused as minors, that suggests that the Catholic Church has more than its fair share of priests who were sexually abused as minors. We have already established that men in the wider community who were sexually abused as minors are no more likely to grow up to abuse minors themselves than are those without a history of abuse. Research reported in The Lancet recently confirms the matter. The author of the study, psychiatrist Arnon Bentovim, says, 'The message here is that sexual victimization alone is not sufficient to suggest a boy is likely to grow up to become a sex offender.'[325] The John Jay report implies that the priesthood particularly attracts individuals who have themselves been abused as minors. We will examine this insight more fully later.

**Report Quote** 'Priest-abusers are similar to sex offenders in the general population. They had motivation to commit the abuse (for example, emotional congruence to adolescents), exhibited techniques of neutralization to excuse and justify their behavior, took advantage of opportunities to abuse (for example, through socialization with the family), and used grooming techniques to gain compliance from potential victims' (p119).

**Reality Check** This conclusion is weak. The similarity between priest-abusers and sex offenders in the general population is questionable. Unlike priest-abusers, child sex offenders in the general population might not inspire trust and authority; might not believe that they are entitled to obtain secretive forgiveness for their abuse; might not have been indoctrinated to believe that their victims are sexually sinful; might not have opportunities for confessional intimacy and might not have access to deferential minors who have been sexually groomed by being made to feel guilty.[326]

The conclusions that open minded readers might well draw from the John Jay report is that some of the points identified above could be making a contribution to cCSA. It would have been problematic for the institute to specifically identify Christian indoctrination as a contributory factor influencing abuse, even if the researchers believed that to be the case. The commissioning body was the United States Conference of Catholic Bishops (USCCB). The Church itself had the final say on whether or not the report was published. The retention of a veto on publication would have made those working on it for five years potentially susceptible to bias, conscious that their report would probably not see the light of day if the bishops did not like it.

In addition to the weaknesses outlined above, this report carefully skirts some obvious factors that might contribute to cCSA. Sherryll Kerns Kraizer, author of *The Safe Child Book* and a pioneer in developing sexual abuse prevention, writes, 'Many (Christian) children tell me that their body belongs to God.'[327] A child who assumes his or her body is not their own, but is 'owned by God' will be vulnerable to abuse by an esteemed 'man of God'. From my perspective as a one-time acolyte, it seems to me that Christian indoctrination provides a consummate underpinning for the subsequent exploitation of a child. Teaching clerics they are Christ in person, telling them children are already stained with sexual sin, stipulating one-to-one hook ups in a confessional box for private discussions with children about sinfulness (and making masturbation a notable sin) and advising them they are assured of forgiveness all seem liable to invite exploitation of a child by someone who might already be inclined to abuse. To complete the recipe for clerical temptation, children are made to feel blameworthy and nurtured to trust and revere the clergy. Disturbingly, the John Jay report admits that it might be impossible to screen novitiates to weed out paedophiles. We have noted that the IICSA still receives over 100 allegations a day and it seems unlikely that cCSA will simply go away (p74).

Based on his conversations with predators who intentionally sought to join religious organisations, former FBI Counterintelligence Agent Joe Navarro lists 15 of the reasons why predators seek to join religious organisations.[328] From getting access to victims to gaining trust and receiving forgiveness, priestly ordination provides an ideal cover for the sexual abuse of minors. German philosopher Martin Buber comments:

> ...*one of the places evil people are most likely to be found is within the church. What better way to conceal one's evil from oneself, as well as from others, than to be a deacon or some other highly visible form of Christian within our culture? ... I do not mean to imply that the evil are anything other than a small minority among the*

*religious or that the religious motives of most people are in any way*
*spurious. I mean only that evil people tend to gravitate toward piety*
*for the disguise and concealment it can offer them.*[329]

Once inside the Church's protective shield, predators are liable to
feel facilitated by Augustine's dogma that children are concupiscent.
This might be why the Catholic Church's own report by the John
Jay institute appears to confirm that a disproportionate number of
clerics are probably paedophiles.

That said, none of the data presented in this book are conclu-
sive. The fact that all sources point in the same direction should
be of concern, but we cannot say with confidence that Christian
indoctrination is a factor in paedophilia. The Vatican has pointed
out that child sex abuse is also rife in other religious denominations, and it is impossible to confirm that Christianity is more
blameworthy than any other religion. [330] Although child sexual
abuse seems to be less prevalent amongst the religious clergy in
other faiths, all religions appear equally unforthcoming with evidence of abuse. Whether that clears the Catholic Church of fault is
a different matter. There is little doubt that religion can be used as
a tool to assist in grooming children, and not just in the Christian
faith.[331]

The proportion of paedophiles in the general population has been
assessed at between 1% and 5%.[306] The number of accused RC clerics has been assessed at 4% in the USA and 7% in Australia, based
on data provided by the Catholic Church. There are no statistics
for the scale of cCSA in the UK, but these figures might give an
indication.[332] However, victims are renowned for their reluctance to
come forward and many cases of cCSA remain undeclared, hidden
in Vatican archives.[333]

Apologists are prone to quote the USA statistic and compare it
with the number of child sexual abuse offenders in the population
at large, which they claim is roughly similar. This is a misleading
comparison in my view, since clerics are in a special position of trust

and authority, demanding high standards of decency and rectitude. 'Position of trust' is a legal term that refers to certain roles and settings where an adult has regular and direct contact with children, for example teachers, childcare workers, doctors, etc. The Office for National Statistics (ONS) provides an analysis of cases of child sexual abuse in England and Wales in 2019. The data show that, given their proportion within the population at large, people in positions of trust and authority perpetrate fewer cases of child sexual abuse compared with other groups.[334]

The John Jay report we have been analysing indicated that a majority of abusive clerics tend to commit multiple offences. From a total of 4,392 priests facing allegations of abuse, 2,512 offenders had two or more allegations (p55). Thus, the prevalence of abuse within the priesthood might be greater than that implied by the number of clerics accused. Although there is no robust study for prevalence in the UK, we can make a working assessment of the extent of cCSA based on publicly available data. The ONS estimates the population of England and Wales in 2018 to be 60 million. The latest available figures provided by church organisations claim 5,250 Catholic and 19,560 C of E men and women are engaged in ministry roles.[335] Together these numbers of clergy constitute 0.0413% of the population. In England and Wales in 2019, the above ONS analysis recorded 73,260 cases of sexual abuse before the age of 16 years. If clerics were no more likely than other individuals to sexually abuse children, they should account for 30 of these cases in a year, proportionate to their numbers in the population. Yet we noted in the introduction that the IICSA claims to have recorded more than 100 allegations of cCSA by clerics every year from 2016 to 2020.[24] (Fig. 6.)

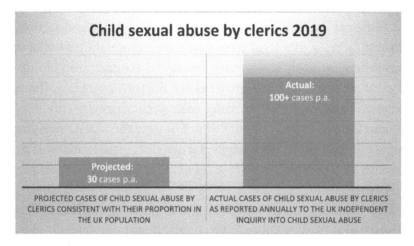

**Figure 6. Chart of child sexual abuse by clerics
in England and Wales 2019**

One would expect cases of child sexual abuse by clerics to be zero, and certainly not significantly more than by other members of society. In chapter 9, we learned from a former FBI investigator why child sexual abuse is more likely to be perpetrated by Christian clerics. Although child sexual abuse is more commonly associated with Catholic clergy, we noted that in 2016 the C of E was dealing with 3,300 complaints of cCSA.[183] Claims that abuse is now under control are not borne out by the facts worldwide. The number of allegations of Catholic clergy sex abuse of minors quadrupled in 2019 compared with the average in the previous five years. In 2018, there were 1,451 allegations of clergy sex abuse against minors and in 2017 the figure was 693.[336] The 2019 report by the US Conference of Catholic Bishops – covering July 2018 through June 2019 – counted 4,434 allegations of clergy sex abuse against minors, and 2,237 were deemed credible by the Church itself.

In light of these statistics, the title **In Persona Christi** seems blasphemously impudent – either Christ is a child abuser or priests do not stand in place of Christ. We have noted that the IICSA records over 100 new cases in the UK every year. No doubt the volume of allegations has been boosted by publicity given to historical claims, but survivors assert that the Catholic Church's structure and culture mean it is 'incapable of delivering the changes survivors need'.[22]

In cases throughout the world, the Christian community has excused, sheltered and covered up for child-abusive priests. In his film *Mea Maxima Culpa: Silence in The House Of God*, Alex Gibney delivers convincing proof to a wide audience that the Vatican had known about it for decades, and had repeatedly chosen not to investigate cases of reported abuse, instead advising that the accused priests be shown compassion.[337] Matthias Katsch, founding member of Ending Clergy Abuse (ECA), points out that thousands of acts of cCSA are filed in Vatican chambers and palaces, kept secret from independent review and investigation. In December 2019, Pope Francis lifted the **Pontifical Secret** providing an opportunity for survivors of clergy sexual abuse to obtain information on their cases.[338] However, up to the date of going to print in May, 2021 no information has yet been shared with victims about the cases of their abusers. Multiple reports confirm that known abusers were allowed to continue to practise their priestly duties, and were even moved around to hinder external interference.[24] Abusers were, and evidently still are, shielded from accountability and blame.[339] The latest reports suggest that the church continues to be reticent in its attitude towards the abuse and exploitation of children. [340]

An academic paper by lawyer Richard Conway LL.B., entitled *The Lawful Argument for the Disestablishment of the Church of England*, considers the Church's special dispensation within UK law via its Enabling Act.[341] The C of E enjoys a 'general' position of power in UK law to enact its own primary and secondary legislation outside that of the current public statutory duty in regards to the safeguarding of vulnerable citizens. Despite the disproportionate number of cases of sexual abuse within church institutions, unlike other public bodies, local authorities or relevant partners, the C of E is not under a statutory duty to make arrangements for safeguarding. Nor is it under any public, secular statutory duty to report or respond to incidences of possible safety issues around children and vulnerable adults. Through the constitutional empowerment of its 'Enabling Act', the Church is afforded the right to make its own arrangements, and only expected to reflect the importance of safeguarding via its own Measures of primary legislation.

Mr Conway describes and documents 'a collusive and psychologically ingrained culture from within the Church's closed institution' to ignore allegations against abusers (clergy) and discredit victims, even when presented with compelling evidence. Relating individual cases of historical and present violent sexual abuse within the C of E the author argues cogently that the Church of England can no longer be trusted to enact its own safeguarding measures or the discipline of its clergy, constitutionally. He calls for the disestablishment of the C of E, which would involve a repeal and abolishment of the Church of England Assembly (Powers) Act 1919, and all other Measures of primary and secondary Church legislation. He points out that disestablishment will not hinder the Church's operation, but will help create a more sustainable standard of excellence in safeguarding. As an abuse victim myself, Mr Conway's report makes a disturbing read and cries out for urgent action.

# 12

# RELIGIOUS TOLERANCE, FAITH SCHOOLS AND SIN

What is 'religious tolerance' and is it compatible at all with faith schools? Many in the UK might say that it is enshrining in law the right to pursue one's own religious or non-religious convictions. Other people might add to that, 'as long as they don't ram it down other people's throats'. Some of the same people enjoy singing Christmas carols at Christmas, and might consider it part of their children's cultural education to be taught them at school, in the same way that this author once taught children the national anthem – not because she is a rampant royalist looking for young minds to shape, but because it is a part of British heritage that one cannot choose to reject or embrace if one knows nothing about. For others, 'religious tolerance' means 'you must respect my religion and the rules that come with it', which can lead to things such as the recent UK disagreements over wearing crosses over a uniform or refusing to bake cakes that celebrate homosexual unions. Individuals will have their own views on these. But as a society, what do we want religious tolerance to mean in schools? At the moment, UK teachers are required to teach in line with 'British values', meaning 'not undermining fundamental British values, including democracy, the rule of law, individual liberty and mutual respect, and tolerance of those with different faiths and beliefs'[342]. The same document also says, 'ensuring that personal beliefs are not expressed in ways which exploit pupils' vulnerability or might lead them to break the law'. This does not forbid a teacher from teaching their religion as correct, with a belief that it will be good for the child, which is of course exactly what faith schools do and they do not hide this. You do not necessarily have to be in a self-confessed faith school, however, to fall under the influence of religious teachers. Some teachers have a personal faith – some do not. Some from each group are tolerant of differing views – some are not. These things are true regardless of where they work. The authors are in no way suggesting that having a view on religion or a personal faith is a problem in itself if you are a teacher. Interestingly, the gov.uk page on 'RE and Collective Worship in Academies and Free Schools'[343] does not mention the word 'teachers'. There is no specific guidance on how they should be presenting facts and opinions; we must fall back on the 'teachers' standards' quoted from above, and remember of course that you do not have to be teaching an RE lesson or taking an assembly to discuss, teach about or influence young people in matters of faith. Many of us would expect a trained professional to be able and willing to differentiate facts from opinion, and in many cases this is true. In the same way that a teacher should not teach pupils their political opinion, by for example telling them to vote for one or other political party (The law forbids teachers promoting partisan political views in the teaching of any subject in the school),[344] it seems logical to expect teachers not to push one religious ideology, or set of beliefs, over another. There is however no such legal restriction on promoting partisan religious views, so how realistic is this expectation in the context of an established church and numerous faith schools that have influence over how important concepts are taught elsewhere?

Once, during a general election campaign, I encouraged my pupils (an above-average group of 9 – 10-year-olds) to read summaries of the policies and manifestos of political parties, discuss them, check the facts and make an independent decision about which they might support. A good teacher of RE (remembering that primary school teachers are unlikely to be RE specialists) will take a similar attitude to religious thinking, bearing in mind of course that religion is often a way of life more than a political position is, and is thus harder to change or abandon. Whether or not anarchy should be taught as a valid political position is a good question, but not one for right now. However, supporting no religious viewpoint at all and/or being actively opposed to them is a valid position and should be taught to children as an idea just like the others. Too often it is not; rather it is left as an absence, nurturing the irritating question often directed at atheists: 'So what do you believe in then?' Already, even in non-faith schools, the idea of not believing as a positive state – one which in my own atheism I would describe as taking responsibility for myself and my actions and trying to have a positive rather than negative effect on the world around me – is rarely presented as a path to take. The National Secular Society (NSS) and Humanists UK have begun to provide resources to teach about secularism (not to be confused with atheism, as explained here[345]) as an approach to life:[346] but schools need to be encouraged, and teachers made to feel confident enough, to bring these resources into the classroom alongside the ones that teach about religious worldviews.

How often are the facts of religious claims checked as part of religious education or any other lessons? In my experience the answer is sometimes. Some teachers (particularly secondary-trained subject specialists) are excellent professionals and in community schools (and more forward-thinking church schools), they and their enquiring approach to religious education can thrive, creating the scenario described earlier this year on the government site 'Get into Teaching': 'As a trainee RE teacher, you'll develop the skills to devise and deliver lessons that excite and intrigue pupils. These will intertwine with their wider learning in other subjects, as well as their understanding of society, culture, and what it means to be human.'[347] This sort of RE is very valuable and is often an enjoyable subject for teenagers, who enjoy a good debate about culture, difference and heritage. But not all young people can access it. Even in schools where they can, certainly at secondary level, potential damage can be done outside RE lessons. Trainee RE teachers, at least at the author's university, were carefully questioned during their interview for the course. How did we feel about teaching 'other' faiths? After stumbling on this one and wanting to ask 'other than what?' (I only fully realised later that they were assuming a religion for me, and because of the context probably a Christian one), I realised that they were vetting me for fundamentalist views, and checking that I wasn't there with some kind of personal conversion mission in mind. All my contemporaries on the RE course were similarly vetted, and we approved of this caution. Not so the geography department, as we discovered at a rare subject-mixing event. A student geography teacher sought us out, thinking we would be like-minded, and was surprised to discover that we hadn't, like him, come into the teaching profession 'to convert' (to Christianity). It would probably be harder now to get away with this, I'm pleased to say, but how many more teachers, having spent decades pushing their version of correctness onto the vulnerable young (and inevitably shaming the uninterested and unbelieving – see chapter 13), are still evangelising in subtler ways? Or working at faith schools, where it is acceptable to tell children that they are sinners and that their religion's way is the only correct way?

You do not have to be a fundamentalist Christian to promote unhealthy views and support discriminatory or shaming behaviour. In this, the only country that requires daily Christian worship in schools, too often, the teacher (particularly the non-RE teachers, and primary teachers with little religious knowledge or experience) and quite possibly parents of the students are happy to whitewash this area with 'it's a faith – what people believe – you can't check it like arithmetic'. This is true with questions such as the existence of a God, but not with something like the existence of Jesus as a person and the events of his life. If I told someone that I believed we should vote Green because wind and solar power had been shown by a number of anecdotes to directly improve mental health, they would want to know where my evidence came from and would not accept 'I strongly feel/know these stories to be true, because they're in the Green Party manifesto and if you allow this idea into your heart, you will feel it too' as an answer. With religion, particularly Christianity, they too often do, or at least, and crucially for a primary school, behave as if they do. In my experience some teachers confuse 'you can't disprove it' with 'you can't question it'.

The document detailing teachers' standards for the UK does not mention the words religion or opinion. It mentions 'respect' five times, but as anyone who has taught pupils from mixed backgrounds knows, what 'respect' means can differ widely. It can mean accepting that some children need to take a day off school for a religious festival; it can mean accepting children being forbidden from learning to swim; it can mean accepting children being prevented from learning about religion from their school syllabus and about the biology of their own bodies and how to keep themselves safe (see following chapter). Somewhere on this scale, I am uncomfortable, well before we get to the end.

Earlier I suggested that we might say (as a society) that we expect teachers to differentiate between fact and opinion. In addition, we might expect teachers to acknowledge the difference between fact and faith, but are these realistic expectations? About one third of UK state (i.e. receiving money from taxpayers) schools have a faith designation, the majority being Christian, as shown in the commons library research briefing available here.[348] This means they are free to discriminate in admissions, employment and the curriculum on the basis of religion. Thus they do not all manage this differentiation satisfactorily. Ofsted has found examples of Islamic and Jewish schools avoiding the teaching of evolution and relationships other than the heterosexual marriage model, segregating pupils by sex and enforcing religious clothing.[349] Catholic schools are less likely to avoid topics altogether but will teach that their belief, or opinion, is correct. Some parents discover too late the extent of the unwanted religious content of their children's education.[350] Non–Catholic Christian faith schools are subjected to SIAMS. The NSS has collected evidence in a recent report[351] that these are leading previously less religious schools to become more so as they are judged not sufficiently Christian. These have been witnessed 'push[ing] an approach to collective worship that was alien to the school' and other observations include 'Some staff found it difficult to separate their personal faith from lessons; or didn't seem to understand that being a "Church school" shouldn't mean proselytising.'

In the NSS report *Unsafe Sex Education: The risk of letting religious schools teach within the tenets of their faith*[352], they find that 77% of the surveyed state-funded secondary faith schools, where an SRE policy was found, are teaching this subject in accordance with religious scripture. This of course will include schools from other faiths, not just Christianity. But another report[353] gives several examples of Christian schools, mostly but not exclusively Catholic, that teach moral judgement on consenting adult choices and harmless acts like masturbation. These are particularly likely to cause feelings of shame in young people questioning their sexuality or gender identity. It is pleasing to find that at least one of the schools highlighted in this report has updated their policy since the report's publication, but there still remains the subheading 'Emotional and **social turmoil** before and after abortion' and this statement does remain the same (emphasis mine): 'the Catholic Church "does not believe that sexual acts between persons of the same sex are morally right in principle".' It adds that 'the possibility of repentance and forgiveness for **sexual sins** is open to all'. I find it hard not to read this as 'even gay people can be forgiven'. Surely this policy, and the numerous others like it, are not compatible with the UK government statutory guidance[354], which under the heading 'Lesbian, Gay, Bisexual and Transgender' states that 'In teaching Relationships Education and RSE, schools should ensure that the needs of all pupils are appropriately met, and that all pupils understand the importance of equality and respect. Schools must ensure that they comply with the relevant provisions of the Equality Act 2010, under which sexual orientation and gender reassignment are amongst the protected characteristics.' We will return to the Equality Act later.

The NSS agrees that these schools misuse taxpayers' money: 'In this way, the Catholic Church uses state funding to promote its anti-LGBT+ and anti-family planning agenda, and inculcate generations of children with the view that same-sex relationships and women who control their own reproduction are shameful and wrong.'[355]

The author has taught briefly in Catholic primary schools whose resources stated that to have sex at any other stage of life than after marriage, being open to the possibility of having children, caused 'serious problems for society'. The resources also failed to mention any hint of pleasure in the sexual act for females, despite including a well-worded explanation of pleasure in the male orgasm. Pupils at Catholic schools are noticing themselves that there are important gaps in their education, the author of the cited article claiming that their Catholic education 'avoids discussion of contraception, abortion or gay sex, ultimately failing students and the development of their knowledge'. In practical terms, they are left with 'very little resources for safe sex practices or contraception'.[356]

The appendix of the school policy mentioned earlier in this chapter contains a summary of official Catholic teaching on relevant topics to aid staff in their teaching. We cannot be surprised that Catholic schools are following Catholic teaching. And this is not to say that there are no teachers who manage to successfully differentiate between the position of the Church and what might be best for an individual. But can we really expect vulnerable young people (and when one's body is mis-behaving the way it does between 12 and 20, who isn't?) to navigate through what might be very strong feelings indeed, with a constant doctrine of how most of what they want is wrong? It is bad enough if the pupil is a straight female (periods, don't do it until you're married, you won't enjoy it anyway, don't use any kind of reliable contraception but also don't have an abortion), but what if they are gay? Heterosexual desires are deemed natural, but must wait until after marriage to a loving partner. Homosexual urges are taboo and you must curb them forever or seek forgiveness every time you weaken. This, despite homosexuals, 'most of them secretly practising' in the Vatican, according to Frédéric Martel.[143] If a young person enjoys aspects of their family faith, gets a lot out of going to church and believes in a god, what kind of a blow must it be to be told of all this sin, on top of that which they must carry just by existing, according to Augustine? If they are not believers, how will this heaped-on sin help them to become so? Could it be that faith schools could increase church 'bums on seats' by easing off on this? But as I write, I realise I am coming at this from the perspective of a non-believer, and someone for whom these principles are not set in stone as they are for Catholics. So it is my proposition that, even if the older practices (like corporal punishment) of Catholic education as detailed in other parts of this book are behind us, this indoctrination of guilt will always continue through literal Catholic teaching of sex and relationships education, and in other religious establishments too, depending on their faith tradition or in the case of the C of E, how fundamentalist they or their teachers might be. There is evidence in Ofsted's equality objectives[357] that inspectors do their best to hold schools to account in respect of the Equality Act, which does not allow teachers to discriminate against pupils because of their own religious views about homosexuality or women's roles, for example, and no doubt would act on any breach of it they found in a school's or teacher's attitude to this topic. But how often will they even be present in a Catholic school's relationships and sex lesson, especially if that school is rated 'good' or 'outstanding' and it is not considered necessary to conduct a very detailed inspection?[358] They might ask to see the policy and evidence that the school follows it, but must rarely witness a sensitive discussion on something like contraception with a class. (Indeed, the inspector I met whilst teaching sex education in primary school asked my permission before observing a lesson, aware of the effect his presence might have on the children's confidence or participation.) In any case, the wording of the appropriate parts of the Equality Act in particular is deliberately open to interpretation, as we will see later.

Bodies exist in the UK to support Christians in education, such as the Association of Christian Teachers.[359] Here is their mission statement:

'ACT is called to glorify God by serving, supporting, inspiring and equipping Christians who work in or care about education. ACT seeks to inspire all Christians in education confidently to live out their faith day by day, positively influencing the culture, values and spiritual environment in the education setting and, ultimately, transforming the nation for the Kingdom of God.'

There's nothing wrong with supporting other members of your faith in what is a difficult and stressful profession. There's also nothing wrong with trying to positively influence the education setting with one's Christian values, if we assume those values are things like compassion, charity and humility. How many of the following 'fundamental truths' are also being wrapped up in that influence? Most open-minded people will find the fundamental truths c – e, g and h in the following list problematic. Several of these also relate directly to the message of this book as a whole. The ideas of **guilt** and **sin** are being presented here as a 'fundamental truth', no doubt one for which 'respect' would be demanded.

The Association of Christian Teachers ascribes to the fundamental truths of Christianity including:

**a** The unity of the Father, of the Son and of the Holy Spirit in the Godhead.

**b** The sovereignty of God in creation, providence, revelation, redemption and final judgement.

**c** The divine inspiration and entire trustworthiness of Holy Scripture and its supreme authority in all matters of faith and conduct.

**d** The sinfulness and guilt of all people since the Fall, rendering them subject to God's wrath and condemnation.

**e** Redemption from the guilt, penalty and power of sin solely through the sacrificial death as our representative and substitute, of the Lord Jesus Christ, the incarnate Son of God.

**f** The bodily resurrection of the Lord Jesus Christ from the dead, and His ascension to the right hand of God the Father.

**g** The necessity of the work of the Holy Spirit to make the death of Christ effective to the individual sinner, granting repentance towards God and faith in our Lord Jesus Christ.

**h** The justification of the sinner by the grace of God through faith in Christ alone.

**i** The indwelling and work of the Holy Spirit in the believer.

**j** The one holy, universal Church which is the Body of Christ, and to which all true believers belong.

**k** The expectation of the personal return of the Lord Jesus Christ.

ACT provide links to resources (they do not claim responsibility for these) that are used by more than just Christian schools. On the 'Lovewise' website[360] is the following:

'Thank you for these fabulous resources. They are excellent quality. I've shared them and I know other schools that are not necessarily [C]hristian using them as they are balanced and easy to follow.'

An inexperienced teacher blindly 'respecting' these views, or an individually religious teacher could thus use them without editing or balance in what parents believed was a non-faith school. This is not to suggest that these resources are all bad – but the sample slides on the website show some gender stereotyping, too often not noticed or questioned by teachers despite its inclusion in the government's RSE statutory guidance[361]: 'Schools should be alive to issues such as everyday sexism, misogyny, homophobia and gender stereotypes and take positive action to build a culture where these are not tolerated, and any occurrences are identified and tackled', and the providers do not hide the fact that they are promoting the Christian perspective.

One of the reasons that the NSS has put together its own resources on secularism for use in schools is that religious groups are prolific in their production of materials to teach about religion from their point of view. Those groups are very happy to share these, and overworked teachers in other schools, particularly primary schools, are happy to take and use them. This piece from the NSS[362] explains the problem well in the context of the Church of England. In chapter 9 we looked at some of the services provided by *RE Today*, (a trading name for the charity Christian Education Movement).[363] This commercial publisher produces two syllabuses that SACREs can use under licence with local authority funding.

> *As part of the licencing agreement, the syllabus is not to be reproduced or published openly. So, unlike the National Curriculum, what children are learning in many schools is hidden behind password protected websites. This is highly unusual and conflicts with the interests of parents, school visitors and the general public who have provided the funding.*

This means that 'a great many community schools nationally are now following a syllabus that is deferential to the C of E's expectations for the subject [RE].' These expectations can be read in the C of E's *Statement of Entitlement*.[364] They are quite balanced and reasonable expectations for a church school, with statements such as 'There should be opportunities for them to understand the role of foundational texts, beliefs, rituals, and practices and how they help form identity in a range of religions and worldviews', but parents deliberately sending their child to a community school might reasonably question the deference to these expectations, such as:

> *All pupils in Church schools should follow a recognised and appropriate qualification or course in RE or Religious Studies at KS 4. This includes pupils who have SEND (Special Education Needs & Disabilities). The study of Christianity will be a significant part of any Religious Studies qualification offered.*

To be fair to the Church of England and authors of the whole statement, it is also reasonable to ask whether educators and SIAMS inspectors are studying it properly in relation to their work.

Then we have the Christian Education.org.uk website, which incidentally contains a link to a 'virtual museum' which questions biological evolution:[365]

'About Us: We are a group of Christians in the United Kingdom, seeking to raise our children to love, know and serve God with all their heart.'

This is their right, of course. Their FAQ[366] page reveals their aims in a little more detail, for example in answer to a question about what God tells us to do with our children. In support of their argument that children must attend a Christian school, they quote Deuteronomy 11 which tells parents to 'Fix these words of mine in your hearts and minds …Write them on the doorframes of your houses and on your gates' and say that 'the education of children and youth must be based on God's Word as absolute truth'. Firstly, this exhortation from Deuteronomy appears to refer to the Jewish mezuzah, a small box containing verses of the Torah which is placed in doorways.[367] While it is not unheard of for Christians to do something similar, it does not appear to be an instruction that they all follow. As for 'God's Word as absolute truth', a whole book could easily be written[368] (and indeed already has, more than once) on how it would be impossible to follow everything written in the Bible as truth, because it contradicts itself and to follow all the instructions would put us in conflict with modern laws, such as murdering someone (by stoning) for working on the Sabbath (Numbers 15:32–36). There are many examples of this; here is not the place for listing all of them. But as this question is about God's wishes for one's children, it is relevant to mention that in at least five places, the Old Testament instructs parents to beat their children[369]. Christian Education does not elaborate on how they adhere to this part of 'God's Word as absolute truth'.

In this further example from the FAQs, in which the emphasis is my own, we see evidence of this group's attitude to St Augustine's teaching on **sin**:

*Q: If I put my children in Christian school, will I be sheltering them from the real world?*

*A: There is a common misconception that Christian schools shield children from every temptation and sinful exposure. This is not true, nor is it even possible. Christian schools have the same types of kids non-Christian schools have – sinners!* **Because all children come into this world with a sin nature, they are all prone to selfishness, anger, malicious talk, coveting, and the list goes on.** *... The difference in the Christian school is that the Christian school brings the Word of God to every situation in the lives of the children.* **The Christian school is able to apply the Word of God to every instance of sinful thought or action, and by God's grace, renew the mind of the child.** *Hence, the goal to produce adults that have been trained unto godly living and thinking in a world full of temptations and* **their own weaknesses as a fallen human being**.

It is noteworthy that there is no mention of forgiveness or compassion here, something I believed was a fundamental part of Christianity. Nor can I find it on any other part of the site. As we have noted time and again in this book, there is also no mention of the victims of 'sinful action'. The best success I have seen in my career in dealing with persistent bad behaviour (rudeness, aggression, refusal to accept adults' authority, frequent disregarding of school rules) involved a 'respect club' which ran at lunchtimes and which those identified were required to attend until the senior member of staff in charge decided they had learned what was necessary and were putting it into practice. Using ideas from restorative justice, they were taught about and given the opportunity to discuss the effects of their actions on others and the likely outcomes of their common behaviours. Most crucially they were supported in the taking of responsibility for their actions as all young people need to do to become fully developed adults. It was not easy for these children but I saw a marked difference in their classroom behaviour and I am confident that my colleague changed some of their lives for the better. God would not have been excluded from these sessions if a child had brought up the idea, but the focus was on personal choice and responsibility.

The document *Learning to Love: An introduction to Catholic Relationship and Sex Education for Catholic Educators*[370] reiterates Augustinian views with the following:

> *The Church considers sinful those who within marriage dishonour their spouses by using their bodies as an instrument for the purpose of self-centred sexual pleasure… when a married couple reject the possibility that their love could bear fruit in children, they fall away from the will of God if they do this out of self-interest, rather than for the good of family. For example, a couple who shun the possibility of having children because they'll interfere with 'career development' or their social life, is thinking sinfully.*

Thus a young person hoping for a career in the performing arts, or as a doctor working in dangerous places overseas for a charity, and all others who might want to limit the size of their family or have no children at all are expected to remain celibate or risk everything they have worked for by using the notoriously unreliable 'rhythm method'.

This document does indeed mention forgiveness, and love many times. I do not suggest that the majority of Catholics are intending to cause harm – quite the opposite. But while encouraging love and support to be shown to trans and gay people, it skilfully glosses over the fact that they are doing it wrong unless they deny the human desires that their fellow humans are allowed to have and express, albeit within a specified framework (marriage). Clever wording and the inclusion of the statutory parts of the curriculum are enough to adhere to the relevant parts of the government guidance document on SRE and equality,[371] which contains statements such as 'schools should ensure that the needs of all pupils are appropriately met' and 'Schools should ensure that all of their teaching is sensitive and age appropriate in approach and content' and the vague 'Schools are free to determine how they do this, and we expect all pupils to have been taught LGBT content at a timely point as part of this area of the curriculum'. But many of us remember teachers who influenced us with their personal opinion, no matter how sensitively or fairly it was expressed.

While some Catholic schools play up the love and acceptance of all people and play down the 'wrong' nature of anyone existing outside the narrow sexually correct box, some are rather more inclined to the *Oranges Are Not the Only Fruit*[372] end of the scale, helping parents to arrange Christian 'gay deliverance'.[373] I wonder, do all parents whose children attend a school like this know about and support this practice? Do the students? In the aforementioned novel and TV adaptation, we see young women in love with each other subjected to exorcisms by their Pentecostal evangelical church, and I remember being horrified that this had happened in my parents' lifetime. At the time I was too naïve to realise it was still happening in mine, and now just remain angry that this is still considered by some in the UK in the 21st century to be acceptable.

Some Catholic resources make some fair points, such as how emotionally devastating sexual relationships can be for young people (though they tend to suggest this is a female response, along with other stereotypes) and how disruptive hormonal contraception can be for women.[374] There are no doubt plenty of non-religious people in British society who might wish they had abstained from sexual relationships for longer, or might wish their children to do so. There are reasons to do this other than religion. A scheme of work that sensitively discusses these points without moral judgement is needed in order to meet the government's guidance, which states, among many other things:

*the Government recognises … that there are strong and mutually supportive relationships outside marriage. Therefore pupils should learn the significance of marriage and stable relationships as key building blocks of community and society. Care needs to be taken to ensure that there is no stigmatisation of children based on their home circumstances.*[375]

It is simply not acceptable that the harmful ideas discussed in this book are being embedded in the minds of our young people, supported by taxpayer funding.

There is no straightforward answer to any of this as long as faith schools exist and are allowed to teach SRE in accordance with their faith. But perhaps requiring them to separate the science (which would include HIV and AIDS, contraception and its side effects, STDs, UTIs, menstruation, puberty and hormones) from the RE (religious teachings on relationship choices and reproduction) might help. It would also help if parents who did not wish their children to be educated within a religion were always able to avoid it: many parents have a restricted primary school choice and can be forced into faith schools.[376] Sometimes it is not easy to tell from the outside whether there is a religious influence in a school, particularly in modern academies.[377]

Current sex and relationship education is the most obvious area in which faith schools, and any schools where teachers intentionally or otherwise convey their religious convictions, contribute to the continued indoctrination of **sin** and **guilt** in young people, especially those without other influences, or those not conforming to religious ideals in terms of sex, gender or sexuality. Recent studies suggest that faith schools represent 'a real and serious threat to children's autonomy, especially their emotional autonomy' and that 'Those who would frustrate, either intentionally or unwittingly, a child's capacity for independent thought, are denying the child right to flourish'.[378] I find this argument compelling, particularly when read in conjunction with the first part of Article 14 of the UNICEF convention on the rights of the child: 'Parties shall respect the right of the child to freedom of thought, conscience and religion.'[379] There is much to read that is relevant to this in the Equality Act advice for schools[380], but this quote illustrates the lack of clarity around teachers giving their opinions: 'it should not be unlawful for a teacher in any school to express personal views on sexual orientation provided that it is done in an appropriate manner and context'. The last four words are an excellent example of government fence-sitting! I am not against teachers expressing personal opinions; it is impossible to avoid sometimes. But counter-opinions should be offered for discussion, as we would expect with politics, and it should be normal for opinions to be challenged. This is tricky for young people when one opinion has the weight of the school, perhaps their family and a large and powerful worldwide pressure group behind it.

'Religious tolerance' means too many things to too many different people, and our children are receiving very different messages while growing up as a result. Despite learning about different religions and worldviews being recommended in UK government guidance, because SACREs usually exclude non-religious people such as humanists, the teaching of non-religious views is patchy and sometimes not included at all. It seems the UK government is willing to recommend, but not enforce. I would like to see an education system in which every child is able to exercise the right to receive balanced, up-to-date, scientifically researched information, including any grey areas, on the biology and psychology of their own bodies and how to get non-partisan support for these. Alongside this, whether in RE lessons or elsewhere in the curriculum, I would like to see a comprehensive and sensitive approach to education on various worldviews including atheist and secularist positions. Respectful language and compassion for others should be taught, the emphasis being on personal responsibility as a child reaches adulthood, whether they choose to do that within a faith tradition or not. As a teacher, I have found that once a pupil trusts you, they will almost always come up with the answer that's right for them when you say, 'Well, what do you think you should do?' The idea of guilt should only arise in the classroom as a name for the feeling when we know we are in the wrong – and a further part of teachers' and parents' jobs is to teach first that everyone makes mistakes, and then how to positively make amends and do better next time. Guilt does not need to be carried around forever, but apologising to a stranger and to a god will not always be enough.

# 13

# FROM PUPIL TO TEACHER – A JOURNEY OUT OF SHAME

Lining a corridor in a modern-day Catholic primary school are images that an alien, having learned the basics about human animals but not yet about religion, might describe as images of torture. As described graphically in chapter 9, in one a close-up of a man's face shows him in obvious pain as blood runs down his face from spikes placed on his head. I find these uncomfortable to walk past, and I remember my acceptance as a child that this was OK, because of the total acceptance and reverence shown by the adults around me in schools. My own first thoughts that perhaps it wasn't OK, because crucifixion actually looked really painful and humiliating, appeared on one of my viewings of the TV show *Jesus of Nazareth*,[381] with its vividly imagined depiction of the suffering involved. I was too young at the time to consider the fact that viewing violence like this would not have been recommended for a primary school-aged child under any other circumstances. Yet here I was, one viewing at least taking place in my committed Christian grandparents' opulent sitting room, with their full approval and encouragement. It is a great source of regret to me that I never, once older, had a proper conversation with my Church of England vicar grandfather about any of the questions that started occurring to me around that time. I tried once or twice with my grandmother, also a devout woman, but gave up quickly when it seemed she would be easily upset by such challenges. I loved her for being a warm, nature-loving, artistic lady, but she was completely immovable on the subject of the Lord, His existence and His plan. In my teaching role I learned that when a refugee child comes to Britain from a war zone, they need patience, kindness and a stable environment in their school. Sometimes it can take months for them to speak or to stop drawing pictures including the violence they have witnessed or even experienced. How can it possibly help them to be presented with these normalised images of violence, part of a religion which might be new to them?

About 20 years after *Jesus of Nazareth*, I was sitting in a staff room with two colleagues. The school was a community school and stuck roughly to the basics of the law, meaning that there were some religious components of assemblies and a minimum of 51% Christianity in the RE curriculum. The colleagues in question were, unlike most of the others, personally committed Christians. Our conversation turned to religion and I mentioned, respectfully, that I actually found the Easter story quite distressing and very unpleasant. I intended to mention the slaughter of the innocents, sometimes tacked on to the more graphic versions of the Christmas story, which I find utterly horrifying (a novel called *The Gospel According to Jesus Christ* includes a very thought-provoking version of this),[382] but before I got that far I was shamed out of the conversation. One colleague was clearly upset that I thought such a wonderful, life-changing revelation was an unpleasant horror story, and gave the impression that she thought I hadn't really understood it properly. She seemed hugely concerned for my welfare in a way that made me feel uncomfortable. The other gave me a patronising look and dismissed me with a roll of the eyes that said immature/uneducated/ungodly and so on. Neither colleague was rude, but my opinion was simply not valid if it involved criticising their religion. This experience, in some form or another, has been repeated throughout my adult life, though thankfully less often with teaching colleagues.

On first approaching this topic, while I was familiar with the teaching of sin in children, I thought it was something by which I had remained mostly unaffected. Then I began to think about it. I had no memories of abuse from teachers – mostly I liked mine – and no memories of being told directly that I was sinful or guilty. In endless repetitions of the Lord's Prayer, although I had asked someone what 'trespasses' meant, I didn't really think about the meaning of any of it. As an adult who has spent time in various roles reading and thinking about religion, I have come to believe that my own experience of Christian-induced shame has come more indirectly. What I would have described as embarrassment or fear of ridicule and being patronised I can now see in the context of this learned premise that humans are inherently 'bad' and must constantly be mitigating this. The Christian without empathy (and this is by no means all of them) will always be the winner in a discussion that goes something like this:

*Evangeliser: Aren't we all sinners?*

*Agnostic/atheist: Well yes, we all do things wrong, of course—*

*Evangeliser: Have you accepted Jesus Christ as your saviour and asked for your sins to be forgiven?*

*Agnostic/atheist: No, because I don't believe that will have any effect.*

*Evangeliser: I have. You really should.*

The evangeliser is not interested in my experience of personal conscience being my moral compass; my atheism has made me a better person because I consider no one but myself in any way responsible for my behaviour. This sort of thing is of course very

175

subjective and I am willing to accept that one of us is not more 'right' than the other. The problem is that followers of religion do not accept that other views might be valid for other individuals.

I also suspect that many other people who might not be consciously aware of these influences have been affected by them and that this contributes to their perpetuation, particularly in primary schools, where assertions are often simply not questioned, out of 'respect'.

When I was in what is now called year six (age 10 – 11), or to everyone else 'the last year of primary school', I had a comparatively young and amusing but at times over-zealously Christian teacher. This was a church school (C of E) and he taught Christian-flavoured RE with great passion. He was also responsible for teaching us sex education, which he did with an emphasis on morals. There was nothing inaccurate in the simplified biological facts we were taught. I do not recall any discussion of the effects of the onset of hormones however, which several of us were already experiencing, or indeed much about hormones at all and their role in making one's brain behave in a way that would, for many, be unrecognisable to their ten-year-old selves. We were basically just told that we shouldn't be doing it. My memory of everything he said is rolled up in this: 'If I hear, in six or seven years' time,' he blustered, in his earnest and slightly red-faced way, my brain immediately calculating how old I would be then, 'if I hear from someone: oh, do you remember that boy and that girl from this class?' [insert pause long enough to sweep a gaze around the room] 'Well, they've had a baby together – I will be VERY DISAPPOINTED.' I strongly suspect that I was not the only girl in the room who thought that the chances of this happening with the boys on offer were slim, but as I said we had not been taught about hormones and how they affect your judgement. More importantly, I remember the feeling of squeezing inside as I wanted to put my hand up and say, but my mum had me when she was that age… what's the problem? (Needless to say, I had been brought up entirely adequately by my young, but perfectly morally sound parents.) I did not say this. Partly because it suddenly appeared that to have a young mum was something to be ashamed of, which I don't think I'd been aware of before, and partly because I simultaneously wondered if she was thus ashamed, and didn't want to increase her embarrassment if she was. The production of a healthy human baby was apparently something to be ashamed of, not celebrated as a miracle of life, as you might expect from a believer. It is not a great stretch from this to Augustine's 'itch of lust' in children. My teacher was already looking at us as if we were considering it. We weren't.

I spent so much of my adolescence and youth feeling embarrassed that I didn't single out this experience, but I never forgot about it, and many years later as a primary teacher myself, in an area where the teenage pregnancy rate was sometimes as high as one in eleven, I made a point of handling this one more appropriately. When presented with facts, more than one opinion and the freedom to ask questions, children often come to the conclusion themselves that having babies very young is not something to be aspired to. It was not up to me as a teacher to encourage them in a moral judgement of people who become young parents (I often taught children who were already uncles or aunts), but to empower them to make the best decisions for themselves, and I always hoped they would also develop some compassion – to my mind a far more desirable aspect of religious belief, for those who have it, than moral judgement. In a small victory, I am confident that like-minded colleagues and I halted the transmission of any sense of shame over one's (legal) sexual choices, and instead developed in children the beginnings of enough self-respect and factual knowledge to make safe decisions but accept that life is not simple.

At all the primary schools I attended, my peers and teachers were shocked if I mentioned that my siblings and I were not christened. Perhaps because of the conversation I had with my parents about it, I always saw christening as a very peculiar thing to do unless you were choosing it for yourself. In my grandmother's one attempt to get me to ask my parents (including her son, who had rejected churchgoing in adolescence) to have me christened, she said, 'You'll belong to

God then'. I was old enough (this was post-*Jesus of Nazareth*) for two things to come to mind. 1) I didn't really want to belong to God. It felt like a narrowing of options. 2) Who did she think I belonged to now? Would her God really treat children differently according to what their parents chose to do? (According to St Augustine, yes.) That didn't sound like a club I wanted to be in, thank you very much, and I now know that thoughts like these were the beginning of my atheism. I was also old and wise enough not to start this conversation with her at the time. With friends at school, I would shrug, often being too wary to say what I thought, which was 'Well why would you get christened?' and 'What if you don't want to be a Christian?' and 'Why does everyone expect me to have a "Christian" name when I wasn't christened and am not a Christian?' (The demise of the term 'Christian name' for 'first name' is surely a positive outcome of the modern world.)

Gradually, as an adult, I have come to the conclusion that those of us who attend even theoretically non-religious schools are infused with an order to 'respect' faith, and in particular the Christian faith, without a good enough examination of what 'respect' does or should mean. One is entitled to be treated courteously by others, regardless of their position; good manners are intrinsic to a civilised society. But let us not confuse courtesy with respect; respect must be earned. Non-believers are tolerated if we do not wish to pray for faith to be given to us. The best teachers, and I have met quite a few, will treat us just the same. But there is an undercurrent of assumption of privilege and monopoly on the truth which I realised eventually had made me, and I think many people, complicit in the idea that we were somehow inferior to the believers. That we should come second in the queue, that our opinions were a little less valid and our objections or even just questions, were a little cheeky or trivial. That perhaps actually we were just seeking attention for ourselves. We were indulged, rather than taken seriously. I have definitely, as a young person, apologised for asking questions and making polite objections concerning religion, which were in fact perfectly within my rights to express. I stopped doing this at around the time when someone I regarded as a friend told me earnestly how sad he felt that all the people he'd met recently (at university), including me and various others he gestured to around the room, were going to hell. He said it in the same manner in which you might express regret that someone couldn't join you in the pub. I stopped being apologetic about my agnosticism (now atheism) and began to challenge religious assumptions about my worth. This has become easier as I have mixed with more diverse people, and since atheist and secular points of view have become more mainstream. But the learned responses are still there, and it is still difficult not to apologise before disagreeing with a Christian.

I think this learned shame and low self-esteem affects many teachers in the UK, and that too few of them give it proper thought. UK teachers are becoming less religious as a group.[383] Nevertheless, how many teachers sit in school assemblies with their hands together and eyes piously closed, thinking about what they're having for dinner but frowning at and shushing any child who wriggles, makes a noise or refuses to participate? How many take assemblies, and regardless of their own beliefs, use the word 'we' to talk about Christian faith, lumping together everyone in the room without their consent? (I have seen this many times even when a significant proportion of the audience identifies as Muslim, Sikh or Hindu.) How many consider the suitability of the content of religious stories presented in primary school assemblies? Would the killing of young children with swords and knives (Matthew 2:16), or a father tying up his son and making him think he was about to stab him (Genesis 22: 1–19, but also in the Quran) or the painful and humiliating torture that is crucifixion be acceptable stories for 4–11-year-olds in another context? Those who have read it will know that these are not the only violent or unpleasant stories in the Bible, but to be fair to teachers and schools, I have no evidence that any of them are telling the story of Lot offering his daughters to a sodomite rapist mob (Genesis 19). At the age of ten, however, I was told the story of Jezebel (1 Kings), who is killed

179

by being thrown from a window, trampled by a horse and is then eaten by dogs. The impression I got from the presentation of this was that women who wore 'too much make up' and were bossy (for women, this means assertive – how religious teaching portrays and affects women is yet another book subject) were considered bad. The same people who teach these stories would, along with me, be horrified to find those same children playing video games with similar levels of violence and remaining untraumatised in the same way. But when I brought this up in a UK primary school, I was faced with a patronising 'it's not quite the same, is it' or the vacant 'oh yes, I don't really know much about the Bible', or the blind 'respect' – 'Yes, it is a bit, isn't it, but we have to respect it'. Asking 'why?' at this point can cause embarrassed shuffling and a rapidly given reason to be elsewhere, or a reversion to one of the other cited responses. Also, to be fair to teachers, none of them has time for a discussion along these lines in their working day. But this is a discussion that should be happening somewhere in the corridors of power.

To return to a theme from the previous chapter: in a humid summer some years back, the school I worked in at the time was juggling the knotty problem of where to house groups of 'the withdrawn' – nomadic Muslims and Christians, or to be more precise, since these children should be considered too young for a permanent label, 'children from Muslim and Christian families'. Clutching reading books and some scruffy bits of paper, these groups would shuffle about the school, often fruitlessly searching for a temporary classroom home in which no one was watching one of Those Videos about relationships and sex education (RSE).[384] Parents have the right in the UK to withdraw children from sex education, though there have been some improvements in this area recently for older students (those who are or will be 16 in the next three school terms can now opt themselves in – this is a positive move from the government but I would question how many 15-year-olds would have the confidence to disobey the kind of parent who does not want their sexually mature child educated in this way with their peers).[385] Partly for our own sanity, we referred to the situation with our classes thus: 'X's parents have decided to educate them at home about this topic.' This no doubt happened in some cases. In others it led to girls as young as eight being terrified by the unannounced onset of menstruation and children being told that members of their faith did not have sex and that babies were a gift from God. An older girl whom I taught when working in secondary school was unable to distinguish between the teaching of her family's religion on abortion (which I and her peers listened to respectfully) and the actual law in the UK, and despite her high level of intelligence, it took a long time for her to understand that as a UK citizen the choice would be hers. Those shuffling children were not being educated about anything during this time; there was no spare member of staff in an already over-stretched school containing many children with additional needs. How did it become acceptable that some children do not learn about the biology of their own body and that they have autonomy over it? I think it is fair to argue that, unless the parents genuinely are providing comprehensive information at home that covers the curriculum, this is punishment of a kind. There is clearer guidance now on SRE in secondary schools and it is moving in the right direction, and primary schools are obliged to teach relationships education. They are not obliged to teach sex education[386], though many choose to. I believe it should be taught in primary school, partly because I have found year after year that 10 –11 is an excellent age to learn about it; primary-aged children are much more inclined to ask questions and get over embarrassment, and are much less affected by adolescent hormones and personal experience than their slightly older counterparts. Furthermore, for some, particularly girls, bodily changes are already a reality and becoming more so as girls reach puberty ever earlier.[387] It can be truly heart-warming to see boys start to understand what girls go through with menstruation and offer them support through their awe-filled curiosity and total acceptance of it as a normal thing. The government could go further in its attempts to ensure every child receives the necessary information by making sex education mandatory by the end of primary school and making parental withdrawal more difficult.

On a poll of hands up, about 90% of the 9 – 11-year-old girls at my school, including those withdrawn, once they knew they would not be asked to elaborate, said yes to the question, 'Have you ever seen something rude on the internet or on a device that made you feel uncomfortable?' And yet, those with religious parents who objected were excluded from the essential education around sex and the media, all the more important now because of the proliferation of easy-access pornography. No child should feel guilty for wanting to know the facts about something that can seriously affect their health and adolescent experience. Failing to arm children with a little knowledge before they go to secondary school, when many of the girls could already pass for about 15 is, I think, neglectful, dangerous and wrong. Nor should they be exposed only to the narrow views of what is acceptable to God through the eyes of Christian doctrine or that of any other religion. Guilt rears its head here in a different way; more than once I have seen the desperate look on a girl's face as she tries to become invisible, hoping that her teacher will not notice that she is still in the room when Those Videos or Those Worksheets appear, only to flush with humiliation if another child piously points it out. As a teacher, I felt ashamed that I could not include those children in the thoughtful, mature and often hilarious discussions arising from primary-style sex education. It used to bring my class together in a way that not many topics did and I hated having to exclude some members.

Education is, I think, moving in the right direction, in that there are plenty of educators who are not guilty of the failings I have described. (However, worrying information is coming to light in 2021 about 'rape culture' in UK schools.[388] It is unclear at this early stage whether St Augustine's teaching contributes to this but religious schools are included in the lists of schools affected[389], and it is surely exacerbated by any unhealthy attitudes to sex from staff that are prevailing.) Corporal punishment is not allowed, and thanks to children arriving at schools from a variety of faiths and backgrounds, schools are forced to use more inclusive language whatever their policies. Faith schools are not just allowed but positively encouraged to exist by those who enjoy the perceived privileges that they offer, but many of these privileges are fallacious, as shown in the NSS's 'Faith School Myth Buster'.[390] There is no mechanism for measuring the effect of this Christian attitude of superiority, or of the effect on young people of the doctrines of the sanctity of heterosexual marriage, sex and reproduction and the idea that children are inherently bad just because of their existence. Their proponents love Christian schools, and understandably so; they are selective and often allow families to ensure that their child mixes mostly with others of a similar tradition, or from certain parts of the world. Ask these parents if they think that there should be more Muslim schools and that children should be taught Islam as correct, having been sent there because they cannot get in to the school of their choice (this happens in the UK to plenty of people with Christian schools),[391] then I know of at least one who would concede that perhaps no faith schools would be better. But there is no sign of a political shift towards this position.

The insistence regarding sin can follow a child into adulthood. Catholic Church elders told a woman 30 years ago that her dead infant son would have gone to hell because she and the father had not been married. This might be a rare incident and might not be typical of what most modern Catholics would say,[392] but this woman still carries that pain with her thirty years later, along with the pain of her lost child. Like the priest who administered a beating to my fellow author, these elders were acting and speaking on behalf of their church, with authority that people used to respecting them would find hard to disregard. This was a moral judgement of the most damaging kind. No adult with a duty of care towards young people should be making moral judgements, either explicitly by teaching that one religion is correct, or implicitly by using exclusive language or expressing personal opinions in a context where those opinions carry too much weight and are not challenged.

Almost all the Catholics I have met, at work and socially, have been delightful people. They appear to be non-judgemental, compassionate, cheerful and self-assured. The power of the community must be very great, because some of the people I know in that community are non-celibate gay people, and few of the others are likely to have used the rhythm method to produce their two sensibly spaced-out children. According to a YouGov poll, only 4% of Catholics questioned believed that artificial contraception was wrong and should not be used.[393] Catholics in particular appear to feel no compulsion to follow the rules set down by their own Church, perhaps using many of the ideas explored in chapter 5 to manoeuvre through this moral maze, yet absolutely consider themselves members of it nonetheless. One hopes that they extend this privilege to others breaking the rules but wishing to be accepted as an equal. I expect the people I know personally do just that, though it is disappointing to me that they continue to align themselves with a religion that they clearly disagree with. However, those who are teachers could be breaking their contracts with faith schools by allowing inclusivity into RSE lessons, so are likely to be promoting a narrow and to some, damaging set of rules about sex and relationships. 'Do as I say, not as I do' seems to be the message. I wonder: do they ever feel guilty about this?

**End**

# ABOUT THE AUTHORS

Michael Moloney is the pseudonym of an acclaimed British writer. He served as altar boy and chorister while attending boarding schools in Ireland and England, where he encountered abuse. With the Vatican decrying critics of the church as 'Friends of the Devil', he thought back to his church schooldays and the harmful situations he had faced.

The UK Independent Inquiry into Child Sexual Abuse reports that abuse continues today, yet nothing in literature explains this deviance credibly. The possible influence of Christian drill and doctrine, on the sexual abuse of children or the callous neglect found in Ireland's mother and baby homes, is unexplored.

Reading about the evasiveness of the churches in response to disclosures of child abuse, Moloney felt driven to record his life experiences and help throw light on the enduring consequences of a faith school education, for certain individuals. In his new book, **Why Punish Me?** he suggests Augustine's ideas on sexual sinfulness and infantile lust might play a more influential role in child sexual abuse and adult mental well-being than has generally been recognised. A teacher's struggles to be objective are spelled out by Lorna Graham, a teacher for 26 years, who brings faith schools to life in the final chapters.

The authors hope you enjoyed reading, but whether you did or not please leave a review at:

*https://Mike-Moloney.com*

# ENDNOTES

1   Worsley, Margret. (1997). *St Philip's from beginning to beginning*. Foreword. ISBN 1862370788, Quotation is from the Book of Proverbs copied out by John Henry Newman into a schoolboy notebook at the age of nine.

2   The Guardian, *Child sexual abuse inquiry criticises lack of cooperation from Vatican*. Retrieved Oct 28, 2019 from *https://www.theguardian.com/uk-news/2019/oct/28/child-sexual-abuse-inquiry-criticises-lack-of-cooperation-from-vatican*

3   Definition of 'concupiscence' courtesy of New World Encyclopaedia, *Christian View*. Retrieved Jun 29, 2020 from *https://www.newworldencyclopedia.org/entry/Concupiscence*

4   St Augustine *The Confessions of St Augustine* (c. 397), Translation by Pusey, Edward B. 'no one is free from sin in (God's) sight, not even an infant whose span of earthly life is but a single day' (Book I, p9); 'The only innocence in infants is the weakness of their frames; the minds of infants are not innocent.' (Book I, p10); 'weltering in filth and scratching off the itch of lust...my infant tongue spake freely to thee' (Book IX, p128); '[infants] being yet little ones and carnal' (Book XII, p213). ISBN: 9781565481541. The full text is also available in the original Latin free under the terms of the Project Gutenberg License, at *www.gutenberg.org*

5   St Augustine *On Merit and the Forgiveness of Sins and the Baptism of Infants* (Book 1) 'In infants it is certain that, by the grace of God, through His baptism who came in the likeness of sinful flesh, it is brought to pass that the sinful flesh is done away. This result, however, is so effected, that the concupiscence which is diffused over and innate in the living flesh itself is not removed all at once, so as to exist in it no longer; but only that that might not be injurious to a man at his death, which was inherent at his birth.' Translated by Peter Holmes and Robert Ernest Wallis, and revised by Benjamin B. Warfield. From Nicene and Post-Nicene Fathers, First Series, Vol. 5. Edited by Philip Schaff. (Buffalo, NY: Christian Literature Publishing Co., 1887.) Chapter 70 [XXXIX.] ASIN: B005FY060U

6   CCC, VII *The Grace of Baptism*. 1264: 'Yet certain temporal consequences of sin remain in the baptized, such as ... concupiscence.'

7   CCC, III *Original Sin*. 411: 'Mary benefited first of all and uniquely from

Christ's victory over sin: she was preserved from all stain of original sin.'

8    The Education Act 1996, section 375 (2), Retrieved Apr 29, 2020 from *http:// www.legislation.gov.uk/ukpga/1996/56/section/375*

9    TeacherTapp. *Teachers are losing their religion – Part.* (2019). Retrieved Apr 29, 2020 from *https://teachertapp.co.uk/ teachers-are-losing-their-religion-how-religious-are-teachers/*

10   DfE, National Statistics *Schools, pupils and their characteristics Academic Year 2019/20, 'State funded primary schools educate 4.71 million pupils'* Retrieved Aug 20, 2020 from *https://www.gov.uk/government/statistics/ schools-pupils-and-their-characteristics-january-2020*

11   Ten:Ten Resources. PowerPoint prayer presentations for Collective Worship annual subscription £588.00 *Penitential Act*, Retrieved Aug 30, 2020 *https://www.tentenresources.co.uk/primary-subscription/prayers-for-home/ sunday-liturgy-for-families/*

12   Church of England. *Common Worship*. Retrieved Mar 11, 2020 from *https://www.churchofengland.org/prayer-and-worship/worship-texts-and-resources/ common-worship/holy-communion#mm7c*

13   British Social Attitudes Survey (2018) *Religion, Identity, behaviour and belief over two decades*, p6. Retrieved Feb 4, 2021 from *https://www.bsa.natcen.ac.uk/ media/39293/1_bsa36_religion.pdf*

14   Harvard University, Center on the Developing Child, *Brain Architecture* Retrieved Feb 4, 2021 from *https://developingchild.harvard.edu/science/key-concepts/ brain-architecture/*

15   Ed. Jane Bybee, (1998), *Guilt and Children,* Chapter 7 ISBN: 9780121486105 – Chapter 7, L Fischer and PS Richards, *Religion and Guilt in Childhood* ISBN: 978-0121486109

16   Jill Mytton interview – Richard Dawkins. YouTube. Retrieved Mar 11, 2020 from *https://www.youtube.com/watch?v=GXA7GA9yntc*

17   National Secular Society (NSS) Retrieved Mar 11, 2020 from *Testimonials https://www.nomorefaithschools.org/testimonials.html*

18   Cooper R. Mail Online *Forcing a religion on your children is as bad as child abuse, claims atheist professor Richard Dawkins* (April 22, 2013) Retrieved Mar 11, 2020 from *https://www.dailymail.co.uk/news/article-2312813/Richard-Dawkins-Forcing- religion-children-child-abuse-claims-atheist-professor.html*

19   Definition of 'punishment' courtesy of Merriam-Webster: 1: the act of

punishing; 2: suffering, pain, or loss that serves as retribution Retrieved Apr 23, 2021 from *https://www.merriam-webster.com/dictionary/punishment*

20   Wikipedia. Anglican Communion sexual abuse cases. Retrieved Sep 28, 2020 from *https://en.wikipedia.org/w/index. php?title=Anglican_Communion_sexual_abuse_cases&oldid=982153252*

21   Jane Corbin, *Scandal in the Church of England* A BBC Panorama documentary (Apr 29, 2019.) Also: *Exposed: The Church's Darkest Secret.* BBC Channel Two short drama documentaries. (Jan 13, 2020 and Jan 14, 2020.)

22   BBC News. Church of England failures 'allowed child sexual abusers to hide'. Retrieved Sep 28, 2020 from *https://www.bbc.co.uk/news/uk-54433295*

23   Sex abuse of minors by priests since AD309: *Sex, Priests, and Secret Codes: The Catholic Church's 2,000 Year Paper Trail of Sexual Abuse.* Thomas P Doyle et al. 2006 ISBN: 1566252652

24   UK IICSA (Nov 10, 2020) *The Roman Catholic Church Investigation-Report* Executive Summary: 'Responses to disclosures about sexual abuse have been characterised by a failure to support victims and survivors in stark contrast to the positive action taken to protect alleged perpetrators and the reputation of the Church.' 'It would be wrong, however, to regard child sexual abuse within the Roman Catholic Church as solely a historical problem. Since 2016, there have been more than 100 reported allegations each year.' Retrieved Oct 12, 2020 from *https://www.iicsa.org.uk/key-doc-uments/23357/view/catholic-church-investigation-report-4-december-2020.pdf*

25   'Children (4 years old) pray four times a day and have RE four days a week, with links made to this in all subjects.' 'When I asked (the teacher) if they teach creationism, she said they talk about all "theories".' National Secular Society *Parent's perspective: We made a mistake sending our child to a faith school* Retrieved Mar 14, 2021 from *https://www.nomorefaithschools.org/testimonials/2020/11/ parents-perspective-we-made-a-mistake-sending-our-child-to-a-faith-school*

26   NATRE *An analysis of the provision for RE in Primary Schools – Autumn Term 2016* Retrieved Mar 3, 2021 from *https://www.natre.org.uk/uploads/Free%20Resources/ NATRE%20Primary%20Survey%202016%20final.pdf*

27   NSS Unsafe Sex Education: The risk of letting religious schools teach within the tenets of their faith Retrieved Mar 20, 2021 from *https://www.secularism.org. uk/uploads/unsafe-sex-report-april-2018.pdf*

28   Ten:Ten Resources, *Relationship and Health Education in Schools (Life to the Full)* annual subscription £456.00 Retrieved Sep 28, 2020 from *https://www.tentenre-sources.co.uk*

29    The Sexual Offences Act 2003, Chapter 42, Paragraph 78 and Paragraph 79 Part 1

30    The Guardian, *Pope Francis decries critics of church as 'friends of the devil'* (Feb 20, 2019) Retrieved Oct 6, 2020 *https://www.theguardian.com/world/2019/feb/20/ pope-francis-decries-critics-of-church-as-friends-of-the-devil*

31    YouGov / Daybreak Survey Results (Sept 13 2010) Retrieved Apr 12, 2021 from *http://cdn.yougov.com/today_uk_import/YGArchives-Life-YouGov-DaybreakReligion-130910.pdf*

32    Toby Helm T and Townsend M. (Jun 14, 2014) The Guardian *Taxpayers' cash should not be used to fund faith schools, say voters* Retrieved Feb 7, 2021 from *https:// www.theguardian.com/education/2014/jun/14/taxpayers-should-not-fund-faith-schools*

33    Guardian Opinion Poll, ICM *Two thirds oppose state aided faith schools* (August 2005) Retrieved Apr 10, 2021 from *https://www.theguardian.com/uk/2005/aug/23/ schools.faithschools*

34    Augustiniana is a peer-reviewed scholarly journal devoted to the study of Saint Augustine, the Augustinian Order, Augustinianism and Jansenism. Online at *https://www.jstor.org/stable/ i40212149?refreqid=excelsior%3A752d3785e8140ea10a3017aeeb865f85*

35    Williams R. (2016) *On Augustine*. India: Bloomsbury Publishing. ISBN: 9781472925275,

36    Lane Fox R. (2016) *Augustine: Conversions and Confessions*. Introduction. Allen Lane ISBN: 9781846144004

37    Percy WA. (May 1, 1996) *Pederasty and Pedagogy in Archaic Greece* ISBN: 978-0252022098

38    Tatius A. *Leucippe and Clitophon*, 2.35-38: 'Menelaus said, '...A woman's every word and every gesture is feigned. If she appears beautiful, it is due to the fussy contrivance of unguents. Her beauty is of scented oil, or hair-dye, or rouge. If you strip her of these many deceits, she is like the jackdaw stripped of feathers in the fable. But the beauty of boys is not watered with scents of unguents or with deceitful and alien smells; the sweat of boys smells sweeter than all the scented unguents of women.'

39    The Warren Cup, shows paederastic sodomy (inlaid) (1st century AD). © The Trustees of the British Museum.

40    Spencer C. (1995) *Homosexuality A History* New York, NY: Harcourt Brace and Company ISBN:9781857021431

41    Quintilian (Original work published 1856) (2006) *Institutes of oratory.* L. Honeycutt, Ed., (J.S. Watson, Trans.). Retrieved Mar 6, 2021 from *http://kairos. technorhetoric.net/stasis/2017/honeycutt/quintilian*

42    Yallop D. (2010) *Beyond Belief: The Catholic Church and the Child Abuse Scandal* UK: Little, Brown Book Group ISBN: 9781849016360,

43    Williams C. (1999) *Roman Homosexuality: Ideologies of Masculinity in Classical Antiquity.* Oxford: Oxford University Press, 1999 ISBN: 9780195125054

44    Internet History Sourcebooks Project Fordham University, *John Chrysostom: (d. 407) Against the Opponents of Monastic Life 3.* Retrieved Jan 20, 2021 from *https:// sourcebooks.fordham.edu/pwh/chrysos-opp3.asp*

45    Crompton, L. (2003) *Homosexuality & Civilization* Cambridge, Mass: Belknap Press of Harvard University Press ISBN: 9780674022331

46    Saint Augustine (1997) *Answer to the Pelagians,* Translation by Roland J Teske 'Who is clean from filth? Not even an infant who has lived one day on earth' (Book six, p622) New City Press ISBN: 978-1565480926

47    Bonner G. (1986) *St.Augustine of Hippo: Life and Controversies* ISBN: 978-0907547525

48    Lössl J. (Jan 2011) *Augustine's Confessions As A Consolation Of Philosophy* ISBN: 9789004195790

49    Kligerman, C. (1957). *A psychoanalytic study of the confessions of St. Augustine.* Journal of the American Psychoanalytic Association, 5, p478. https://doi. org/10.1177/000306515700500306

50    Dittes, J.E. (1965). *Continuities in the life and thought of St. Augustine.* Journal for the scientific Study of Religion 5, p134. Republished in D. Capps & J. E. Dittes (Eds.).

51    Beers, W. (1988) *The 'Confessions' of Augustine: Narcissistic Elements.* American Imago, 45(1), 107-125. Retrieved Jan 30, 2021, from *http://www.jstor.org/ stable/26303960*

52    Study.com. *Reaction Formation in Psychology: Definition & Example.* Retrieved Jan 28, 2021 from *https://study.com/academy/lesson/reaction-formation-in-psychology-defi-nition-example.html*

53    Lanning K. (Dec 1992) National Center for Missing & Exploited Children *Child Molesters: A Behavioral Analysis* Retrieved Apr 20, 2021 from *https://www. ojp.gov/pdffiles1/Digitization/149252NCJRS.pdf*

54  Hammel-Zabin, Dr A. (May 12, 2003) *Conversations with a Pedophile: In the Interest of Our Children* Barricade Books (Aug. 2013) ISBN: 9781569802472

55  Brown P. (Sep 2, 2012) *Through the Eye of the Needle: Wealth, the Fall of Rome, and the Making of Christianity in the West* (P 160) ISBN: 9780691152905

56  Lane Fox R. (Nov 24, 2015) *Augustine: Conversions to Confessions.* Chapter 3 Infancy, Order and Sin. ISBN: 9780465061570

57  'Therefore, just as sin entered the world through one man, and death through sin, and in this way death came to all people, because all sinned' New Testament, Paul the Apostle, Romans 5:12-21 and 'For as in Adam all die, so in Christ all will be made alive.' 1 Corinthians 15:22

58  'Every soul that is born into flesh is soiled by the filth of wickedness and sin...' Homilies on Leviticus 8:3 [A.D. 248]

59  Cauley K. GEWATKINS.NET *The Argument Against the False Doctrine of Original Sin* Retrieved Jan 18, 2021 from *https://gewatkins.net/ the-argument-against-the-false-doctrine-of-original-sin/*

60  The extent to which humans have freedom of will is still in hot dispute. Compare Augustine's notion of free will requiring God's grace with concepts of free will (versus determinism) defined in modern debate. Further reading: Dennett D. (Feb 1985) *Elbow Room: The Varieties of Free Will Worth Wanting* ISBN: 978-0198247906. Another view: Harris S. YouTube (Mar 28, 2012) *Sam Harris on "Free Will"* Retrieved Apr 19, 2021 from https://www.youtube.com/watch?v=pCofmZlC72g

61  CCC, In Brief, 419: 'We therefore hold, with the Council of Trent, that original sin is transmitted with human nature, "by propagation, not by imitation" and that it is. . . "proper to each".' (Paul VI, CPG § 16).

62  CCC, Article 3, He was Conceived by the Power of the Holy Ghost and Born of the Virgin Mary, 484: 'To her question, "How can this be, since I know not man?", the divine response was given: "The Holy Ghost will come upon you."'

63  Office of Attorney General (Jul 27, 2018) Commonwealth of Pennsylvania *Report I of the 40th Statewide Investigating Grand Jury, Pennsylvania*

64  Pepinster C, The Guardian (Feb 21, 2019) *For Pope Francis, the moment of truth on sexual abuse has arrived* Retrieved Dec 11, 2020 from *https://www.theguardian.com/ commentisfree/2019/feb/21/pope-francis-truth-sexual-abuse-summit*

65  Editorial. Boston Globe (Aug 20, 2018) *After latest shocking sex abuse report, Pope Francis must lead* Retrieved Jan 18, from *https://www0.bostonglobe.com/opinion/ editorials/2018/08/20/after-shocking-pennsylvania-abuse-report-pope-francis-must-lead/*

*W0pxwZDhWsEmyBTHQ1ytRP/story.html?p1=Article_Inline_Bottom*

66   Kincaid J. (1998) *Erotic Innocence: The Culture of Child Molesting* p13, p20, ISBN: 9780822321934

67   Boyce J. (2016) *Born Bad: Original Sin and the Making of the Western World* ISBN: 9781619027183

68   Rich TR. Judaism 101, *Kosher Sex* Retrieved Apr 19, 2021 from *https://www. jewfaq.org/sex.htm*

69   Wikipedia (Apr 30, 2021) *Religion in the United Kingdom* Eurostat's Eurobarometer survey (May 2019) Retrieved May 01, 2021 from *https://en.wiki- pedia.org/w/index.php?title=Religion_in_the_United_Kingdom&oldid=1020755457*

70   YouGov Survey (Jun 24, 2013) *British Youth reject Religion https://yougov.co.uk/ topics/politics/articles-reports/2013/06/24/british-youth-reject-religion*

71   Wikipedia (Apr 30, 2021) *Religion in the United Kingdom* Retrieved May 01, 2021 from *https://en.wikipedia.org/wiki/Religion_in_the_United_Kingdom*

72   Redmond J. Info Bloom *What is Catholic Guilt?* Retrieved Dec 09, 2020 from *https://www.wisegeek.com/what-is-catholic-guilt.htm*

73   Sheldon K. (2006) Research: *Catholic Guilt? Comparing Catholics' and Protestants' Religious Motivations.* The International Journal for the Psychology of Religion 76(3):209-223.DOI: 10.1207/s15327582ijpr1603_5

74   Albertsen E., O'Connor L. and Berry J. Mental Health, Religion & Culture (2006) *Religion and interpersonal guilt: Variations across ethnicity and spirituality* 9:1, 67-84, DOI: 10.1080/13694670500040484

75   Tangney J P. and Dearing R L. (2002). *Emotions and social behaviour. Shame and guilt.* Guilford Press. Retrieved Nov 19, 2020 from *https://doi. org/10.4135/9781412950664.n388*

76   Walinga, P, et al. (2005). *Guilt and Religion: The influence of orthodox Protestant and orthodox Catholic conceptions of guilt on guilt-experience.* Archive for the Psychology of Religion, 2005(27), 113-136. Retrieved Nov 19, 2020 from *https://doi. org/10.1163/008467206774355330*

77   Quinn B. The Guardian (Feb 26, 2013) *Catholic guilt 'is a myth', poll finds,* Retrieved Nov 10, 2020 from *https://www.theguardian.com/world/2013/feb/26/ catholic-guilt-myth-poll*

78   Work of God Catholic information. *Holy Eucharist - Order of the Mass.* Retrieved Mar 11, 2020 from *https://www.theworkofgod.org/Devotns/Euchrist/guide.htm*

79   Roman Catholics recite the rosary prayers appealing to The Holy Virgin Mary to intercede with her son, Jesus Christ, to grant favours.

80   The version of the Penitential Rite (prayer) that I recited. Summarised by the Vatican in 1962, but a version, including confession and self-castigation, is in common usage today in schools and Latin churches throughout Christendom – see notes 11 and 12 above.

81   NSPCC, *Grooming*, retrieved May 24, 2020 from *https://www.nspcc.org.uk/what-is-child-abuse/types-of-abuse/grooming/#types*

82   In the past, the term 'orphan' had a wider meaning than today. Just having a father who was permanently absent could qualify a child as an orphan.

83   Mommaerts JL, Devroey D. *The placebo effect: how the subconscious fits in.* Perspect Biol Med. 2012;55(1):43-58. doi:10.1353/pbm.2012.0005. PMID: 22643715.

84   Psychology Wiki (Oct 19, 2011) *Autosuggestion* Retrieved Mar 11, 2020 from *https://psychology.wikia.org/wiki/Autosuggestion*

85   Cohen N. New Statesman (Aug 2, 2004) *How church schools brainwash children* Retrieved Dec 13, 2020 from *https://www.newstatesman.com/node/195087*

86   GP Taylor Yorkshire Post (Nov 21, 2018) *I'm a priest, and I say it's time to end faith schools.* 'I have never been able to understand why taxpayers' money should go towards funding schools with an ethos based on a particular faith. Surely, if a religion wants to subliminally proselytise children, it should pay for it itself. Better still, it should not be allowed to do it at all.' Retrieved Dec 13, 2020 from *https://www.yorkshirepost.co.uk/news/politics/gp-taylor-im-priest-and-i-say-its-time-end-faith-schools-208461*

87   Iles-Caven Yasmin et al, Frontiers in Psychology (2020) *The Relationship Between Locus of Control and Religious Behavior and Beliefs in a Large Population of Parents* Retrieved Dec 09, 2020 from *https://www.frontiersin.org/article/10.3389/fpsyg.2020.01462* DOI=10.3389/fpsyg.2020.01462, ISSN=1664-1078

88   Lewis HB. (1971) *Shame and guilt in neurosis.* New York: International Universities Press. ISBN: 9780823626076

89   Wikipedia (Mar 29, 2021). *Guilt–shame–fear spectrum of cultures* Retrieved Apr 20, 2021 from *https://en.wikipedia.org/w/index.php?title=Guilt%E2%80%93shame%E2%80%93fear_spectrum_of_cultures&oldid=1014951569*

90   ReShel, Azriel. (2018) *Neuroscience and the 'Sanskrit Effect'* Retrieved Nov 20,

2020 from *https://upliftconnect.com/neuroscience-and-the-sanskrit-effect/*

91   Simon, R., Pihlsgård, J., Berglind, U. et al. (2017) *Mantra Meditation Suppression of Default Mode Beyond an Active Task: a Pilot Study.* J Cogn Enhanc 1, 219–227 Retrieved Aug 19, 2020 from *https://doi.org/10.1007/s41465-017-0028-1*

92   Powledge T. BioScience (Aug 2011) *Behavioral Epigenetics: How Nurture Shapes Nature*, Volume 61, Issue 8, Pages 588–592, https://doi.org/10.1525/bio.2011.61.8.4

93   Scott E. Very Well Mind *The Toxic Effects of Negative Self-Talk*, Retrieved Aug 19, 2020 from *https://www.verywellmind.com/negative-self-talk-and-how-it-affects-us-4161304*

94   Imi Lo. Eggshell Transformations. *...For the Emotionally Intense.* Retrieved Aug 19, 2020 from *https://www.eggshelltherapy.com*

95   Leith, K. P., & Baumeister, R. F. (1998) *Empathy, shame, guilt, and narratives of interpersonal conflicts: Guilt-prone people are better at perspective taking.* Journal of Personality, 66(1), 1–37. Retrieved Aug 19, 2020 from *https://doi.org/10.1111/1467-6494.00001*

96   Dr Peter Brierley (2018) Brierley Consultancy *Nominal Christians* Retrieved Dec 5, 2020 from *https://europeanmission.files.wordpress.com/2018/10/nominal-cians-0218.pdf*

97   Independent Schools Council. Retrieved Apr 29, 2020 from *https://www.isc.co.uk/schools/*

98   UK House of Commons Briefing Paper Number 06972 (Dec 20, 2019) *Faith Schools in England: FAQs* Introduction. Retrieved Apr 29, 2020 from *https://commonslibrary.parliament.uk/research-briefings/sn06972/*

99   UK House of Commons Briefing Paper Number 06972 (Dec 20, 2019) *Faith Schools in England: FAQs,* p18 'In January 2019, around 1.9 million pupils were taught in state-funded faith schools (28% of primary and 18% of secondary pupils) Retrieved Apr 29, 2020 from *https://commonslibrary.parliament.uk/research-briefings/sn06972/*

100  Article 14 of the UNCRC says that children and young people are free to be of any or no religion. Their parents can help them make decisions around religion, but a parent cannot force a child or young person to adopt a religion, and a parent cannot force a child or young person to stop following a religion.

101  Peg Streep, Psychology Today (Jan 10, 2018) *Tackling Self-Blame and Self-Criticism: 5 Strategies to Try* Retrieved Aug 27, 2020

from *https://www.psychologytoday.com/gb/blog/tech-support/201801/ tackling-self-blame-and-self-criticism-5-strategies-try*

102 Cikanavicius D. Psych Central (15 Dec. 2018) *6 Ways Childhood Abuse and Neglect Leads to Self-Blame in Adulthood* Retrieved Aug 27, 2020 from *https://blogs. psychcentral.com/psychology-self/2018/07/abuse-neglect-blame/*

103 Hidalgo M. (2007) *Sexual Abuse and the Culture of Catholicism: How Priests and Nuns Become Perpetrators*, New York, Haworth Press ISBN: 0789029561

104 Dawkins, R, (2006) *The God Delusion*, 'Give me the child for his first seven years, and I'll give you the man' ISBN: 978 0618918249

105 McLeod, S. A. (Jun 06, 2018,). *Jean Piaget's theory of cognitive development.* Simply Psychology. Retrieved Sep 28, 2020 from *https://www.simplypsychology.org/piaget.html*

106 Recovering from Religion, Retrieved May 08, 2021 from *https://www.recovering-fromreligion.org*

107 Tarico V. AlterNet. *Religious Trauma Syndrome: How Some Organized Religion Leads to Mental Health Problems* Retrieved Aug 19, 2020 from *https://truthout.org/articles/ religious-trauma-syndrome-how-some-organized-religion-leads-to-mental-health-problems/*

108 Dein S. (2018). *Against the Stream: religion and mental health - the case for the inclusion of religion and spirituality into psychiatric care.* BJPsych bulletin, 42(3), 127–129. https://doi.org/10.1192/bjb.2017.13

109 Nieuw Amerongen JC van. et al. (2018) Mental Health, Religion & Culture *The "religiosity gap" in a clinical setting: experiences of mental health care consumers and professionals,* 21:7, 737–752, DOI: 10.1080/13674676.2018.1553029

110 Curlin FA. Lawrence RE., Odell S. et al., (2007) *Religion, spirituality, and medicine: psychiatrists' and other physicians' differing observations, interpretations, and clinical approaches,* American Journal of Psychiatry, vol. 164, no. 12, pp1825–1831.

111 Rettner R. - Senior Writer, LiveScience, *God Help Us? How Religion is Good (And Bad) For Mental Health*, Retrieved Sep 23, 2020 from *https://www.livescience. com/52197-religion-mental-health-brain.html*

112 Cornah Dr D. Mental Health Foundation (2006) *The impact of spirituality on mental health*, (Review of literature). ISBN: 978-1-903645-85-7

113 Kirwan Institute, The Ohio State University *Understanding Implicit Bias* Retrieved Sep 8, 2020 from *http://kirwaninstitute.osu.edu/research/ understanding-implicit-bias/*

114 Koenig HG. Research Gate (Dec 2012) *Religion, Spirituality, and Health: The*

*Research and Clinical Implications* (review of 93 studies) Retrieved Sep 23, 2020 from *https://www.researchgate.net/publication/237200852_Religion_Spirituality_and_Health_The_Research_and_Clinical_Implications*

115  Marshall J, Pew Research Center (Jan 31, 2019) *Are religious people happier, healthier? Our new global study explores this question.* Retrieved Dec 12, 2020 from *https://www.pewresearch.org/fact-tank/2019/01/31/are-religious-people-happier-healthier-our-new-global-study-explores-this-question/*

116  Bains S. (2011) *Questioning the Integrity of the John Templeton Foundation,* Evolutionary Psychology – ISSN 1474-7049 – Volume 9 (1) Retrieved Dec 12, 2020 from *https://journals.sagepub.com/doi/full/10.1177/147470491100900111*

117  Baker J., Stroope S. and Walker M. (2018) Secularity, religiosity, and health: Physical and mental health differences between atheists, agnostics, and non-affiliated theists compared to religiously affiliated individuals Social Science Research, Volume 75, ISSN 0049-089X Retrieved May 5, 2020 *https://doi.org/10.1016/j.ssresearch.2018.07.003*

118  Bartkowski J, Xiaohe Xu, Bartkowski S. (2019) *Mixed Blessing: The Beneficial and Detrimental Effects of Religion on Child Development among Third-Graders.* Religions, 10 (1): 37 DOI: 10.3390/rel10010037

119  QuestionPro. *Religion survey questions for questionnaires.* Retrieved May 5, 2020 from *https://www.questionpro.com/blog/religion-survey-questions/*

120  BBC News. *How many Catholics are there in Britain?* Retrieved Sep 29, 2020 from *https://www.bbc.co.uk/news/11297461*

121  Winell Dr M. British Association for Behavioural and Cognitive Therapies, *Understanding Religious Trauma Syndrome: Trauma from Leaving Religion* Article 3 of 3, Retrieved Dec 12, 2020 from *https://legacy.babcp.com/Review/RTS-Trauma-from-Leaving-Religion.aspx*

122  Ward Prof. K. (2011) *Is religion dangerous?* ISBN 9780745955308

123  Ed. Bybee J. (1998), *Guilt and Children,* Chapter 7, ISBN: 9780121486105

124  Klass P. Independent (Dec 13, 2017) *A healthy dose of guilt can actually be good for your child's development* Retrieved Mar 11, 2021 from *https://www.independent.co.uk/news/science/guilt-child-development-parenting-a8094491.html*

125  Stossel J. ABC News (Jan 6, 2006) *Is Guilt Good for You?* Retrieved Aug 28, 2020 from *https://abcnews.go.com/2020/story?id=123763&page=1*

126  Shreve-Neiger AK, Edelstein BA. *Religion and anxiety: a critical review of*

*the literature.* Clin Psychol Rev. 2004 Aug;24(4):379-97. doi: 10.1016/j. cpr.2004.02.003. PMID: 15245827

127  Mohdin A, Walker P and Parveen N. (Mar 21, 2021) The Guardian *No 10's race report widely condemned as 'divisive'* Retrieved Mar 30, 2021 from *https://www.theguardian.com/world/2021/mar/31/deeply-cynical-no-10-report-criticises-use-of-institutional-racism*

128  The Children's Society (2020) *Good Childhood Report* Retrieved Apr 21, 2021 from *https://www.childrenssociety.org.uk/sites/default/files/2020-09/PRE022a_Good%2520Childhood%25202020_V6_LR.pdf*

129  Timpson review of school exclusion (May 2019) Controller of Her Majesty's Stationery Office CP92 ISBN 978-1-5286-1272-2 Retrieved Apr 20, 2021 from *https://assets.publishing.service.gov.uk/government/uploads/system/uploads/attachment_data/file/807862/Timpson_review.pdf*

130  Wynch G. Psychology Today *Why Do We Punish Ourselves?* Retrieved Sep 28, 2020 from *https://www.google.com/amp/s/www.psychologytoday.com/gb/blog/the-squeaky-wheel/201407/why-do-we-punish-ourselves%3famp*

131  Bodkin H. health correspondent. The Telegraph (Jan 27, 2019) *Molly Russell: The 'caring soul' who died after exploring her depression on Instagram* Retrieved Sep 28, 2020 from *https://www.telegraph.co.uk/news/2019/01/27/molly-russell-caring-soul-died-exploring-depression-social-media/*

132  Commission on Religious Education *Religion and Worldviews: The way forward* Retrieved Feb 6, 2021 from *https://www.commissiononre.org.uk/wp-content/uploads/2018/09/Final-Report-of-the-Commission-on-RE.pdf*

133  Ministry of Housing, Communities & Local Government *Independent Faith Engagement Review: call for evidence* Retrieved Nov 14, 2020 from *https://www.gov.uk/government/consultations/independent-faith-engagement-review-call-for-evidence/independent-faith-engagement-review-call-for-evidence*

134  DfE (Nov 25, 2010) *Nick Gibb to the Catholic Education Service diocesan school commissioners conference* Retrieved May 08, 2021 from *https://www.gov.uk/government/speeches/nick-gibb-to-the-catholic-education-service-diocesan-school-commissioners-conference*

135  Holness M. Church Times *EDUCATION - New intake limbers up* (Jun 09, 2009) Retrieved May 08, 2021 from *https://www.churchtimes.co.uk/articles/2009/12-june/features/education-new-intake-limbers-up*

136  Simons J. and Porter N. (eds.) *Knowledge and the Curriculum* (London: Policy Exchange, 2015) Gibb N. *'How E. D. Hirsch Came to Shape UK Government*

*Policy'* ISBN: 978-1-910812-01-3

137  Hirsch ED. *The Schools We Need: and Why We Don't Have Them* (Dec 31, 1996) ISBN: 9780385484572

138  Parallel Parliament (Mar 26,2018) *Religion: Education* Retrieved May 08, 2021 from *https://www.parallelparliament.co.uk/question/133483/religion-education*

139  Humanists UK (Mar 4, 2021) *New survey reveals how Census question leads people to tick a religious answer* Retrieved Mar 14, 2021 from *https://humanism.org.uk/2021/03/04/ new-survey-reveals-how-census-question-leads-people-to-tick-a-religious-answer/*

140  YouGov Survey (Mar 22, 2021) *Do you think the House of Lords should or should not continue to have places for Church of England bishops* Retrieved Mar 25, 2021 from *https://yougov.co.uk/topics/politics/survey-results/daily/2021/03/22/e0986/3*

141  Greer G. (Dec 04, 2003) *Convent Girls* (edited by Jackie Bennett and Rosemary Forgan) ISBN: 9781844080991

142  Seltzer L Ph.D *The Rebellion of the Over-Criticized Child* Retrieved Oct 12, 2020 from *https://www.psychologytoday.com/gb/blog/evolution-the-self/201904/ the-rebellion-the-over-criticized-child*

143  A vintage BBC documentary examining Freud's ideas about the unconscious mind. The story of the convent girls appears about halfway through. Courtesy of Onderkoffer (2013) *The Century Of The Self - There is a Policeman Inside All Our Heads* Retrieved Jan 26, 2021 from *https://www.dailymotion.com/video/x17b3lw*

144  Wikipedia (Jan 23, 2020) *Moral scepticism* Retrieved Oct 12, 2020 from *https:// en.wikipedia.org/w/index.php?title=Moral_skepticism&oldid=937119873*;

145  Cikanavicius D. *The Trap of External Validation for Self-Esteem* Retrieved Jul 01, 2018 from *https://blogs.psychcentral.com/psychology-self/2017/08/validation-self-esteem/*

146  Definition of 'casuistry' courtesy of Dictionary.com Retrieved Oct 11, 2020 from *https://www.dictionary.com/browse/casuistry*

147  Hartnett EA. University of St. Thomas Law Journal (2007) *Catholic Judges and Cooperation in Sin*, 4 U. St. Thomas L.J. 2, 221 at 253 (citing 1 Henry Davis, Moral and Pastoral Theology 346 (L.W. Geddes ed., 8th ed. 1959) (1935». at 252)

148  Tamanaha BZ. University of St. Thomas Law Journal (2006) *Good Casuistry and Bad Casuistry: Resolving the Dilemmas Faced by Catholic Judges* Volume 4, Issue 2 Fall Article 6

149  Skopeliti C. The Guardian *Lord Sumption tells stage 4 cancer patient her life is 'less*

*valuable'* Retrieved Feb 7, 2021 from *https://www.theguardian.com/law/2021/jan/17/jonathan-sumption-cancer-patient-life-less-valuable-others*

150  Martel F. *In the Closet of the Vatican: Power, Homosexuality, Hypocrisy* (Feb 2019) ISBN: 9781472966148

151  Simmons L. *Desert ascetics or sexual aesthetics?: an exploration into the place of sexuality within our spirituality* Retrieved Feb 7, 2021 from *https://www.biblesociety.org.uk/uploads/content/bible_in_transmission/files/2005_summer/BiT_Summer_2005_Simmons.pdf*

152  Gleeson K. (Nov 2015) *The Money Problem: Reparation and Restorative Justice in the Catholic Church's Towards Healing Program.* Current Issues in Criminal Justice, 26:3, 317-332, DOI: 10.1080/10345329.2015.12036024

153  Jessica Abrahams, *'Equality' divides Christianity* Retrieved Oct 12, 2020 from *https://www.theguardian.com/commentisfree/belief/2012/may/25/same-sex-marriage-christian-divisions-equality*

154  Aronson R. (Sept. 2009) *Living Without God: New Directions for Atheists, Agnostics, Secularists, and the Undecided* ISBN: 9781582435305

155  Johnson C. (May 2014) *A Better Life: 100 Atheists Speak Out on Joy & Meaning in a World Without God* ISBN: 9780989936002

156  Sheldrake P A (2007) *Brief History of Spirituality* ISBN: 9781405117708

157  Shenhav et al. (2012) *Divine Intuition: Cognitive Style Influences Belief in God.* Journal of Experimental Psychology: General. (Sep 2011) American Psychological Association, Vol. 141, No. 3, 423– 428

158  Farias M. Coventry University. (Nov 8, 2017). *Why do we believe in gods? Religious belief 'not linked to intuition or rational thinking'* Retrieved Oct 12, 2020 from *https://www.coventry.ac.uk/primary-news/why-do-we-believe-in-gods-religious-belief-not-linked-to-intuition-or-rational-thinking-new-research-suggests-/*

159  McGreal S. Psychology Today *Reason Versus Faith? The Interplay of Intuition and Rationality In Supernatural Belief,* Retrieved Sep 23, 2020 from *https://www.psychologytoday.com/us/blog/unique-everybody-else/201209/reason-versus-faith-the-interplay-intuition-and-rationality-in*

160  Ottati V. et al. (2015) *When self-perceptions of expertise increase closed-minded cognition: The earned dogmatism effect* Journal of Experimental Social Psychology, Volume 61ISSN 0022-1031

161  Wikipedia (Dec 27, 2020) *Seven deadly sins.* Retrieved Jan 13, 2021 from *https://en.wikipedia.org/w/index.php?title=Seven_deadly_sins&oldid=996506798*

162 Definition of 'brainwash' courtesy of the Cambridge English Dictionary © Cambridge University Press Retrieved Oct 12, 2020 from *https://dictionary.cambridge.org/dictionary/english/brainwash*

163 Fair Admissions Campaign *Number of schools by type* Retrieved Feb 9, 2021 from *https://fairadmissions.org.uk/why-is-this-an-issue/number-of-schools-by-type/*

164 The National Archives *Criminal Justice System Aims and Objectives* Retrieved Feb 7, 2021 from *https://webarchive.nationalarchives.gov.uk/20100920201828/http://www.cjsonline.gov.uk/aims_and_objectives/*

165 Restorative Justice Council *Criminal justice* Retrieved Feb 6, 2021 from *https://restorativejustice.org.uk/criminal-justice#:~:text=Government%20research%20demonstrates%20that%20restorative,in%20the%20frequency%20of%20reoffending.&-text=For%20victims%2C%20meeting%20the%20person,and%20recovering%20from%20the%20crime.*

166 Sherman L and Strang H. *Restorative Justice: The Evidence* The Smith Institute ISBN: 1905370164

167 Centre for Justice & Reconciliation *Albert Eglash and Creative Restitution: A Precursor to Restorative Practices* Retrieved Feb 7, 2021 from *http://restorativejustice.org/rj-library/albert-eglash-and-creative-restitution-a-precursor-to-restorative-practices/4068/*

168 Webster R. (Oct 2, 2017) *The Lifelong Impact Of Child Abuse* Retrieved Jun 13, 2020 from *http://www.russellwebster.com/the-lifelong-impact-of-child-abuse/*

169 Stand By Me *Manifesto* Retrieved Jul 23, 2020 from *https://www.standby.me/manifesto*

170 St Philip's Roman Catholic Home for Boys, Edgbaston run by the Order of Daughters of St Vincent De Paul, Sisters of Charity. (Fig. 2).

171 Worsley, Margret. (1997). *St Philip's from beginning to beginning.* p253. ISBN 1862370788.

172 Thompson Gershoff E. American Psychological Association (2002) *Inc Corporal Punishment by Parents and Associated Child Behaviors and Experiences: A Meta-Analytic and Theoretical Review* DOI: 10.1037//0033-2909.128.4.539

173 Hansard HL Deb (May 20, 2004) vol 661 cc890-914, Retrieved Mar 2, 2021 from *https://api.parliament.uk/historic-hansard/lords/2004/may/20/reasonable-chastisement*

174 Rowland, A., FRCPCH FRCEM FRSA, Gerry, F., Qc, & Stanton, M., MSW. (2017). *Physical Punishment of Children* The International Journal of Children's Rights, 25(1), 165-195. doi: https://doi.org/10.1163/15718182-02501007

175 End Violence Against Children *Country Report for the United Kingdom* Retrieved Apr 12, 2021 from *https://endcorporalpunishment.org/ reports-on-every-state-and-territory/uk/*

176 Black and Tan was a nickname for the Royal Irish Constabulary Special Reserve. Clad in black cap and khaki uniform (hence Black and Tans) this force of poorly trained temporary constables was formed in 1919 to help maintain law and order, but they became notorious for attacks on civilians.

177 Between 1864 and 1906, when all Ireland was under English rule, public money was advanced as loans at low annuities for civic works, including the erection of labourers' cottages to replace the pre-existing insanitary hovels widespread in Ireland at the time. In the first major social housing scheme in the British Isles, nearly 50,000 labourer-owned cottages were erected, each with a small allotment, housing over a quarter of a million landless rural labourers and their families. Further reading: The rehousing of rural labourers in Ireland under the Labourers (Ireland) Acts, 1883–1919. Frederick HA Aalen 1986, Journal of Historical Geography, Elsevier Ltd.

178 Until 1970, a non-Catholic was obliged to take up the faith when marrying someone in the Roman Catholic Church, a rule based on the 1908 papal decree 'Ne Temere' (Pope Pius X, Sacred Congregation of the Council). The Roman Catholic Church permits Catholics to marry non-Christians now, but creates division by referring to such unions as non-sacramental marriages. Further reading: Collins, B. (2010). Mixing Marriages. BBC Radio Ulster documentary.

179 CCC, II The Lord's Day, 2181: 'The Sunday Eucharist is the foundation and confirmation of all Christian practice. For this reason, the faithful are obliged to participate in the Eucharist on days of obligation, unless excused for a serious reason (for example, illness, or the care of infants). Those who deliberately fail in this obligation commit a grave sin.'. A grave sin is a mortal sin and if the perpetrator fails to confess it and obtain forgiveness before he dies, he will go straight to hell.

180 Dad obtained copies of Roman coins from the British Museum, inscribed with the words Pontifex Maximus (supreme priest). This was the title given to the Imperial Roman Emperor, Caesar – who, through the procurator, Pontius Pilate, decreed the execution of Christ. RC popes claim to succeed Christ's disciple St Peter, but they also adopt the title of Pontifex Maximus. Dad proposed to ask the priest how the pope could claim both titles. By an extraordinary quirk of history the pope can, and does, represent both Christians and their pagan Roman persecutors. Constantine converted to Christianity in the fourth century, and reconnected the Roman Empire, split under Diocletian 50 years

earlier. In 380 AD, Emperor Theodosius I made Christianity the official religion, so Christ's executioners became his followers, and the pope represents both. The three crowns of the papal tiara symbolise the Kingdom of Heaven, the Roman Empire and the Vatican. That said, several alternative explanations of its meaning have been published and a dozen or more papal crowns are in existence.

181 Interchangeable with 'priest' in some denominations, the word *pastor* originates from the Latin noun '*pastor*', which means 'shepherd'.

182 CCC, III The Effects of Confirmation, 1303: 'Recall then that you have received the spiritual seal, the spirit of wisdom and understanding, the spirit of right judgment and courage, the spirit of knowledge and reverence, the spirit of holy fear in God's presence.'

183 The Tridentine Mass, sometimes called 'The Latin Mass', is the old form of Roman Rite Mass that was celebrated throughout the Roman Catholic Church from 1570 until it was replaced in 1962. Responses are given by a deacon, a lay minister or an altar boy, in Latin, and the congregation does not participate.

184 CCC, II The Sacrament of Holy Orders in the Economy of Salvation, 1548: 'In the person of Christ the Head. In the ecclesial service of the ordained minister, it is Christ himself who is present to his Church as Head of his Body, Shepherd of his flock, high priest of the redemptive sacrifice, Teacher of Truth. This is what the Church means by saying that the priest, by virtue of the sacrament of Holy Orders, acts *in persona Christi Capiti*s.' Pius XII, encyclical, Mediator Dei: AAS, 39; 1947.

185 Najim M. The Seminarians *The Roman Catholic Priest: In Persona Christi Capitis* Retrieved Sep 26, 2020 from: *http://www.cfpeople.org/SeminarianWritings/Sem033. html*

186 '*Unlimited power is apt to corrupt the minds of those who possess it; and this I know, my lords: that where law ends, tyranny begins.*' Speech to Parliament by William Pitt, 1st Earl of Chatham and former Prime Minister of Great Britain from 1766-1768.

187 The Honourable S.H.S. Hughes, Q.C. Commissioner (May, 1991) *Royal Commission of Inquiry into the Response of the Newfoundland Criminal Justice System to Complaints*

188 National Crime Agency (Oct 2013) *CEOP Thematic Assessment The Foundations of Abuse: A thematic assessment of the risk of child sexual abuse by adults in institutions*

189 Heikens J. Crux Catholic Media Inc. (Mar 20, 2020) *Theologian says clerical sexual abuse 'always about abuse of power'* Retrieved on

Sept 27, 2020 from *https://cruxnow.com/church-in-europe/2020/03/theologian-says-clerical-sexual-abuse-always-about-abuse-of-power/*

190 Religion Media Centre, *Sex Abuse in UK Christian Churches* Retrieved on Sept 27, 2020 from *https://religionmediacentre.org.uk/factsheets/sex-abuse-in-christian-churches-in-the-uk/*

191 CCC, V The Sacramental Sacrifice, Thanksgiving, Memorial, Presence, 1376: 'There takes place a change of the whole substance of the bread into the substance of the body of Christ our Lord and of the whole substance of the wine into the substance of his blood. This change the holy Catholic Church has fittingly and properly called transubstantiation.' Roman Catholics continue to teach that the bread and wine of Holy Communion are not just representative, but really are the body and blood of Christ. The miracle of transubstantiation is that what looks, feels, smells, and tastes like bread and wine is in fact the physical flesh and blood of Christ.

192 Jaswal VK. Association for Psychological Science *Young Children Are Especially Trusting of Things They're Told* Retrieved Oct 10, 2020 from *https://www.psychologicalscience.org/news/releases/young-children-are-especially-trusting-of-things-theyre-told.html*

193 The First Vatican Council of 1870 made the pope infallible when 'he defines... a doctrine of faith and morals'. Prior to 1870, Pope Gregory VII claimed the papacy 'never will err to all eternity'. Retrieved May 12, 2020 from *https://www.bbc.co.uk/religion/religions/christianity/pope/infallibility.shtml*

194 Office of Attorney General (Jul 27, 2018) Commonwealth of Pennsylvania *Report I of the 40th Statewide Investigating Grand Jury, Pennsylvania*

195 Dr Jodi Death, Crime and Justice Research Centre, Queensland University of Technology (2013) *'They Did Not Believe Me': Adult Survivors' Perspectives of Child Sexual Abuse by Personnel in Christian Institutions.* Retrieved Dec 10, 2020 from *https://eprints.qut.edu.au/59565/*

196 Wikipedia (Feb 27, 2021) *Sacrament of Penance* Retrieved Mar 4, 2021, from *https://en.wikipedia.org/w/index.php?title=Sacrament_of_Penance&oldid=1009246714*

197 Rev. Johnston e-Catholic 2000 *Penance* Retrieved Mar 3, 2021 from *https://www.ecatholic2000.com/cts/untitled-341.shtml*

198 CCC, Article 8, Sin, In Brief, 1871: 'Sin is an utterance, a deed, or a desire contrary to the eternal law (St. Augustine, Faust 22:PL 42, 418).'

199 CCC, IV The Gravity of Sin: Mortal and Venial Sin, 1861/1862: 'Mortal sin... causes exclusion from Christ's kingdom and the eternal death of hell.' Whereas, 'Venial sin is

... a less serious matter.' Since St Augustine, the Roman Catholic Church has ranked sins in two levels of seriousness: grave or mortal sins and minor or venial sins.

200 The Council of Trent (Session 14, Chapter I) quoted John 20:22-23 as the primary scriptural proof for the doctrine on the Sacrament of Penance.

201 These instructions accord with the guidance contained in CCC VII The Acts of the Penitent, 1454, and with the instructions prior to penitential prayers given to school children today, see note 11 above.

202 A booth with two compartments in one of which the confessor (priest) sits, behind a separating partition, to hear the confessions of penitents in the other compartment. Some booths have three compartments and the confessor occupies the central compartment. Denominations other than Catholic have diverse arrangements for hearing confessions but all offer God's absolution from sin. The confessional box was designed by 16th century Cardinal Charles Borromeo, who was alarmed by the many complaints of sexual abuse lodged against priests. Borromeo's box put a physical partition between penitent and confessor, but priests have continued to abuse their power. Further reading: see note 203 below.

203 Code of Canon Law Book IV, Can. 983: Title IV, The Sacrament of Penance (Cann. 959 - 997) 'The sacramental seal is inviolable; therefore it is absolutely forbidden for a confessor to betray in any way a penitent in words or in any manner and for any reason.' S2: 'All others who have knowledge of sins from confession are also obliged to observe secrecy.'

204 Code of Canon Law Book IV, Can. 980: Title IV, The Sacrament of Penance (Cann. 959 - 997) 'If the confessor has no doubt about the disposition of the penitent, and the penitent seeks absolution, absolution is to be neither refused nor deferred.'

205 The Church claims that Christ gave limitless authority to priests to forgive transgressions when he told the Apostles: 'Amen I say to you, whatsoever you shall bind upon earth, shall be bound also in heaven; and whatsoever you shall loose upon earth, shall be loosed also in heaven.' (Matthew 18:18.)

206 CCC, VII The Acts of the Penitent, 1452: 'When it arises from a love by which God is loved above all else, contrition is called "perfect" (contrition of charity). Such contrition remits venial sins; it also obtains forgiveness of mortal sins if it includes the firm resolution to have recourse to sacramental confession as soon as possible.'

207 Friedman J. Ph.D. MentalHelp.net *Resolving Guilt Once and For All, Time After Time* Retrieved Mar 14, 2021 from *https://www.mentalhelp.net/blogs/ resolving-guilt-once-and-for-all-time-after-time/*

208 Bragg M. BBC Podcast - In Our Time (Nov 1, 2007) *Guilt* Melvyn Bragg

discusses the moral conscience and takes a long hard look at the idea of guilt. Retrieved Feb 23, 2021 from *https://www.bbc.co.uk/programmes/b0084kd8*

209  Thufail PT, Outlook (Jul 09, 2018) *Kerala Church Scandal: Sin In The Box,* Retrieved Dec 11, 2020 from *https://magazine.outlookindia.com/story/ kerala-church-scandal-sin-in-the-box/300325*

210  Cornwell J. (Feb 10, 2014) *The Dark Box: a Secret History of Confession* ISBN: 9781781251089

211  Secretariat of State of the Holy See, Vatican City State (Nov 10, 2020) *Report on the Holy See's Institutional Knowledge and Decision-Making Related To Former Cardinal Theodore Edgar Mccarrick* Retrieved Apr 23, 2021 from *https://www.vatican.va/resources/resources_rapporto-card-mccarrick_20201110_en.pdf*

212  The Roman Catholic Church Investigation Report, Part D: The Nolan and Cumberlege reviews, D.1: The Nolan report (2001) Part I: Reporting of child sexual abuse cases, 1I.4: *The seal of the confessional* 'Monsignor Read … explained that a priest could not refuse absolution if a perpetrator refused to report a matter to the police.'

213  Death J (2015) *Bad apples, bad barrel: Exploring institutional responses to child sexual abuse by Catholic clergy in Australia.* International Journal for Crime, Justice and Social Democracy 4(2): 94-110. doi: 10.5204/ijcjsd.v3i2.229.

214  Robert Kaiser (2015) *Tom Doyle's Steadfast Witness For Victims Of Clerical Sexual Abuse* ISBN: 9781514327616

215  Franz T (2002) *Power, patriarchy and sexual abuse in churches of Christian denomination.* Traumatology 8(1): 4- 17. Retrieved Apr 23, 2021 from *https://doi.org/10.1177/153476560200800102*

216  Rowe P (Aug 4, 2019) San Diego Union-Tribune. California State Bill 360 would have required clergy to alert authorities of child abuse confessed by priests or church employees. Retrieved Jun 21, 2020 from *https://www.sandiegouniontribune.com/lifestyle/people/ story/2019-08-02/i-confess-should-the-confessional-be-a-safe-space-for-pedophiles*

217  Wilkinson P, Church Times (Dec 4, 2020) *Ampleforth College banned from taking on new pupils owing to safeguarding concerns* Retrieved Apr 23, 2021 from *https://www.churchtimes.co.uk/articles/2020/4-december/news/uk/ ampleforth-college-appeals-dfe-ban-on-taking-new-pupils*

218  Rashid F and Barron I, University of Massachusetts Amherst (2020) *Clerical Child Sexual Abuse in the Catholic Church of England and Wales: A Commentary of child safeguarding.* Retrieved Apr 23, 2021 from *https://scholarworks.umass.edu/cgi/*

*viewcontent.cgi?article=1000&context=cie_materials*

219 Australian Royal Commission into Institutional Responses to Child Sexual Abuse (2017) ISBN: 9781925622492

220 Pepinster C, The Guardian (Feb 21, 2019) *For Pope Francis, the moment of truth on sexual abuse has arrived* Retrieved Dec 11, 2020 from *https://www.theguardian.com/commentisfree/2019/feb/21/pope-francis-truth-sexual-abuse-summit*

221 Bloom P. The New York Times Magazine (May 5, 2010) *The Moral Life of Babies* Retrieved Feb 8, 2021 from *https://www.nytimes.com/2010/05/09/magazine/09babies-t.html*

222 Daily Mail (Feb 12, 2012) *Research shows toddlers understand right from wrong at just 19 months* Retrieved Feb 8, 2021 from *https://www.dailymail.co.uk/news/article-2103849/Research-shows-toddlers-understand-right-wrong-just-19-months.html*

223 Boyer P. (2001) *Religion Explained: The Evolutionary Origins of Religious Thought* ISBN 0-465-00695-7

224 Shultz S, Opie C, Atkinson QD. Nature (Nov 9, 2011) *Stepwise evolution of stable sociality in primates* 479(7372):219-22. doi: 10.1038/nature10601. PMID: 22071768.

225 Dr Scott Curry O. *What is morality? Where does it come from? How does it work?* Retrieved Feb 10, 2021 from *https://www.oliverscottcurry.com/research*

226 de Waal F. (Oct 15, 1997) *Good Natured: The Origins of Right and Wrong in Humans and Other Animals* ISBN 9780674356610

227 Allan D. CNN (Dec 11, 2018) *Breaking news alert: People are inherently good, non-violent* Retrieved Feb 12, 2021 from *https://edition.cnn.com/2018/12/11/health/nonviolence-good-wisdom-project/index.html*

228 Wikipedia (Feb 5, 2021,) *Dark triad.* Retrieved Feb 25, 2021 from *https://en.wikipedia.org/w/index.php?title=Dark_triad&oldid=1004938429*

229 Medscape (Note: NPD holds a fragile place in the diagnostic universe and could be excluded from the forthcoming edition of DSM) *DSM-5 diagnostic criteria for narcissistic personality disorder (NPD)* Retrieved Mar 10, 2021 from *https://www.medscape.com/answers/1519417-101764/what-are-the-dsm-5-diagnostic-criteria-for-narcissistic-personality-disorder-npd*

230 Anderson S. Psychology Today *Don't Let Narcissists Ruin Your Health* Retrieved Mar 10, 2021 from *https://www.psychologytoday.com/gb/blog/mood-microbe/201905/*

*dont-let-narcissists-ruin-your-health*

231  Ashley A. Hansen-Brown & Stephanie D. Freis (2019) *Assuming the worst: Hostile attribution bias in vulnerable narcissists, Self and Identity* DOI: 10.1080/15298868.2019.1609574

232  Fredriksen, P. Soundings: An Interdisciplinary Journal (1978) *Augustine and his Analysts: The Possibility of a Psychohistory.* 61(2), 206-227. Retrieved Feb 28, 2021, from *http://www.jstor.org/stable/41178077*

233  O'Brien C. Irish Times (Feb 16, 2017) *One in five baptised child just to gain entry to school* Retrieved Feb 7, 2021 from *https://www.irishtimes.com/news/education/ one-in-five-baptised-child-just-to-gain-entry-to-school-1.2975741*

234  Johnes R and Andrews J. LSE (Jan 11, 2017) *Faith schools do better chiefly because of their pupils' backgrounds* Retrieved Feb 14, 2021 from *https://blogs.lse.ac.uk/religionglobalsociety/2017/01/ faith-schools-do-better-chiefly-because-of-their-pupils-backgrounds/*

235  K12Academics *Faith Schools in the United Kingdom* Retrieved Feb 23, 2021 from *https://www.k12academics.com/Education%20Worldwide/Education%20in%20the%20 United%20Kingdom/faith-schools-united-kingdom*

236  Allen-Kinross P. Schools Week (Sep 30, 2019) *20,000 sent to faith schools despite requesting secular education* Retrieved Feb 9, 2021 from *https://schoolsweek. co.uk/20000-pupils-assigned-to-faith-schools-despite-requesting-secular-education/*

237  Dr David Lundie, (2018) *Religious Education and The Right Of Withdrawal* Retrieved Oct 12, 2020 from *https://davidlundie.files.wordpress.com/2018/04/report-on-re-opt-out-wcover.pdf*

238  Busby E. Independent (Nov 10, 2019) *Faith schools contribute millions of pounds less towards own costs, figures suggest* Retrieved Oct 12, 2020 from *https://www. independent.co.uk/news/education/education-news/faith-schools-funding-money-reli-gion-voluntary-aided-accord-coalition-a9192296.html*

239  Sherwood H. The Guardian (Apr 17, 2021) *Radical proposals to Church of England call for bishops to declare extra income* Retrieved Apr 21, 2021 from *https://www.theguardian.com/world/2021/apr/17/ radical-proposals-to-church-of-england-call-for-bishops-to-declare-extra-income*

240  Office for National Statistics (ONS) *Measures of employee earnings, using data from the Annual Survey for Hours and Earnings (ASHE)* Retrieved Apr 20, 2021 from *https://www.ons.gov.uk/employmentandlabourmarket/peopleinwork/ earningsandworkinghours/bulletins/annualsurveyofhoursandearnings/2020*

241 Lutzer E. (1977) *The Doctrines That Divide: A Fresh Look at the Historic Doctrines That Separate Christians* ISBN 9780825431654

242 Skinner F. Hodder & Stoughton (1 April 2021) *A Comedian's Prayer Book* ISBN: 9781529368956

243 Hewstone M et al. (2018). *Influence of segregation versus mixing: Intergroup contact and attitudes among White-British and Asian-British students in high schools in Oldham, England. Theory and Research in Education.* 16. 147787851877987. 10.1177/1477878518779879

244 DfE (Feb 2015) *Reformed GCSE and A level subject content Government consultation response* Retrieved Apr 12, 2021 from *https://assets.publishing.service.gov.uk/ government/uploads/system/uploads/attachment_data/file/403347/Reformed_GCSE_ and_A_level_subject_content_Government_response.pdf*

245 Fox v Secretary of State for Education, Case No: CO/2167/2015. Royal Courts of Justice, Strand, London, WC2A 2LL, 25 Nov. 2015

246 Asthana A. The Guardian (Sep 23, 2007) *Crisis of faith in first secular school* Retrieved Feb 23, 2021 from *https://www.theguardian.com/uk/2007/sep/23/schools.faithschools*

247 NHS Specialist Pharmacy Service (Oct 2017) *Clinical evidence for homeopathy* Retrieved Dec 30, 2020 from *https://www.england.nhs.uk/wp-content/ uploads/2017/11/sps-homeopathy.pdf*

248 UK DfE Academy and free school funding agreement (Dec 01, 2020) 'The Academy Trust must not allow any view or theory to be taught as evidence-based if it is contrary to established scientific or historical evidence and explanations. This clause applies to all subjects taught at the Academy.' In addition, 'The Academy Trust must provide for the teaching of evolution as a comprehensive, coherent and extensively evidenced theory' Ref: DfE-00213-2020, Retrieved Mar 26, 2021 from *https://www.gov.uk/government/publications/ academy-and-free-school-funding-agreements*

249 Humanists UK *Collective Worship and school assemblies: your rights* Retrieved Oct 11, 2020 from *https://humanism.org.uk/education/parents/ collective-worship-and-school-assemblies-your-rights/*

250 DfE Department for Children, Schools and Families (2010) *Religious education and collective worship* (Circular 1/94)

251 National Secular Society (NSS). Jan 03, 2018. *Case study: Difficulty exercising the right to withdraw from collective worship.* Retrieved Apr 29 2020 from *https://www.secularism.org.uk/opinion/2018/01/ case-study-difficulty-exercising-the-right-to-withdraw-from-collective-worship*

252 Gillard D (2018) *Education in England: a history* Retrieved Apr 02, 2021 from *www.educationengland.org.uk/history*

253 The 1944 Education Act was arguably the most significant aid to social mobility of the 20th century. Academic students went to grammar schools, others to secondary modern and some went on, as I did, to technical colleges to qualify in technology and the sciences. This arrangement, known as the tripartite system, was controversial mainly because the continuation of grammar schools created a sense of division. The system was dismantled in 1976, but it had enabled bright kids who were not academically minded to obtain a university education in craft skills. Unfortunately, money was short after the war. Technical secondary schools were seriously underfunded and 80% of children who should have gone to technical schools were unable to do so. Nevertheless, the results produced a generation of highly qualified technicians who helped rebuild Britain's WWII damage. Further reading: Sir Michael Barber, BBC *Rab Butler's 1944 act brings free secondary education for all. https://www.bbc.co.uk/schoolreport/25751787*

254 Moore E. NSS *The surprising origin of Collective Worship in schools* Retrieved Feb 07, 2021 from *https://www.secularism.org.uk/opinion/2016/03/the-surprising-origin-of-collective-worship-in-schools*

255 YouGov Survey (Nov 2013) Retrieved Feb 07, 2021 from *http://cdn.yougov.com/cumulus_uploads/document/3s35pyaa5c/YG-Archive-131125-Prospects.pdf*

256 Reddit.com *An Ethical Critique of the Ten Commandments* Retrieved Feb 07, 2021 from *https://www.reddit.com/r/DebateAChristian/comments/285657/an_ethical_critique_of_the_ten_commandments/*

257 Humanists UK (Mar 11, 2021) *'Violent', 'sexist' Bible story video for primary schools pulled after complaints* Retrieved Mar 12, 2021 from *https://humanism.org.uk/2021/03/11/violent-sexist-bible-story-video-for-primary-schools-pulled-after-complaints/*

258 Humanists UK (Jan 24, 2021) Exposed: Catholic school resources say 'man was created to be the initiator in sexual relationships', women 'receiver-responders' Retrieved Mar 12, 2021 from *https://humanism.org.uk/2021/01/24/exposed-catholic-school-resources-say-man-was-created-to-be-the-initiator-in-sexual-relationships-women-receiver-responders/*

259 Rev. Johnson B. Acton Institute (Mar 06, 2018) *Crushing religious schools with state funding* Retrieved Mar 12, 2021 from *https://www.acton.org/publications/transatlantic/2018/03/06/crushing-religious-schools-state-funding*

260 Ferguson D. The Guardian (May 26, 2019) *'We can't give in': the*

*Birmingham school on the frontline of anti-LGBT protests* Retrieved Mar 10, 2021 from *https://www.theguardian.com/uk-news/2019/may/26/ birmingham-anderton-park-primary-muslim-protests-lgbt-teaching-rights*

261  NSS (May 8, 2018) *NSS renews call to end faith schools' 'religiosity inspections* Retrieved Apr 12, 2021 from *https://www.secularism.org.uk/news/2018/05/ nss-renews-call-to-end-faith-schools-religiosity-inspections*

262  BBC News (Apr 19, 2021) *Clergy speak out over 'racism in Church of England'* Retrieved Apr 19, 2021 from *https://www.bbc.co.uk/news/uk-56779190*

263  Selway C. National Secular Society *Understanding Christianity and the Study of Religion and Worldviews* Retrieved Feb 09, 2021 from *https://www.secularism.org. uk/uploads/understanding-christianity-and-the-study-of-religion-and-worldviews.pdf*

264  NCBI Paediatrics & child health (2003) *Impact of media use on children and youth* 8(5), 301–317. Retrieved Mar 02, 2021 from *https://doi.org/10.1093/pch/8.5.301*

265  Bushman BJ, Huesmann LR. (2006) *Short-term and Long-term Effects of Violent Media on Aggression in Children and Adults.* Arch Pediatr Adolesc Med. 2006;160(4):348–352. doi:10.1001/archpedi.160.4.348

266  Gallop Poll (Jul 26, 2019) *40% of Americans Believe in Creationism…only 22% believe in natural selection* Retrieved Mar 02, 2021 from *https://news.gallup.com/ poll/261680/americans-believe-creationism.aspx*

267  Wikipedia (Feb 28, 2021) *Veracity of statements by Donald Trump* Retrieved Mar 22, 2021, from *https://en.wikipedia.org/w/index. php?title=Veracity_of_statements_by_Donald_Trump&oldid=1009323316*

268  Dean, J. (2006) *Conservatives without Consciousness.* New York: Viking ISBN-13: 9780670037742

269  Elmore JM. Power and Education (2014) *Exclusion, Alienation and the Sectarian Mind: Critical Education versus Dogmatic Training*; 6(1):73-83. doi:10.2304/ power.2014.6.1.73

270  Hugill D. Local Schools Network (Dec 09, 2010) *Five reasons why Religious Studies MUST be in the English Bacc* Retrieved Mar 20, 2021 from *https://www.localschoolsnetwork.org.uk/2010/12/ five-reasons-why-religious-studies-must-be-in-the-english-bacc-by-a-top-rs-teacher*

271  Jackson C. Birmingham Live (Jul 25, 2019) *LGBT teaching row blamed on academisation and 'broken' school system* Retrieved Mar 01, 2021 from *https://www.birminghammail.co.uk/news/midlands-news/ lgbt-teaching-row-blamed-academisation-16646938*

272 Sherwood H. The Guardian (Feb 21, 2021) *Church of England land should be used to help tackle housing crisis, says report* Retrieved Feb 22, 2021 from *https://www. theguardian.com/society/2021/feb/21/church-of-england-land-should-be-used-to-help-tackle-housing-crisis-says-report?CMP=Share_AndroidApp_Other*

273 Mount H. The Spectator (Jan 20, 2018) *Holy Lands* Retrieved Apr 02, 2021 from *https://www.spectator.co.uk/article/holy-lands*

274 Verkaik R. The Independent *The Church of England makes more money than McDonald's. So why is it struggling financially?* Retrieved Apr 02, 2021 from *https:// inews.co.uk/news/uk/church-england-struggling-financially-178826*

275 Martin Bashir, one-time journalist on American and British television and a former presenter of the BBC's Panorama programme, is a staunch Christian. Retrieved May 30, 2021 from *https://www.radiotimes.com/tv/bbcs-religion-editor-martin-bashir-why-christianity-is-still-relevant-this-easter/* In 1995 he used forgery and deception to obtain an interview with Diana, Princess of Wales. In 2003 he presented an ITV documentary about Michael Jackson, which was also proven to be fraudulent. Later, he justified his actions with arguments that some think specious. Despite his recourse to such casuistry, his knowledge of doctrine was extensive and he was appointed BBC religious affairs correspondent in 2016. At the time of writing, Bashir's CBBC video promoting his principles of journalism to children remains available from the BBC. Retrieved May 30, 2021 from *https://www.thetimes.co.uk/article/ martin-bashir-a-broken-man-who-cant-quite-admit-he-wronged-diana-mps7rh2bx*

276 de Castella T and Heyden T. BBC News Magazine (Feb 27, 2014) *How did the pro-paedophile group PIE exist openly for 10 years?* Retrieved Feb 07, 2021 from *https://www.bbc.co.uk/news/magazine-26352378*

277 @CASSANDRACOGNO Bits of Books *Sir Harold Hayward* Retrieved Feb 07, 2021 from *https://bitsofbooksblog.wordpress.com/tag/sir-harold-haywood/*

278 Booth R and Pidd H. (Feb26, 2014) *Lobbying by paedophile campaign revealed* Retrieved Feb 07, 2021from *https://www.theguardian.com/society/2014/feb/26/ lobbying-paedophile-campaign-revealed-hewitt*

279 Adams G. Daily Mail (Feb 26, 2014) *Labour's deputy leader Harriet Harman expresses 'regret' over links to paedophile lobby – but STILL won't apologise* Retrieved Feb 07, 2021 from *https://www.dailymail.co.uk/news/article-2567329/ Call-apology-Harriet-Harman-Labours-deputy-leader-expresses-regret-civil-liberties-groups-links-paedophile-lobby.html*

280 Pidd H and Mason R. The Guardian (Feb 28, 2014) *Patricia Hewitt backed*

*NCCL policy of lowering age of consent* Retrieved Feb 07, 2021 from *https://www. theguardian.com/politics/2014/feb/28/patricia-hewitt-age-of-consent*

281  Harman H. Daily Mail (Feb 25, 2014) *Not one hint of remorse: Harman and Dromey's statements, and the Mail's replies* Retrieved Apr 02, 2021 from *https:// www.dailymail.co.uk/news/article-2567098/Not-one-hint-remorse-Harriet-Harman-Jack-Dromeys-statements-Mails-replies.html*

282  IICSA (Feb 2020) *Allegations of child sexual abuse linked to Westminster Investigation Report* Introduction (3) Retrieved Feb 7, 2021 from *https://www.iicsa.org. uk/publications/investigation/westminster/part-g-paedophile-information-exchange/ g1-introduction*

283  Doward J. The Guardian (Mar 02, 2014) *How paedophiles infiltrated the left and hijacked the fight for civil rights* Retrieved Apr 22, 2021 from *https://www.theguardian. com/politics/2014/mar/02/how-paedophiles-infiltrated-the-left-harriet-harman-patricia-hewitt*

284  Woodhead L. *The rise of 'no religion' in Britain: The emergence of a new cultural major-ity* Journal of the British Academy, 4, 245–61. DOI 10.5871/jba/004.245

285  North American Man/boy Love Association, website available here: *https://www. nambla.org*

286  Edemariam A. The Guardian (Feb 20, 2010) *'People should sort this mess'* Retrieved Feb 14, 2021 from *https://www.theguardian.com/theguardian/2010/feb/20/ margaret-humphreys-child-migrants-trust*

287  House of Commons, Select Committee on Health, Third Report (Jul 30, 1998) *The Welfare of Former British Child Migrants* Retrieved Mar 14, 2021 from *https:// publications.parliament.uk/pa/cm199798/cmselect/cmhealth/755/75507.htm*

288  IICSA (Mar, 2018) *Child Migration Programmes Investigation Report* Retrieved Feb 08, 2021 from *https://www.iicsa.org.uk/publications/investigation/child-migration/ michael-o-donoghue*

289  Symonds T. BBC News (Feb 26, 2017) *The child abuse scandal of the British children sent abroad* Retrieved Feb 07, 2021 from *https://www.bbc.co.uk/news/uk-39078652*

290  Daly M. BBC News (Sep 17, 2018) *The sisters who survived the evil at Lagarie* Retrieved Feb 14, 2021 from *https://www.bbc.co.uk/news/resources/idt-sh/ sisters_who_survived_the_evil_at_lagarie*

291  Brocklehurst S. BBC Scotland News (Jun 27, 2018) *Children of God cult was 'hell on earth'* Retrieved Mar 22, 2021 from *https://www.bbc.co.uk/news/ uk-scotland-44613932*

292  Pettifor T. The Mirror (Sep 3, 2014) *'He groomed the nation': Jimmy Savile was*

*UK's most prolific paedophile, police report reveals* Retrieved Nov 06, 2020 from *https://www.mirror.co.uk/news/uk-news/jimmy-savile-uks-most-prolific-1529071*

293  Cockerton P. The Mirror (Oct 27, 2012) *The dark knight: Jimmy Savile could be first person ever to be stripped of Papal Knighthood* Retrieved 01 Dec, 2020 from *https://www.mirror.co.uk/news/uk-news/jimmy-savile-papal-knighthood-could-1402033* (At time of going to print (Jun 2021) Savile had not been stripped of his Papal Knighthood)

294  Freeman H. The Guardian (Mar 4, 2019) *The Michael Jackson accusers: 'The abuse didn't feel strange, because he was like a god'* Retrieved Feb 08, 2021 from *https://www.theguardian.com/tv-and-radio/2019/mar/04/the-michael-jackson-accusers-the-abuse-didnt-feel-strange-because-he-was-like-a-god*

295  BBC News (Jun 19, 2015) *Jehovah's Witnesses to compensate woman over sex abuse* Retrieved Feb 08, 2021 from *https://www.bbc.co.uk/news/uk-33201010*

296  Buckley J. Daily Mail (Oct 16, 2018) Cambridge graduate who is one of Britain's worst paedophiles and whose abuse on the 'dark web' left four of his victims trying to kill themselves has his jail sentence CUT from 32 to 25 years Retrieved Feb 14, 2021 from *https://www.dailymail.co.uk/news/article-6281653/Cambridge-graduate-one-Britains-worst-paedophiles-jail-sentence-cut.html*

297  2 Hare Court (Jun 03, 2016) *Brian O'Neill QC prosecutes 'Britain's worst ever paedophile'* Retrieved Feb 9, 2021 from *https://www.2harecourt.com/2016/06/03/brian-oneill-qc-prosecutes-britains-worst-ever-paedophile/*

298  McGreal C. The Guardian (May 26, 2011) *Elizabeth Smart tells rapist after nine years: 'I have a wonderful life now'* Retrieved Feb 25, 2021 from *https://www.theguardian.com/world/2011/may/26/elizabeth-smart-faces-rapist*

299  Sutton C. New York Post (Jun 14, 2018) *Infamous pedophile smiles as he gets life in prison* Retrieved Feb 09, 2021 from *https://nypost.com/2018/06/14/infamous-pedophile-smiles-as-he-gets-life-in-prison/*

300  Dunn M. News.com.au (Feb 20, 2016) *FBI describe dark net paedophile kingpin as one of the most prolific child sex offenders ever* Retrieved Feb 09, 2021 from *https://www.news.com.au/technology/online/security/fbi-describe-dark-net-paedophile-kingpin-as-one-of-the-most-prolific-child-sex-offenders-ever/news-story/eb468fcdb238a09883a1a6fe3b69d0a2*

301  Hampson S. E. (2008). *Mechanisms by Which Childhood Personality Traits Influence Adult Well-being.* Current directions in psychological science, 17(4), 264–268. https://doi.org/10.1111/j.1467-8721.2008.00587.x

302 Chapman G. The Guardian (May 4, 2018) *Nature or nurture: unravelling the roots of childhood behaviour disorders* Retrieved Feb 14, 2021 from *https://www.theguardian.com/science/head-quarters/2018/may/04/nature-or-nurture-unravelling-the-roots-of-childhood-behaviour-disorders*

303 Wikipedia (Feb 19, 2021 *Christianity by country* Retrieved Feb 27, 2021 from *https://en.wikipedia.org/w/index.php?title=Christianity_by_country&oldid=1007656703*

304 The EU commissioned a report through the Safer Internet Plus Programme. The report included maps and analysis of P2P activity against paedophile content in Europe in 2009. The authors reported that relationships between the variables were unclear. Latapy M. et al. *Maps of paedophile activity.* Retrieved Apr 02, 2021 from *http://antipaedo.lip6.fr/T24/TR/maps.pdf*

305 The Mail (Nov 3, 2011) *Hacker group Anonymous publishes internet addresses of 190 paedophiles in hi-tech 'sting'* Retrieved Nov 23, 2021 from *https://www.dailymail.co.uk/sciencetech/article-2057068/Hacker-group-Anonymous-publishes-internet-addresses-190-paedophiles-hi-tech-sting.html*

306 Ryan C. New York Times (May 25, 2011) *Irish Church's Forgotten Victims Take Case to U.N.* Retrieved Nov 29, 2020 from *https://www.nytimes.com/2011/05/25/world/europe/25iht-abuse25.html*

307 Sixsmith M. Daily Mail (June 2014) *I found nuns' secret grave for 800 babies in Tuam* Retrieved Jun 25, 2020: *https://www.dailymail.co.uk/news/article-2651484/I-thought-Id-seen-Philomena-And-I-nuns-secret-grave-800-babies-By-Martin-Sixsmith-exposed-Sisters-sold-children-fallen-girls.html*

308 Finnerty D. BBC News (Apr 24, 2019) *The Girls of Bessborough* Retrieved Dec 01, 2020 from *https://www.bbc.co.uk/news/resources/idt-sh/the_girls_of_bessborough*

309 Travers N. William & Mary Journal of Race, Gender, and Social Justice (2006) *A Brief Examination of Pedophilia and Sexual Abuse Committed by Nuns Within the Catholic Church*, Volume 12, Issue 3, Article 10

310 Clarke-Billings L. The Mirror (Apr 24, 2015) *Catholic girls' school tells pupils sex outside marriage makes their 'bodies sick' and will 'destroy their souls'* Retrieved Feb 23, 2021 from *https://www.mirror.co.uk/news/uk-news/catholic-girls-school-tells-pupils-5575674*

311 CCC, IV Offences Against the Dignity of Marriage, 2390: 'The sexual act must take place exclusively within marriage. Outside of marriage it always constitutes a grave sin...' (See note 192 above – a grave sin merits 'the eternal death of hell.')

312 Lanning K. FBI National Center for Missing and Exploited Children

(Dec 1992) *Child Molesters: A Behavioral Analysis For Law Enforcement Officers Investigating Cases of Child Sexual Exploitation* (Extracts from this publication are regularly misquoted to support the claim that most child abusers are 'situational offenders'. Please refer to the original document available here: Retrieved Feb 7, 2021 from *https://www.ojp.gov/pdffiles1/Digitization/149252NCJRS.pdf*)

313 Daydreamer of Oz, Absolute Zero United (Jul 11, 2006) *Deception* Retrieved Feb 22, 2021 from *http://absolutezerounited.blogspot.com/2006/07/deception.html*

314 Seto M. American Psychological Association (Aug 30, 2018) *Pedophilia and Sexual Offending Against Children Theory, Assessment, and Intervention* ISBN: 9781433829260

315 Cantor, J. M., Kabani, N., Christensen, B. K., Zipursky, R. B., Barbaree, H. E., Dickey, R., … Blanchard, R. (2008). Cerebral white matter deficiencies in pedophilic men. Journal of Psychiatric Research, 42(3), 167–183. *https://doi.org/10.1016/J.JPSYCHIRES.2007.10.013*

316 Wikipedia (April 19, 2020) *Debate on the causes of clerical child abuse* Retrieved May 06, 2020, from *https://en.wikipedia.org/w/index.php?title=Debate_on_the_causes_of_clerical_child_abuse&oldid=951944021*

317 John Jay College Research Team (May 2011) *The Causes and Context of Sexual Abuse of Minors by Catholic Priests in the United States, 1950-2010* ISBN 978-1-60137-201-7

318 Stephenson W. BBC News (Jul 30, 2014) *How many men are paedophiles?* Retrieved Feb 23, 2021 from *https://www.bbc.co.uk/news/magazine-28526106*

319 The First Lateran Council, held under Pope Calistus II in 1123, forbade clerical marriage and required priests already married to renounce their wives. Pope Innocent II decreed clerical marriages to be invalid in the Second Lateran Council of 1139.

320 Manuel, GS. (2012) *Living celibacy: Healthy pathways for priests.* Paulist Press. ISBN: 9780809147847

321 Davidson, JD. (Aug 16, 2018) *The Catholic Church's Sex Abuse Scandal is a Crisis of Faith.* The Federalist. Retrieved May 13, 2020 from *https://thefederalist.com/2018/08/16/catholic-churchs-sex-abuse-scandal-crisis-faith/*

322 France-Presse A. The Guardian *Polish clerical child abuse documentary casts shadow on John Paul II centenary* Retrieved Feb 22, 2021 from *https://www.theguardian.com/world/2020/may/17/*

polish-clerical-child-abuse-documentary-casts-shadow-on-john-paul-ii-centenary

323  Gunn B. and Burges R. Acadiana Advocate *Documents shed light on old scandal* Retrieved Feb 23, 2021 from *https://www.theadvocate.com/acadiana/news/article_ ee007ac9-3d70-567c-86fa-22e36e7024e0.html*

324  Carroll M. and the investigative staff of the Boston Globe (2016) *Betrayal: The Crisis In the Catholic Church: The Findings of the Investigation That Inspired the Major Motion Picture Spotlight* ISBN: 978-0316271530

325  Boyles S. WebMD *Do Sexually Abused Kids Become Abusers?* Retrieved Feb 22, 2021 from *https://www.webmd.com/mental-health/news/20030206/ do-sexually-abused-kids-become-abusers*

326  Infants in faith schools are ritually taught to confess misdeeds and repent, often by a cleric. The NSPCC cites guilt and shame, used by a figure of authority, as a method of child sexual grooming. (See note 80 above.)

327  Kraizer S. (Apr 01, 1985) *The Safe Child Book* ISBN: 978-0385294034

328  Psychology Today (Apr 20, 2014) *Why predators are attracted to careers in the clergy.* Retrieved Aug 20, 2020. *https://www.psychologytoday.com/gb/blog/ spycatcher/201404/why-predators-are-attracted-careers-in-the-clergy*

329  Buber M. (1997) *Good and Evil: Two Interpretations* ISBN: 9780023162800

330  Butt R and Asthana A. The Guardian (Sep 28, 2009) *Sex abuse rife in other religions, says Vatican* Retrieved Feb 08, 2021 from *https://www.theguardian.com/ world/2009/sep/28/sex-abuse-religion-vatican*

331  Raine S and Kent SA. Science Direct (2019) The grooming of children for sexual abuse in religious settings: Unique characteristics and select case studies. Aggression and Violent Behavior, 48, 180–189. *https://doi.org/10.1016/j. avb.2019.08.017*

332  IICSA Research Team (Nov 2017) *Child sexual abuse within the Catholic and Anglican Churches.* p8 Key Findings Retrieved Feb 23, 2021 from *https://www.iicsa.org.uk/research-seminars/research/research-projects/ child-sexual-abuse-within-catholic-and-anglican-churches#614681908*

333  Concordat Watch *Secret archives at the Vatican and in each diocese worldwide.* Retrieved on Oct 01, 2020 from *http://www.concordatwatch.eu/topic-50010.834*

334  ONS (Jun 2020) *Child sexual abuse in England and Wales: year ending March 2019* Retrieved Apr 02, 2021 from *https://www.ons.gov.uk/peoplepopula- tionandcommunity/crimeandjustice/articles/childsexualabuseinenglandandwales/ yearendingmarch2019#:˜:text=contact%20sexual%20abuse-,In%20the%20*

year%20ending%20March%202019%2C%20the%20CSEW%20estimated%20
that,contact%20sexual%20abuse%20(6%25)

335  Number of clerics in the UK:

Male C of E clergy = 19,560: *https://www.churchofengland.org/sites/default/files/2020-06/
Ministry%20Statistics%202019%20report%20FINAL_0.pdf*

Male Catholic clergy = 5,250: *https://faithsurvey.co.uk/catholics-england-and-wales.html*

336  The Washington Post (Jun 26, 2020) *Scandals, compensation programs lead Catholic
clergy sex abuse complaints to quadruple in 2019* Retrieved Sep 30, 2020 from
*https://www.washingtonpost.com/religion/2020/06/26/scandals-compensation-pro-
grams-lead-catholic-clergy-sex-abuse-complaints-quadruple-2019/*

337  Gibney A. Documentary film (Oct 2013) *Mea Maxima Culpa: Silence in the
House Of God*

338  Katsch M. ECA *Has anyone got their files from the CDF?* Retrieved Jul 25, 2020
from *https://archive.aweber.com/awlist4986531/P5Ra7/h/ECA_GLOBAL_
NEWS_ECA.htm*

339  Wikipedia *Catholic Church sexual abuse cases* Retrieved
Apr 22, 2020 from *https://en.wikipedia.org/w/index.
php?title=Catholic_Church_sexual_abuse_cases&oldid=951695391*

340  BBC Correspondent (2020) Cardinal Pell 'knew of' clergy abuse', says
Australian royal commission Retrieved May 07, 2020 from *https://www.bbc.co.uk/
news/world-australia-52569092*

341  Mr. R. J. Conway (LL.B.) The Lawful Argument for the Disestablishment
of the Church of England  (2018) Retrieved May 28, 2020 from *https://www.
academia.edu/37932680/The_Lawful_Argument_for_the_Disestablishment_of_the_
Church_of_England?email_work_card=abstract-read-more*

342  Department for Education (DfE) Teachers' Standards, p14. Retrieved Apr 16,
2021 from *https://www.gov.uk/government/publications/teachers-standards*

343  DfE Religious education (RE) and collective worship in academies
and free schools. Retrieved Apr 16, 2021 from *https://www.gov.uk/gov-
ernment/publications/re-and-collective-worship-in-academies-and-free-schools/
religious-education-re-and-collective-worship-in-academies-and-free-schools*

344  Education Act 1996, Section 406. Retrieved Apr 16, 2021 from *https://www.
legislation.gov.uk/ukpga/1996/56/section/406*

345  NSS. *What is Secularism?* Retrieved Apr 16, 2021 from *https://www.secularism.org.*

uk/what-is-secularism.html

346 NSS. Exploring Secularism *Homeschooling resources* Retrieved Apr 16, 2021 from *https://humanism.org.uk/homeschooling/*

347 DfE *Training to Teach Religious Education.* Retrieved Jan 29, 2021 from *https:// getintoteaching.education.gov.uk/explore-my-options/training-to-teach-secondary-subjects/ training-to-teach-religious-education*

348 UK House of Commons Briefing Paper Number 06972 *Faith Schools in England: FAQs* Introduction: what is a faith school? The Government funds many different types of 'faith school' – i.e. schools which are designated as having a faith character. Currently, around one third of state-funded schools in England have a faith designation. (Dec 20, 2019) Retrieved Apr 16, 2021 from *https://commonslibrary.parliament.uk/research-briefings/sn06972/*

349 NSS search results. Retrieved Apr 16, 2021 from *https://www.secularism.org. uk/search.html?query=Jewish+schools* and *https://www.secularism.org.uk/search. html?query=Islamic+schools*

350 NSS *Parent's perspective: We made a mistake sending our child to a faith school* Retrieved Apr 16, 2021 from *https://www.nomorefaithschools.org/testimonials/2020/11/ parents-perspective-we-made-a-mistake-sending-our-child-to-a-faith-school*

351 NSS *Religiosity Inspections: The case against faith-based inspections of state schools* Retrieved Apr 16, 2021 from *https://www.secularism.org.uk/uploads/religiosity-inspections-the-case-against-faith-based-inspections-of-state-schools.pdf*

352 NSS Unsafe Sex Education: The risk of letting religious schools teach within the tenets of their faith Retrieved Apr 16, 2021 from *https://www.secularism.org. uk/uploads/unsafe-sex-report-april-2018.pdf*

353 NSS *Most faith schools distorting sex education, NSS study finds* Retrieved Apr 16, 2021 from *https://www.secularism.org.uk/news/2018/05/ most-faith-schools-distorting-sex-education-nss-study-finds*

354 DfE. *Relationships Education, Relationships and Sex Education (RSE) and Health Education Statutory Guidance* Retrieved Apr 16, 2021 from *https://assets.publishing.service.gov.uk/government/uploads/system/uploads/attachment_data/file/908013/ Relationships_Education__Relationships_and_Sex_Education__RSE__and_Health_ Education.pdf*

355 NSS. *Human rights should not be at the mercy of the pope's pontifications* Retrieved April 16, 2021 from *https://www.secularism.org.uk/opinion/2020/10/ human-rights-should-not-be-at-the-mercy-of-the-popes-pontifications*

356 This is Local London Young Reporter. *The problem with sex education in catholic schools* Retrieved Apr 16, 2021 from *https://www.thisislocallondon.co.uk/youngreporter/18828026.problem-sex-education-catholic-schools/*

357 Ofsted. *Ofsted's equality objectives 2017 - 2020* Retrieved Apr 16, 2021 from *https://assets.publishing.service.gov.uk/government/uploads/system/uploads/attachment_data/file/860514/Ofsted_s_equality_objectives_2017-2020_gov_for_publication_Annex_A-amd.pdf*

358 Ofsted. *Inspecting schools: guide for maintained and academy schools* Retrieved Apr 16, 2021 from *https://www.gov.uk/guidance/inspecting-schools-guide-for-maintained-and-academy-schools#timings-of-inspections*

359 Association of Christian Teachers Retrieved Jan 29, 2021 from *https://christian-teachers.org.uk/*

360 Lovewise. Retrieved Apr 16, 2021 from *https://lovewise.org.uk/relationships-matter.html*

361 DfE. *Relationships Education, Relationships and Sex Education (RSE) and Health Education Statutory Guidance* Retrieved Apr 16, 2021 from *https://assets.publishing.service.gov.uk/government/uploads/system/uploads/attachment_data/file/908013/Relationships_Education__Relationships_and_Sex_Education__RSE__and_Health_Education.pdf*

362 NSS *RE shouldn't be a vehicle for the Church of England's interests* Retrieved Apr 16, 2021 from *https://www.secularism.org.uk/opinion/2020/12/re-shouldnt-be-a-vehicle-for-the-church-of-englands-interests*

363 Charity Commission for England and Wales. *Christian Education Movement* Retrieved Apr 16, 2021 from *https://register-of-charities.charitycommission.gov.uk/charity-search/-/charity-details/3977812/charity-overview*

364 The Church of England Education Office. *A Statement of Entitlement* Retrieved Apr 16, 2021 from *https://www.churchofengland.org/sites/default/files/2019-02/RE%20Statement%20of%20Entitlement%20for%20Church%20Schools.pdf*

365 Christian Education Retrieved Apr 16, 2021 from *https://christian-education.org.uk/*

366 Christian Education FAQ Retrieved Apr 16, 2021 from *https://christian-education.org.uk/faq/*

367 My Jewish Learning. *Why Jews Hang a Mezuzah on the Doorpost* Retrieved Apr 16, 2021 from *https://www.myjewishlearning.com/article/mezuzah/*

368 Goodreads (summary). *All That's Wrong with the Bible: Contradictions, Absurdities, and More* by Jonah David Conner Retrieved Apr 16, 2021 from *https://www.goodreads.com/book/show/36257900-all-that-s-wrong-with-the-bible*

369 Huffpost. James D. Tabor *Spanking Children: Does the Bible Tell Me So?* Retrieved Apr 16, 2021 from *https://www.huffpost.com/entry/ spanking-children-does-th_b_5888520*

370 Department of Catholic Education and Formation Catholic Bishops' conference of England and Wales *Learning to Love, An introduction to Catholic Relationship and Sex Education (RSE) for Catholic Educators* Retrieved Apr 16, 2021 from *https:// www.catholiceducation.org.uk/images/Learning2love.pdf.pdf*

371 DfE. *Relationships Education, Relationships and Sex Education (RSE) and Health Education Statutory Guidance* Retrieved Apr 16, 2021 from *https://assets.publishing.service.gov.uk/ government/uploads/system/uploads/attachment_data/file/908013/Relationships_Education__ Relationships_and_Sex_Education__RSE__and_Health_Education.pdf*

372 Goodreads (summary) Oranges Are Not the Only Fruit by Jeanette Winterson Retrieved Apr 16, 2021 from *https://www.goodreads.com/book/show/15055. Oranges_Are_Not_the_Only_Fruit*

373 Faith Schoolers Anonymous. *Deliver us from Evil: 'Gay Deliverance' in an English Christian School* Retrieved Apr 16, 2021 from *https://faithschoolersanonymous. uk/2016/11/deliver-us-from-evil-gay-deliverance-in-an-english-christian-school/*

374 The i news *Catholic school sex education resource says men are the 'initiators' and women are 'receiver-responders'* Retrieved Apr 16, 2021 from *https://inews. co.uk/news/education/faith-school-sex-education-pupils-men-initiators-women-receiv- er-responders-842785?fbclid=IwAR1-R7tHLI2do26XAHjoxm1U3Ih-QX26_ SGdhaanvPHcmPAmerB783lX5bM*

375 DfE. *Sex and Relationship Education Guidance*, updated July 2019, p4 Retrieved Apr 16, 2021 from *https://www.gov.uk/government/publications/sex-and-relationship-education*

376 NSS The choice delusion: how faith schools restrict primary school choice in England Retrieved Apr 16, 2021 from *https://www.secularism.org.uk/faith-schools/ choicedelusion.html*

377 NSS blog. *When is a community school not a community school?* By Alastair Lichten Retrieved Apr 16, 2021 from *https://www.secularism.org.uk/opinion/2016/07/ when-is-a-community-school-not-a-community-school*

378 Taylor & Francis online, International Journal of Children's Spirituality *Against faith schools: a philosophical argument for children's rights* Retrieved Apr 16, 2021 from *https://www.tandfonline.com/doi/abs/10.1080/13644360500154177*

379 UNICEF *Convention on the Rights of the Child text* Retrieved Apr 16, 2021 from *https://www.unicef.org/child-rights-convention/convention-text#*

380 DfE The Equality Act 2010 and schools Departmental advice for school leaders, school staff, governing bodies and local authorities May 2014 Retrieved Apr 16, 2021 from *https://assets.publishing.service.gov.uk/government/uploads/system/uploads/attachment_data/file/315587/Equality_Act_Advice_Final.pdf*

381 ITC Films *Jesus of Nazareth* Retrieved Apr 16, from *https://www.imdb.com/title/tt0075520/*

382 The Gospel According to Jesus Christ by José Saramago Retrieved Apr 16, 2021 from *https://www.goodreads.com/book/show/28859. The_Gospel_According_to_Jesus_Christ*

383 Teacher Tapp *Teachers are losing their religion* Retrieved Apr 16, 2021 from *https://teachertapp.co.uk/teachers-losing-religion/*

384 TV Channel 4. *All About Us: Living and Growing* Retrieved Apr 16, 2021 from *http://archive.teachfind.com/ttv/www.teachers.tv/series/all-about-us-living-and-growing.html*

385 DfE Government response *Relationships education, relationships and sex education (RSE) and health education: FAQs* Retrieved Apr 16, 2021 from *https://www.gov.uk/government/news/relationships-education-relationships-and-sex-education-rse-and-health-education-faqs*

386 DfE Guidance Relationships education (Primary) Retrieved Apr 16, 2021 from *https://www.gov.uk/government/publications/relationships-education-relationships-and-sex-education-rse-and-health-education/relationships-education-primary*

387 The Guardian. (Feb 10, 2020) *Girls beginning puberty almost a year earlier than in 1970s* Retrieved Apr 16, 2021 from *https://www.theguardian.com/society/2020/feb/10/girls-puberty-year-earlier*

388 Independent. (Mar 29, 2021) *MP calls for inquiry into 'rape culture' at independent schools* Retrieved Apr 16, 2021 from *https://www.independent.co.uk/news/education/education-news/rape-culture-independent-schools-inquiry-b1823689.html*

389 Mail Online. (Mar 27, 2021) *We were victims of private school rape culture… Britain's citadels of privilege* Retrieved Apr 16, 2021 from *https://www.dailymail.co.uk/news/article-9408165/We-victims-private-school-rape-culture-wont-silent-more.html*

390 NSS *Faith school myth buster* Retrieved Apr 16, 2021 from *https://www.nomore-faithschools.org/#grp-182056*

391 NSS The choice delusion: how faith schools restrict primary school choice in England Retrieved Apr 16, 2021from *https://www.secularism.org.uk/faith-schools/*

*choicedelusion.html*

392  BBC Religions *Original sin* Retrieved Apr 16, 2021 from *https://www.bbc.co.uk/ religion/religions/christianity/beliefs/originalsin_1.shtml*

393  YouGov survey (Aug – Sept 2010) Retrieved Apr 16, 2021 from *http://cdn. yougov.com/today_uk_import/YG-Archives-Pol-YouGovITV-PapalVisit-020910.pdf*

Lightning Source UK Ltd.
Milton Keynes UK
UKHW020008280921
391277UK00002B/159